CARLOS C

*In the business of truth, it is
forbidden to put words in handcuffs*

– Carlos Cardoso, 1985

*Carlos Cardoso has this particular quality – when
we look at him we see everything clear and
transparent. Few of us have this quality, this
purity. He is a man of causes. So he is a man who
can see further ahead than the rest of us. And
when we go into battle, in a formation that has its
hierarchies and positions, since Cardoso is carrying
the standard, he is more easily targeted.*

– José Luís Cabaço

CARLOS CARDOSO

TELLING THE TRUTH
IN MOZAMBIQUE

Paul Fauvet and Marcelo Mosse

DOUBLE
STOREY
a juta company

First published in English in 2003 by Double Storey Books,
a Juta company, Mercury Crescent, Wetton, Cape Town

Second Impression 2006
© 2003 Paul Fauvet and Marcelo Mosse

ISBN 1-919930-31-0

The writing of this book has been sponsored by the United States Agency
for International Development (USAID) and by the Royal Norwegian
Embassy, Maputo.

Editing by Priscilla Hall
DTP and layout by Claudine Willatt-Bate
Cover design by Toby Newsome
Printing by ABC Press, Epping, Cape Town

Contents

Acknowledgements

This book was born out of discussions shortly after the assassination of Carlos Cardoso, when friends and colleagues were considering what would be appropriate ways of honouring one of Mozambique's most remarkable journalists.

Right from the start Cardoso's widow, Nina Berg, gave her full support to the project. Indeed, without Nina's help it would have been quite impossible, for Nina is the guardian of Cardoso's personal archives, which are an extraordinary treasure trove of notebooks, diaries, letters, articles (published and unpublished), poems, and other jottings. This archive is the main primary source for this book, and without it we would be reduced to guessing about Cardoso's position on many of the events in the 1970s and '80s.

Thanks are also due to Gustavo Mavie, director of the Mozambique News Agency (AIM), for allowing access to Cardoso's personal files at AIM.

A wealth of published sources have been used – particularly the articles by Cardoso that appeared in the weekly magazine *Tempo*, the daily paper *Notícias*, the wire service of AIM, and the two privately owned fax papers that Cardoso edited, *Mediafax* and *Metical*.

The book also draws on the personal experience of its authors. Paul Fauvet worked under Cardoso at AIM from 1981 to 1989, and Marcelo Mosse was a senior journalist under Cardoso first at Mediafax, then at Metical, between 1993 and 2000.

A large number of people agreed to be interviewed, to share their memories of Cardoso. Others who could not meet personally with the authors sent in valuable contributions by e-mail. Cardoso's brother José Manuel, his sister-in-law Milena, and his cousin Helena Nicolau provided information on his childhood and education.

Stelios Comnenos provided details of life at Witbank High School in the 1960s. Several former students of the University of the Witwatersrand recalled the days of Cardoso's student radicalism and his deportation from South Africa, among them Erica Emdon, Alan Fine, Patrick Fitzgerald, Stephen Friedmann, Dee Malcomess, Glenn Moss, Karl Muller and Glynis O'Hara.

The three former Mozambican ministers of information with whom Cardoso worked closely – José Luís Cabaço, Teodato Hunguana and Jorge Rebelo – all agreed to be interviewed, as did the former education minister and widow of the country's first president, Graça Machel; the former security minister, Sérgio Vieira; and onetime director of Samora Machel's office, Luís Bernardo Honwana. Two former national directors of information made valuable contributions: Arlindo Lopes in person, and José Mota Lopes by e-mail.

Many of Cardoso's friends, colleagues and fellow journalists delved into their memories. They included Frances Christie, Mia Couto, Machado da Graça, Calane da Silva, Maria de Lourdes Torcato, Odete do Carvalho, Sol do Carvalho, Polly Gaster, Cassimo Ginabay, Alves Gomes, Fernando Gonçalves, António Gumende, Joseph Hanlon, Lourenço Jossias, Gil Lauriciano, Fernando Lima, Albino Magaia, Gustavo Mavie, Orlanda Mendes, Salomão Moyana, Kok Nam, Rui Alves Pereira, Manuela Soares, and António Souto.

We would like to thank all of them. Any errors of fact or interpretation, of course, are entirely the responsibility of the authors.

This book was also made possible through support provided by the Office of Program Development's Bureau for Mozambique, the US Agency for International Development (USAID), and the Royal Norwegian Embassy in Maputo. Opinions expressed are those of the authors, and do not necessarily reflect the views of USAID or of the Royal Norwegian Embassy.

Since this book is intended for a wide audience, we have decided not to burden it with large numbers of footnotes. Only a few essential notes are given at the end of each chapter. Unless otherwise stated, the sources are the writings of Cardoso himself or interviews with the persons named.

Abbreviations

Aicajú	Associação de Industrias de Cajú (Cashew Industry Association)
AIM	Agência de Informação de Moçambique (Mozambique News Agency)
Angop	Angolan News Agency
Apie	Administração de Parque Imobiliário do Estado (Mozambican state housing agency)
BCM	Banco Comercial de Moçambique (Commercial Bank of Mozambique)
BPD	Banco Popular de Desenvolvimento (People's Development Bank)
CAS	Country Assistance Strategy of the World Bank
CCF	Comissão de Cessar-Fogo (UN-chaired Ceasefire Commission)
CSC	Comissão de Supervisão e Controle (UN-chaired Supervisory and Control Commission)
DTI	Departamento do Trabalho Ideologico (Frelimo Ideology Department)
FADM	Forças Armadas de Defesa de Moçambique (Mozambican Defence Force), the unified army of volunteers from FAM and Renamo set up in 1994
FAM	Forças Armadas de Moçambique (Mozambican Armed Forces)
Fapla	Forças Armadas Populares de Libertação de Angola (People's Armed Forces for the Liberation of Angola), the Angolan army
FAR	Forças Armadas Revolucionárias (Revolutionary Armed Forces of Cuba)

FPLM	Forças Populares de Libertação de Moçambique (People's Forces for the Liberation of Mozambique), the Frelimo guerrilla army, later transformed into the FAM
Frelimo	Frente de Libertação de Moçambique (Mozambique Liberation Front)
JPC	Juntos pela Cidade (Together for the City)
MFA	Movimento das Forças Armadas (Armed Forces Movement)
Micoa	Ministério de Coordenação de Acção Ambiental (Environment Ministry)
MPLA	Movimento Popular de Libertaçao de Angola (People's Movement for the Liberation of Angola)
MNR	Mozambique National Resistance (Resistência Nacional Moçambicana), later known as MNR/Renamo or Renamo
Norad	Norwegian government development aid agency
ONJ	Organização Nacional de Jornalistas (National Journalists Organisation)
Onumoz	UN peacekeeping mission for Mozambique
Pana	Pan-African News Agency
PF	Patriotic Front, used in the combinations Zanu-PF and PF-Zapu
PGR	Procurador-Geral da República (Attorney-General), and also Procuradoria-Geral da República (Attorney-General's Office)
Pic	Polícia de Investigação Criminal (Criminal Investigation Police)
Pide	Polícia Internacional de Defesa do Estado (International Police for the Defence of the State), the secret police of the Portuguese colonial-fascist regime, abolished immediately after the 25 April 1974 coup in Lisbon
Renamo	see MNR
SADCC	Southern African Development Coordination Conference
Sintic	Sindicato Nacional de Trabalhadores de Cajú (National Cashew Workers Union)

Sise	Serviço de Informação e Segurança do Estado (the State Information and Security Service), which is not paramilitary and has no powers of arrest or detention
Snasp	Serviço Nacional de Segurança Popular (People's National Security Service), the paramilitary security body from 1975 until 1991, when it was replaced by Sise (see above)
Unita	União Nacional para a Indepêndencia Total de Angola (National Union for the Total Independence of Angola)
USAID	United States Agency for International Development
Zanla	Zimbabwean African National Liberation Army, the armed wing of Zanu
Zanu	Zimbabwe African National Union
Zapu	Zimbabwe African People's Union
Zipa	Zimbabwe People's Army
Zipra	Zimbabwe People's Revolutionary Army, the armed wing of Zapu

Introduction: 22 November 2000

When Carlos Cardoso, the owner and editor of the independent Maputo newsheet *Metical*, went to work on 22 November 2000, Mozambique was still reeling from the bloodiest scenes since the peace accord of 1992. On 9 November the former rebel movement Renamo, once a docile instrument of apartheid, now the major opposition party, had organised nationwide demonstrations against the results of the December 1999 elections, which they claimed were rigged. In several northern cities and towns, the demonstrations degenerated into clashes between Renamo and the police. In all, about 40 people – demonstrators and police – died. *Metical*, rather than take the claims and counter-claims of Renamo and the police at face value, did its own investigation, concluding that, while Renamo had staged a mini-insurrection in the town of Montepuez, in other places the police appeared to have opened fire first.

Now disturbing reports were trickling in of police reprisals in Montepuez, of beatings, and of mass arrests. That day, Cardoso pondered over a report from an envoy sent by the Mozambican Human Rights League to Montepuez. Parts of the report were barely legible, but Cardoso decided that what could be deciphered was important enough to appear in the next day's paper. As he sat at his desk, Cardoso could not imagine that at that very moment they were counting the bodies in Montepuez, where at least 83 people had died of asphyxiation in a grotesquely overcrowded police cell. That story would not hit the Maputo media until the following morning; by which time Carlos Cardoso would not be alive to write about it.

Cardoso was also a member of the Maputo municipal assembly, elected on the ticket of the independent citizens' group Juntos pela

Cidade (Together for the City), and he spent much of the morning on assembly affairs. What he learnt angered him. 'They can't do this!' he exclaimed as he arrived at the *Metical* office. He had received information that the mayor of Maputo, Artur Canana, was negotiating the allocation of municipal land without the knowledge of the assembly. He vowed he would fight to the end against Canana's land deals. Cardoso feared that prime municipal land would be delivered to members of the political elite, and next to nothing would enter the state's coffers.

Two other items were on Cardoso's agenda that day. One was the disastrous situation of the vegetable oil industry. Over the past five years, Cardoso had repeatedly written in defence of Mozambican industries facing extinction due to government or World Bank policies, or because of unfair competition. He had fought for the beleaguered cashew-processing industry, and now he argued that the government must take measures to support the local cooking-oil factories which 'purely and simply cannot compete with the illegal imports and with the extremely low prices of the Asian exports that benefit from the sharp devaluations of their currencies'. The local industry had asked the government to exempt it from value-added tax, but had received no reply. In the last editorial of his life, Cardoso declared: 'It is not coherent for the government, on the one hand, to call for an economic debate, and specifically for a debate on taxes, but on the other to say neither yes nor no to the request made by the edible oil industry.' By persisting on its current path, the government was driving companies to bankruptcy and 'killing off its own sources of revenue'.

The other matter on Cardoso's mind was the city's rubbish. He knew that Maputo was on the brink of another of its regular rubbish collection crises. In the last article he ever wrote, Cardoso warned that the capital might 'once again face mounds of rubbish accumulating on its street corners, because the City Council hasn't paid for the service for six months, and the owner of the trucks has ordered them off the streets'. He knew this because, the previous day, a representative of the private consortium hired by the city council to collect the garbage had come to the *Metical* office and told him that the council had not paid for the last six months. This man, Christian Lenferna, had flown from Durban to Maputo 'to contact in person the municipal officials responsible, but no City Councillor has bothered to receive him'. So he went to the press. Cardoso's reputation was such that Lenferna did not choose the main daily paper *Notícias*, but headed straight for the *Metical* offices in order that 'the citizens of Maputo may know why their rubbish collection could stop'.

On 22 November, all in the office seemed normal. But a few days earlier, *Metical* staff had been worried about a mysterious client calling himself Rachid, who visited the premises every evening to buy the paper. He never had the right money, and while the *Metical* staff were looking for change for inconveniently large banknotes, he had plenty of time to observe the office – and Cardoso in particular. On one occasion a *Metical* guard noted Rachid in a red Citi-Golf apparently pursuing the *Metical* vehicle, a Toyota Corolla, as it took Cardoso to a meeting. The last day on which the mystery client bought the paper was 17 November. He did not return in the next few days, so the staff felt that perhaps it was nothing to worry about.

In the afternoon of 22 November, two colleagues rang Cardoso to ask if he would put his name to a civil society movement being formed in response to the 9 November violence. The columnist João Machado da Graça was in the office of the weekly paper *Savana*, delivering his copy for the next issue; he took the opportunity to discuss with its editor, Salomão Moyana, what could be done to put a brake on the spiral of violence. They decided to call a meeting at the headquarters of the journalists' union with representatives of civil society organisations, to form a broad front against political violence. They rang Cardoso at about 16.30. *Savana* was sponsoring the meeting – would *Metical* add its name? Cardoso agreed at once. This was the start of what would become the Movement for Peace and Citizenship.

Cardoso's second cousin, Dalila Lawrence, called at the office. She was an intermediary between the city council and the consortium dealing with the garbage, and they discussed the consortium's contract. At about 18.30 Cardoso rang Teodoro Waty, who chaired the municipal assembly. Waty recalled Cardoso asking what he

Mourners file past the coffin of Carlos Cardoso in Maputo City Hall, 24 November 2000.

AIM: Ussene Mamudo

intended to do with the information he now had about the impending crisis, and Cardoso's last words: 'See what you can do. It would be bad for us to have the city filthy again. You know what I think about this, but tomorrow this will come out in my paper. You'll read it there. See you tomorrow.' But for Carlos Cardoso there would be no tomorrow.

Cardoso had to go home earlier than normal that evening: he was looking after his two children, Ibo and Milena, since their mother, Nina Berg, was working in Zambezia province. The next day's paper was ready, and he left the office, walking Dalila Lawrence to her car. Then, chauffeured by the *Metical* driver, Carlos Manjate, he followed her up the road. As Cardoso left, a red Citi-Golf that had been waiting on the other side of the road glided after the *Metical* Toyota. Two hundred metres further up Avenida Martires da Machava, in front of the city's main athletics stadium, the Parque dos Continuadores, the Citi-Golf pulled in front of the Toyota, forcing it to a halt. A hail of bullets rang out from an AK-47 assault rifle. One bullet struck Carlos Manjate in the head, severely injuring him. But he was not the main target. At least five bullets struck Carlos Cardoso in the head, neck, chest and upper arm, killing him instantly. The Citi-Golf sped off into the night.

As the news spread, a wave of shock and revulsion surged through Mozambican society. Prime Minister Pascoal Mocumbi's voice was cracking with emotion as he condemned the assassination on that night's television news. Colleagues who visited the morgue broke into tears on seeing the ruined body. That night the murder site became an impromptu shrine. The *Metical* Toyota had come to a halt beside a tree stump; on this were placed candles and messages. Over the next few days, flowers were piled high and more messages of grief and indignation were taped to the nearby wall. Messages of condolence poured in from all over the world. Perhaps Cardoso's friend Teresa Lima, a Mozambican journalist then working on the BBC Portuguese service in London, summed up the feeling: 'There is no coffin large enough for the heart of this man.'

For over a quarter of a century, in a working life that coincided almost exactly with the life of Mozambique as an independent nation, Cardoso had come to embody all that was best in Mozambican journalism, all that was honest, questioning, combative. He was admired, respected and loved – even among some of those subjected to withering criticism in his paper. All the key figures of state – the president of the Republic, the speaker of parliament, the president of the Supreme Court – attended Cardoso's funeral on 24 November in Maputo city hall. Addressing the mourners, President Joaquim Chissano said:

> We were used to arguing with Cardoso. We argued with him because he raised pertinent questions that demand the attention of all of us. He forced us all to think. Today, when he is no longer with us, we can no longer argue. Who else will raise the questions with the force that he raised them?

Giving the main funeral eulogy, the country's best-known writer, the novelist Mia Couto, declared: 'We are not merely weeping for the death of a man. It wasn't just Carlos Cardoso who died. They didn't just kill a Mozambican journalist … a piece of the country has died, a part of all of us.'

Who was this man who could inspire such an extraordinary out-pouring of grief? How did a journalist, just 49 years old when the assassins' bullets silenced him, come to symbolise all that was most generous, noble, and utopian in the Mozambican revolution? The rest of this book tries to provide some answers.

PART I

Against all Orthodoxies

by Paul Fauvet

AIM: Anders Nilsson

President Samora Machel in conversation with Carlos Cardoso (centre) and Paul Fauvet (right) at a reception in 1985.

CHAPTER 1

The Natural Order of Things

In 1951, when Carlos Cardoso was born, colonial rule in Africa was at its peak. With the anomalous exceptions of Liberia and Ethiopia, all of sub-Saharan Africa was under colonial and white minority rule. For ruling elites in London, Paris or Lisbon, nothing seemed more natural. Although the Second World War had been fought against the most murderous form of racism the world had ever seen, it did not appear to bring freedom and self-determination any nearer for most people living in Africa. Indeed, at the southern tip of the continent, the prospect of majority rule was kicked into the indefinite future in 1948 when a party that drew inspiration from Nazism took power. This was South Africa's National Party. Its core policy, which the new regime set about implementing, was designed to empower the white population, particularly the Afrikaans speakers, and was proudly called 'apartheid'. Within a few years, South African blacks would lose what few rights they possessed. They would be told they were only temporary sojourners in the cities, and that their real place was in the 'homelands' (usually referred to derisorily as 'bantustans'), barren fragments of land covering no more than 13 per cent of South Africa's territory.

Surrounding South Africa were a ring of dependencies and satellites. To the west lay the former German colony of South West Africa (known to its own people as Namibia), then under South African occupation. There were the three British protectorates of Swaziland, Bechuanaland (now Botswana) and Basutoland (now Lesotho), which avoided absorption into South Africa but remained heavily dependent on their large and powerful neighbour. To the north was

Southern Rhodesia, where much of the local white political elite looked approvingly to Pretoria and swore that blacks would never share, let alone take, power. And there were the two Portuguese colonies of Mozambique and Angola, completing the buffer around the mineral wealth of South Africa.

Some colonialisms are more benighted than others, and the Portuguese variant was remarkable for its combination of repression and stagnation. Lisbon basked in a glorious and largely fictional past. Portugal, so the story went, was a 'pluricontinental' nation, spreading Christianity and civilisation across the globe since the fifteenth century. The regime liked to claim that Portugal had been in Africa for almost five centuries – so Mozambique and Angola were not colonies at all: they were 'overseas provinces', part of the one and indivisible Portuguese nation. It was indeed true that Vasco da Gama had landed at various points on the Mozambican coast in 1498, but that had been entirely incidental. For the Portuguese seamen, Africa was not their goal; it was just a large obstacle on the route to the fabled wealth of the Indies. That was the real treasure, and the Portuguese crown showed its true priorities by running Mozambique from Goa for several centuries.

Africa produced two things the Portuguese were interested in: slaves and ivory. Deals were done with local kingdoms in which live people and dead elephants were the prizes. This extractive activity did not need direct control, and right up until the late nineteenth century, in both Mozambique and Angola, the writ of the Portuguese crown ran scarcely further than a few coastal towns and up some of the main rivers. So feeble was Portuguese control that Britain and Germany toyed with the idea of carving up Portugal's African possessions between them; but in the end mutual distrust between the two great powers prevailed, and at the 1885 Berlin conference Portugal could hang on to its rickety empire. Huge tracts of Mozambique were handed over to chartered companies, mostly owned by British capital, which ran them, to all intents and purposes, as separate states with their own currencies and with customs posts separating them from the rest of Mozambique. For only 34 years – from 1941, when the last charter expired, to 1975, the date of independence – did Portugal run its sprawling East African colony as a unitary state.

As for the 'civilising mission' that Portugal boasted of, the harsh reality was that almost no education was available for blacks. Even in the mid-1970s, the illiteracy rate in Mozambique was around 93 per cent. Christianity arrived in Mozambique with Vasco da Gama – but the first black Mozambican priest was not ordained until the 1950s. Portugal itself was the least developed country in western Europe, and from 1928 had been under the authoritarian, clerical rule of António de Oliveira Salazar. There were enough similarities between Salazar's regime and that of Mussolini for it to be labelled 'fascist', though Salazar was canny enough to stay out of World War II. Thus, in 1945 when Italy lost its colonies, Portugal kept its African empire.

The Mozambican economy was heavily dependent on South Africa. Since the end of the nineteenth century, the southern third of the country had been a labour reserve for the South African mines. Rare indeed were the households south of the Save river where the men did not serve one or more contracts on the gold mines. As for the capital, Lourenço Marques, this expanded around its port, which had been built explicitly to serve the Transvaal. Central Mozambique had a similar relationship to Rhodesia: migrant labourers went to work on Rhodesian farms, and the country's second city, Beira, was built (on top of a swamp) because its harbour was a convenient outlet to the sea for Rhodesia.

It was in Beira that Carlos Cardoso was born on 10 August 1951, the second son of Jaime and Maria Luísa Cardoso. Jaime Cardoso was one of the fairly small group of local white business people whose roots were more in Mozambique than in Portugal. He too had been born in Mozambique and was thus not a settler in the strict sense of the term. He owned the Savoy Hotel in Beira, but the business was not successful. In 1956, with Carlitos (as his family always called Carlos) just four years old, the family moved to what was then Lourenço Marques. Here Jaime Cardoso set up an import–export company dealing mainly in condensed milk and competing with the Nestlé brand Cruz Azul. His firm merged with the major Lourenço

Marques dairy products company, Protal, best known for its Belarosa processed cheese, where Jaime became managing director. The Cardoso family owned two three-storey buildings in central Lourenço Marques, in what is now Avenida Armando Tivane. Jaime, Maria Luísa and their three sons, José Manuel, Carlos and Nuno, lived in one of the houses, while the other was split into flats and rented out.

Carlos Cardoso's childhood was strict. His father was stern, his mother less so, but both, according to José Manuel, 'were totally dedicated to their careers. This meant that in our early years, we were left in the care of domestic staff under the supervision of our paternal grandmother, Maria de Jesus Cardoso.' Avo Maria, as the children called their grandmother, taught in the Rainha Dona Isabel (now 3 Fevereiro) Primary School in the heart of Lourenço Marques. This was where Carlos went to school, as did his cousin, Helena Nicolau. Helena recalled her grandmother as 'terrifying – a big, tall person, and very overpowering. She scared the living daylights out of us.' Years later Carlos remembered how he once filched 25 escudos from his grandmother's purse. He didn't want it all for himself: instead he bought ice cream for all his friends in the street. When his grandmother saw Carlos in the midst of a group of young boys strolling along licking ice-creams, her suspicions were aroused. Having discovered their source, she thrashed her grandson so severely that Cardoso resolved he would never steal again. But when a beggar came to the Cardoso house and his mother told Carlos to give him some money, she found that Carlos had emptied her purse of all its coins. 'When confronted, Carlos simply told her that she should not grumble, because she had everything and they had nothing,' his brother recalled.

The Cardoso children's strict upbringing moderated when their maternal grandparents moved in. Carlos was then seven years old. 'They were very affectionate, easy-going and extremely protective of us and balanced the strict approach our father took,' recalls José Manuel. They had to endure Carlos taking risks. He was inquisitive from an early age: sometimes too much so for his own good, as when, before his second birthday, he drank a bottle of DDT and had to be rushed to hospital. Various pranks and falls meant that, as his brother put it, 'before the age of 12 he had to have stitches on his head five times. The hospital staff got to know him pretty well.'

By the standards of colonial society, the Cardosos were not particularly rich – just well-to-do. And by all accounts, Jaime Cardoso worked hard at building up his businesses and earning the money that would later be used to educate his children. Carlos later recalled that his childhood in Lourenço Marques was 'paradise'. He had no illusions, though – it was paradise because he was lucky enough to be born with a white skin. Black politics went largely unnoticed among the whites of Lourenço Marques. They were insulated socially from the black majority: for most urban whites, the only blacks they knew were their servants. Even then, they were unlikely ever to visit their servants' homes in the suburbs or to speak their language. So they had no idea what black Mozambicans were thinking, and the censored Mozambican press did not enlighten them. Very few whites knew that Mozambican political organisations were being formed in neighbouring countries – the Makonde African National Union (later the Mozambique African National Union, Manu) in Tanganyika, or the Democratic National Union of Mozambique (Udenamo) in Rhodesia.

Few whites (outside the secret police, the Pide) paid much attention when the only black Mozambican with a doctorate, Eduardo Mondlane, came home briefly in 1961 and quietly mobilised others for the nationalist cause. Nor were there any splash headlines in the Lourenço Marques press when the nationalists formed a single organisation, the Mozambique Liberation Front (Frelimo), with Mondlane as president, in Dar es Salaam on 25 June 1962. A couple of years later it became harder to ignore the nationalist movement. On 25 September 1964 an attack against a small Portuguese garrison at Chai, in the northern province of Cabo Delgado, signalled the start of Frelimo's war for independence. Initially, however, this had precious little impact on colonial society in Lourenço Marques. Chai was 2000 kilometres to the north. For plenty of white businesses, it might as well have been on another planet.

Carlos started his secondary school studies at the Salazar High School (today's Josina Machel Secondary School). For the first two years he was doing well, but then, in his own words, 'I replaced my books with five-a-side football matches, and my school curriculum went into mourning. I failed the third year of high school twice. Seeing that the frequent discipline of the shout and the blow was no longer working, my father sent me to South Africa.' This was a crucial decision, since it was eventually to bring Cardoso into contact with revolutionary politics via the anti-apartheid struggle.

Witbank High was a South African government school, and it was therefore supposed to teach 'Christian National Education'. 'Christian Nationalism' was the official ideology of the apartheid state. The 1960s and '70s were the high point of racial segregation. As Cardoso remarked later, 'Whenever a white was seen speaking in a friendly manner with a black, the other whites and other blacks thought it very strange and the police immediately thought about arresting both of them.' At Witbank Cardoso found himself with some 600 other teenage pupils, all white and mostly English-speaking South Africans. Day pupils came from the English-speaking community of Witbank. But Cardoso was in the boarding section with pupils who came from Johannesburg or further afield. They were children of white miners or farmers, and some were tough kids expelled from other schools. There was a smattering of foreigners – mostly Mozambicans, but some from Zambia or Kenya.

Cardoso did well academically, but disliked the school intensely. He recalled his school days in a series of articles entitled 'The natural order of things' published in the Maputo daily Notícias in 1983:

> At morning assembly on the first day of classes, my
> feelings were the same as those of many other pupils,
> especially the younger ones: we wanted the classes to
> pass quickly so that we could go on holiday again. To
> be at school, and a boarding school at that, was a kind
> of calvary. Holidays were the regular escape from the
> almost militarised world that school life imposed on us.

Cardoso did not fit in well with the school's 'regime of iron discipline', with the result that he was beaten regularly. 'In my four years at Witbank High I must have received some 300 strokes of the cane.' Under South African law, only the school director or hostel father were entitled to apply corporal punishment, but in reality 'all the teachers, and even the prefects, used to do it. The teachers who were most fond of this type of punishment had "special" canes. The most feared canes were made of fibreglass, sheathed in leather.' The instrument of torture struck the child's buttocks, drawing blood, and the weals would last for several days. 'The law ordered the punishment to be administered "without emotion."' Thus a pupil caught red-handed might be punished a few hours later, or even the next day. 'The anxiety of waiting made the punishment much more severe for those not used to it.'

There was some free time, and one way of escaping the boredom and violence of the school was to go deep into the bushes surrounding the hostel. There rebellious students had a small 'hide', used not for bird-watching but for smoking cigarettes. This was an entirely illicit activity. Cardoso recalled that in his final year he was caught smoking. A teacher then took him to his room and gave him two packets of Texan, a very strong brand, and ordered him to smoke them all, one after another. 'After 10 cigarettes, I began to feel giddy, by the twentieth I had clouds in my head, and with number 30 came the first vomiting. For the next two days I didn't touch a cigarette.' The effect did not last long – Cardoso was a chain smoker for the greater part of his adult life.

The institutionalised violence that characterised Witbank High is confirmed by Stelios Comninos, a South African of Greek origin who entered the school in 1968 and in later life was to become a firm friend of Cardoso. Comninos recalled that evening 'inspection' followed 'the mandatory "silent time," when we were supposed to read the Bible'. During the inspection 'everything was checked – rooms, beds, cupboards, shoes, uniform, etc. Of course, if anything was found wrong, we were whipped.' The evenings were a time of terror, when the Witbank pupils learnt what it meant to be powerless in the face of irrational tyranny. For the juniors, Comninos says, the inspections consisted of three teachers going from room to room searching for any infraction, however minor, of the rules. 'We would hear them coming down the corridor – stopping in each room, shouting and then whipping with the cane,' he recounts. 'Once in

Cardoso the schoolboy sportsman, holding a rugby cup, after a victory at Witbank High.

my room I got whipped for having squashed a mosquito on the wall – leaving a small blood stain.'

As Cardoso found, violence is infectious. School bullies took out their frustrations on younger boys and would visit their rooms for the sole purpose of beating them. Nearby there was a railway training college. Occasionally pupils from this college would slip into the Witbank High grounds and attempt to enter the girls' hostel. This called forth what were literally manhunts. Teachers formed the older boys into gangs of vigilantes to track down the intruders. Those caught were brought into the quad, forced to lie on the grass face down, and then whipped. Comninos found these scenes frightening to watch, and recalled some of the victims screaming for mercy.

There were four houses at Witbank High, each with its own songs and war cries. Sport was compulsory, but most pupils were enthusiastic about sporting activities and the prizes for individuals and houses. Cardoso played soccer as goalkeeper, and was athletic enough (despite the cigarettes) to represent Witbank High in rugby and gymnastics competitions. Yet he and Comninos were both outsiders. Thanks to their vaguely Mediterranean origins, they were not regarded as real whites, and were regularly insulted. Those of southern European ancestry were 'dagos' or, in the case of the Portuguese, 'sea-kaffirs'. And behind all the sporting spirit 'an ideology was inexorably consolidated', Cardoso remarked. On sports days there were no blacks anywhere to be seen – which consolidated the idea of South Africa as 'a country of whites'.

Apartheid looked stronger than ever. It had survived the post-Sharpeville crisis, and South Africa had consolidated an informal regional alliance with Portugal, and with Rhodesia, where the ultra-racist Rhodesian Front of Ian Smith had come to power and in 1966 had made a Unilateral Declaration of Independence (UDI), contemptuously ignoring the bleatings of Britain's impotent Labour government. The ANC (African National Congress) had been decapitated. Its leadership was either in jail or exile. Nelson Mandela was the moral victor in the Rivonia trial, but the movement seemed crushed, and the chances of organising armed struggle from distant capitals such as Lusaka and Dar es Salaam minimal. But there is no indication that any of this impinged on the lives of the white teachers and pupils at Witbank High.

For the last two years of school, Cardoso discovered, pupils enjoyed certain privileges such as 'regular authorisation to remain awake later than nine o'clock at night'. Prefects were chosen from those in Standard 9 (now Grade 11) who would actually make it into matric, and in November 1968 Cardoso was appointed prefect for the 1969 school year, after an interview by seven teachers. 'They wanted to know my opinion about a whole range of subjects. They asked me, for example, what I thought about the role of prefects. I said something confused such as "to keep order and represent the pupils." This talk of representing the pupils did not go down well with some teachers.' But he was still appointed.

Prefects had individual study rooms, and the right to 'skivvies' – the most junior pupils, who performed menial tasks such as cleaning their rooms, carrying their bags, and polishing their shoes. Prefects were allowed to hit younger students:

> So they were now part of the power structure. I recall
> that I didn't want to use some of the rights I now had,
> but I hit pupils frequently. I and the other prefects did
> so with perfect peace of mind. And the pupils would
> rather be caned by us than sent to the teachers, because
> in general we didn't hurt much.

The prefects behaved 'like people of power ... They were the depositories of future fascist behaviour begun at school.'

Cardoso was also enrolled in the school cadets, a paramilitary body for pupils. This involved a military uniform, a military band,

and marching once a week. Some of the more enthusiastic pupils learnt how to handle guns. Along with the military training went the apartheid propaganda. In the name of 'youth preparedness', the pupils were taught of the dangers of 'communism'. Cardoso's first published work – at any rate the first that I have discovered – saw the light of day in the Witbank High School magazine of December 1968. He wrote a poem entitled 'The Patriot', which took a pacifist position, querying the values of 'patriotism' drummed so frequently into the heads of white South Africans, in verses such as:

> To kill those that I don't know
> Will it be worthy, will it or not
> But I know I must show
> I am a patriot

Back home in Mozambique, the war had spread bit by bit, engulfing large areas of Cabo Delgado, Niassa and Tete provinces. Wars were also raging in Angola, and in Portugal's small West African colony of Guinea-Bissau. So the Portuguese army became larger, and the economy groaned under the burden of three wars. Some of the whites of Lourenço Marques could see the writing on the wall – the exodus of the Portuguese settlers began in 1970.

That year Cardoso entered the University of the Witwatersrand in Johannesburg, universally known as Wits. He opted to take a BA in economics, for no better reason than that his accountancy results at Witbank were good. He soon found this was a mistake, and in February 1971 switched to philosophy and political science. Cardoso embarked upon the philosophy course with some enthusiasm, apparently enjoying Plato's discourses, wrestling with such questions as 'How do we know that we know?' and designing syllogisms.

A diary from 1973 has survived. Switching from Portuguese to English and back again, Cardoso jotted down concerns that many students would find familiar. He worries about his health, he admits to smoking too much, he is concerned about not receiving letters from his girlfriend – and he experiments with cannabis. 'Last Friday night I went to a party and had too much Malawi grass. I resolved, after the effects had worn off, to be very careful about that sort of thing.' He was angered to read of a four-month jail sentence for a

Johannesburg boy and a Lourenço Marques girl caught committing unspecified 'indecent behaviour in some park in Beira'. 'It's a bloody shame for the human race to have narrow-minded people telling others how to behave, setting up a timetable for their lives,' he wrote. 'I felt like appearing in the centre of Beira totally naked. That would surely scandalise the decent ladies of the town.'

Occasionally he would stay up all night, playing the guitar with friends. He had arguments with other Mozambicans, whom he described as 'blind patriots' – those in favour of Portuguese rule. 'Sometimes I understand quite clearly why people like Socrates were and are sentenced to death,' he remarked. As a Portuguese citizen, against his will he was expected to do military service. In January 1973 he had to visit the Portuguese consulate in Johannesburg to arrange his 'exemption from the army until 1975'. Cardoso could now grow his hair as long as he liked; with hair flowing beyond his shoulders, plus a substantial beard, he began to look like the archetypal hippie. Cardoso recalls how, as he hitched a lift down to the Mozambican border, Afrikaners would yell from their open car windows, '*Jou kaffir boetie!*' ('You brother of a black!') Such motorists believed that Cardoso's hair plus his Wits T-shirt summed him up.

Wits was, in fact, far from a communist institution. It was a classically liberal university, and jealous of its academic freedoms. A minority of students were indeed vociferously opposed to apartheid. 'We protested, and we called strikes, whenever our student leaders were imprisoned or banned,' Cardoso later recalled.

> We marched through the streets, and we boycotted lectures when black student leaders were thrown out of their universities. All this sometimes resulted in some heads being broken or some days in a Johannesburg police cell. Only a minority of this minority undertook any serious work with the clandestine black union organisations. This small minority was constantly threatened by the police, and periodically its ranks, never very large, were thinned still further when the state banished or detained some of them.

The mainly white student demonstrations would make the front pages in a way that strikes by black workers, or the development of the black student movement, did not.

Only later did I understand what was at the root of this excessive publicity. It was that, whether they supported or opposed apartheid, history had to be made by whites. Involved in a game of opposition from within the system, and inebriated with the romanticism of street demonstrations, we were blind and deaf to anything that might have constituted genuine grass-roots work. Rich liberals and the children of rich liberals stayed at home condemning "police excesses" – most of the police were boers – but they didn't lift a finger against the might and designs of the regime's military and police apparatus. Only later did I come to understand that liberalism meant an excuse for not doing anything.

Understandably, Cardoso became a leading light in the Philosophy Society. It held 'Speakers' Forums' in the open air, on the Wits library lawn, which were a focus for political debate. It also arranged 'Alternative Philosophy' classes, introducing students to 'Continental' philosophers who were not on the official syllabus (such as Hegel or Sartre). One of the enormous advantages of taking the philosophy and political science courses was that banned literature suddenly became available. Under apartheid, the works of Marx, Lenin and other socialist thinkers were prohibited – unless you happened to be studying politics. At Wits, Marxist literature was kept in 'the locked room' to which only politics students were, on request, admitted. There, under lock and key, were not only the classics of Leninism, but also, and much more relevant, the key documents of the ANC and the South African Communist Party. Books, the possession of which would have earned an ordinary South African a spell in jail, were readily available to Cardoso in the Wits library. The university's erratic defence of academic freedom had created bubbles of open learning in a deeply repressive society.

CHAPTER 2

Revolution and Deportation

In 1974, the Portuguese regime collapsed. Tired of fighting three unwinnable colonial wars, the Portuguese army staged a lightning coup on 25 April, and the oldest dictatorship in Europe crumbled away in a matter of hours.

Right from the start, the coup had Mozambican links. One of the key figures in the coup, Otelo Saraiva de Carvalho, was born in Mozambique and had clear pro-Frelimo sympathies. Another Mozambican could claim credit for setting the coup in motion. He was the journalist Teodomiro Leite Vasconcelos, then working as a disc jockey on the Lisbon Catholic radio station Radio Renascença. He was in contact with some of the discontented young officers who formed the Armed Forces Movement (MFA). They needed a signal for the coup, and chose the banned song 'Grândola Vila Morena' by the left-wing singer José Afonso. It was thus a Mozambican who put 'Grândola' on the turntable at exactly midnight on 24 April. Vasconcelos would later become a leading figure in the Mozambican media, and a close friend of Cardoso.

The immediate task for the new regime in Lisbon was to end the African wars. The first post-coup president, António Spinola, wanted to end them on Portugal's terms: he had no intention of handing power over to the liberation movements. But only in Angola was the Portuguese army in a comfortable position, thanks largely to damaging splits within the main liberation movement, the People's Movement for the Liberation of Angola (MPLA). In Guinea-Bissau the military situation was hopeless, and the African Party for the Independence of Guinea and Cape Verde (PAIGC) had declared independence in 1973 – by the time of the April coup, more countries had recognised the nascent Guinean state than had diplomatic relations with Portugal. And in Mozambique Frelimo held the military initiative. It was striking deep into the centre of the country, threatening the Rhodesia–Beira railway.

By then, Cardoso was taking a course on African government as part of his philosophy and politics degree, which gave him the chance to write about the rapid changes taking place in his home-land as Portuguese colonial rule crumbled. His first essay on Mozam-bique was entitled 'Frelimo: Birth, growth and possible end of a revolution'. His tutor was not much impressed, scribbling in the margin: 'As a summary of Mozambique's revolution this (rather short) essay just suffices. Your analysis is rather thin, though, with the tendency to unsupported generalisations. 55%.'

But the downfall of the Portuguese empire could hardly be restricted to polite debate in university lecture rooms. Suddenly the flanks of white minority rule were exposed. Even the South African media understood that much immediately. On the very afternoon of 25 April, the Johannesburg *Star* wrote: 'If the young Portuguese offi-cers manage to hold on to power – and this seems likely – there will certainly be profound changes in southern Africa, leaving South Africa and Rhodesia increasingly isolated.'[1] It became obvious that, sooner rather than later, Mozambique would be independent and ruled by Frelimo. Led since 1970 by Samora Machel, one of the most charismatic figures produced by the southern African liberation movements, Frelimo brushed aside all of Spinola's attempts to per-petuate colonial rule. 'All or nothing' is not usually a good negotiat-ing stance; but in Mozambique in 1974 the Portuguese position was so weak that Machel knew no compromise was necessary. There would be no referendum ('You don't ask slaves if they want to be free,' Frelimo remarked). Instead the war would continue until Por-tugal accepted the principle of unconditional independence under Frelimo rule. Details of the handover and the transition period could be negotiated later.

The Portuguese revolution veered leftwards, Spinola fell, and the officers of the MFA, dragging the civilian politicians behind them, decided that it was in Portuguese as well as African interests to recognise reality and hand over power to the liberation movements. This would prove tricky in Angola, where the liberation movement was badly divided, but in Mozambique it was a relatively simple matter to arrange the transfer of power to Frelimo. The agreement to this effect was signed in Lusaka on 7 September 1974.

From the far right came cries that Portugal had been betrayed by its own soldiers. But in reality the recognition of Guinea-Bissau's independence and the agreement with Frelimo restored some honour to the Portuguese armed forces – the only alternative was to continue wars, which the great majority of Portuguese citizens had no interest in paying, let alone dying, for. Immediately the Lusaka agreement was signed – on the very same day, 7 September – far-right settlers calling themselves the 'Dragons of Death' or 'Moçambique Livre' ('Free Mozambique') staged a brief revolt, seizing the radio station in Lourenço Marques. Blacks in the Maputo suburbs rose, not against Frelimo but against those in the *putsch*. The Portuguese army, with Frelimo backing, had little difficulty in restoring order. For a few months, political parties had sprouted in the streets of Lourenço Marques, some of them openly colonialist (such as Fico, Portuguese for 'I'm staying' – they didn't), and others last-minute attempts to stop Frelimo, such as Gumo (Mozambican United Group). But 7 September was a turning point. The botched coup was a catastrophe for the anti-Frelimo parties. Most of them evaporated leaving little trace. Those of their leaders who stayed in Lourenço Marques were arrested. No one came to their defence.

The impending independence of Mozambique had a dramatic impact on its powerful neighbour, South Africa. Blacks there was elated, as were the handful of whites – notably among students – who actively opposed apartheid. The South African press could no longer ignore Frelimo. Cardoso noted that photos began to appear of Frelimo leaders in military uniform. They sometimes carried dismissive captions referring to Frelimo as 'terrorists'. But the word 'terrorism' did not strike fear into the heart of black South Africans. Cardoso later recalled: 'In Soweto and the other townships the black population cut out the photographs, threw away the captions, and hung them on the walls of their houses.' Cardoso himself stuck a newspaper photo of Samora Machel on his student wall. It was still among his possessions at the time of his death.

There were open pro-Frelimo demonstrations. Thus, two weeks after the botched September coup, black students in Durban and at the University of the North, in Turfloop, took to the streets to express their support for Frelimo. Summing up this period later, Cardoso wrote:

> In a matter of months, the name of Samora Machel was being painted on city walls, on the trains to Soweto, all over the place. The white establishment, normally more intellectually concerned with events in western Europe and in the US, suddenly realised it was in Africa. From one day to the next, the white left dropped its readings of Marx and Gramsci, and instead read voraciously the texts of Amilcar Cabral[2] or of Samora Machel.

Cardoso found a new role in this. As one of the few left-wing intellectuals in Johannesburg who was bilingual in Portuguese and English, he was called upon to translate Frelimo documents into English. They were used in public meetings and study groups, and were published in student magazines. Thus in mid-1975 *Wits Student*, the paper of the university students' union, published in full Cardoso's translation of Samora Machel's speech proclaiming Mozambican independence on 25 June. Initially, texts by Samora Machel were read out at well-attended public meetings. Then the South African police realised the implications of a revolution next door and began to crack down on Frelimo literature. Frelimo texts were now read in smaller study groups, to avoid police spies.

The 1974–75 period saw Cardoso move to the forefront of Wits politics. For perhaps 18 months, he was the best-known face of radical politics on campus. Alan Fine, who later also became a journalist, recalls: 'The Nusas [National Union of South African Students] left was on the defensive. Carlos came as a breath of fresh air, as someone who spoke his mind. He didn't give a damn about his image.' One close friend, Glynis O'Hara, who later also became a journalist, says, 'What separated Carlos from the other politicos on campus was his enormous warmth and passion. Although he was perfectly capable of holding his own in impenetrable, arcane debates about communism, capitalism, development, modernisation, and so on, he was actually a man of the people.' She thought Cardoso was eventually deported 'because he was so effective – he was busy converting a good proportion of the campus to communism'. Cardoso's friend Patrick Fitzgerald thought he brought to the Wits campus 'a realisation that there was an Africa beyond South Africa, with a liberation movement going on'. He even talked about the likelihood of guerrilla warfare. This was an extraordinary, not to mention dangerous, thing to say on a predominantly white university campus in 1974. 'He told people there would be an armed struggle in South Africa, if they weren't careful,' recalled Fitzgerald.

Wits had a students' representative council (SRC) that was not held in high regard by many of the students. In 1973, 14 candidates were elected unopposed to the 14-member SRC; they included three government spies, the most notorious of whom was Craig Williamson, who later proved to be an undercover officer of the security police. But by early 1975 the political situation on the campus had been transformed, and Cardoso decided it was worth running for the SRC in the March by-election. He distributed a roughly cyclostyled manifesto rejecting the line that students should just pass their exams and keep their noses out of politics. He called on his fellow students to 'transform the meaningless representative capacity of the SRC into a platform of conscious participation and hence into a source of political awareness'.

Cardoso's manifesto touched on none of the parochial issues which, according to conventional wisdom, were the key to winning student elections. More parking space for student cars, or the installation of pinball machines – these were supposed to be the winning issues. But the candidates promising parking facilities and pinball machines were thrashed. Not only did Cardoso top the poll, but he received the highest percentage of votes in the history of the Wits SRC elections, a record that was to stand for a decade.

Cardoso soon found SRC work deeply bureaucratic: one overwhelming by-election victory was not enough to change the culture. And with the approach of Mozambican independence on 25 June 1975, Cardoso was increasingly engrossed in Frelimo documents and attempting to give his English-speaking audience some feel for the Mozambican revolution. José Manuel believes that Cardoso's pro-Frelimo activities 'attracted the attention and rage of Portuguese right-wing individuals', who had him followed. For a time his life seemed to be in danger – but when the attack did come it was from the South African state, not the Portuguese vigilantes.

On 24 August 1975 he was detained, in a general clampdown on student activitists. The police handed Cardoso a blunt letter declaring: 'I have to inform you that the Honourable the Minister of the Interior has, by warrant under his hand, ordered your removal from the Republic of South Africa in terms of section 45 of the Admission of Persons to the Republic Regulation Act no. 59 of 1972.' This was a typically authoritarian piece of apartheid legislation allowing the minister of the interior to deport any foreigner if he considered this to be 'in the public interest'. There was no appeal procedure, and the minister was not obliged to give any reason. Cardoso had lived in South Africa for 10 years, his residence papers were in order, and he was not accused of any crime. None of this mattered: the apartheid law gave the minister absolute power over foreign nationals.

The police seized Cardoso, but did not bother to tell his family, his friends, or the university authorities. For three days nobody knew where he was; fearing the worst, students checked local hospitals and morgues. Eventually they found him in the notorious police headquarters in Johannesburg's John Vorster Square. He had been transferred there after a brief period in police cells in the suburb of Hillbrow.

It was in prison that Cardoso suddenly understood something that the apartheid regime had been successful in hiding from domestic public opinion. While on his way to the shower, he found a cell where the inmates were speaking Portuguese. They too were waiting for deportation – they had been arrested after fleeing from Angola and entering Namibia illegally. So why were they running away from Angola? Cardoso asked. 'Unita's killing whites now,' said one.

Another added. 'You can't live there any more, it's war everywhere, with Unita and the South Africans advancing northwards.' 'What South Africans?' asked the astonished Cardoso. 'What, you don't know? The South Africans are there inside Angola with battalions, tanks, artillery, and I don't know what else.' This was Pretoria's first major assault on the region. It was a massive military adventure which had been kept entirely secret, even from the whites whose children were fighting in Angola. Later, when the South Africans could hide their involvement no longer, they claimed they had gone into Angola in response to 'Cuban aggression'. But in fact the apartheid armed forces, the SADF, had occupied swathes of southern Angola months before Fidel Castro responded to the calls for help from the embattled MPLA. From that moment on, Cardoso was to follow events in Angola closely; at the peak of the Angolan war, his reporting was so accurate that it was reviled by both the South African and the Angolan governments.

At Jan Smuts airport on 1 September 1975, 50 students sang 'We shall overcome' as Cardoso was deported. With his hair flowing over his shoulders, smoking cigarette after cigarette, he talked quietly with a few friends until the time came to board the plane. It would be nine years before he set foot on South African soil again. In a typically petty act of revenge against this upstart foreign radical, the apartheid government deported him not to Mozambique but to Portugal, using the excuse that he held a Portuguese passport. In what may have been the first time that Cardoso came to Frelimo's attention, the new Mozambican authorities offered to pay for his air ticket from Lisbon to Maputo, but Jaime Cardoso turned the offer down. The family paid the fare. Eleven days after the deportation, Cardoso was back in Maputo, a Maputo in the first euphoric glow of revolution.

The university authorities had done nothing to stop the deportation, but they offered to allow Cardoso to continue his studies by correspondence and sit his exams outside South Africa. Patrick Fitzgerald wrote him a brief note with instructions about the type of letter he should write and where to send it. He offered to send him notes or tapes of lectures. The Wits deputy registrar wrote asking for a reply by 5 December 1975 as to whether he wanted the university 'to make special arrangements' for him to sit the exam in Mozambique in January–February 1976. Cardoso sent the university a polite refusal. Rather than resume his studies, he had entered the effervescent world of Mozambican journalism.

CHAPTER 3

'The New World is Already Being Built'

In 1975, when Cardoso took his first steps in journalism, he shared
with many of his colleagues a strong commitment to the ideas of
Frelimo and of its president. He fought for a journalism of intervention, a journalism that was openly political and ideological, and not
merely reporting. Looking back in 1990, he explained:

> I am speaking of a period that today is very difficult to
> understand if you did not live through it. There was no
> 'me' the journalist and 'them' the leaders. At the centre
> of the strongest feeling in the initial post-independence
> years there was the idea ... that journalists, party cadres
> and leaders were all comrades at their various posts,
> each responsible to the others in the struggle for the
> elimination of misery in Mozambique. They were years
> that will perhaps never be repeated in the life of the gen-
> eration to which I belong, now that today's accelerated
> stratification will certainly open breaches in the ideolog-
> ical fabric that was previously more or less homogenous.

In September 1975 Carlos Cardoso was an unusual phenomenon –
a white Mozambican flying into Maputo. Most of the white population was heading the other way. The exodus had begun in the last
years of the colonial war, but picked up speed after the fall of fascism
in Lisbon, and particularly after the failure of the 7 September 1974
coup. Within perhaps 18 months, as much as 90 per cent of the
white population left. Very few were thrown out by the new government. It was just a handful of Portuguese regarded as economic saboteurs who were given the '24/20' order (24 hours to leave the

country with 20 kilos of luggage). The vast majority left of their own free will, despite Frelimo's very public position that Mozambique was for all Mozambicans of whatever racial origin. The exodus split families; in general, the minority of whites who took Mozambican nationality were young. Frequently their parents left.

Cardoso found himself in just such a situation. His immediate personal drama was the breakup of his family. José Manuel was already living in South Africa, and by the time Carlos returned to Maputo his parents were preparing to leave. As far as Frelimo was concerned, the Cardoso family was Mozambican: Jaime and his three sons had been born in Mozambique. Furthermore, skilled managers such as Jaime Cardoso were in short supply, and Frelimo wanted them to stay. But Jaime had made his mind up, and nothing that his rebellious son Carlos said would change it. Jaime always maintained that he and Maria Luísa were not racists: they were leaving not because Frelimo was black but because it was 'communist'.

Carlos was together with his parents for just two months. Jaime, Maria Luísa, younger brother Nuno, and the beloved family dog Negrita left for Johannesburg on 5 December 1975. Maria Luísa wrote to Carlos shortly after Christmas. She missed him, and wanted to meet him in Swaziland (since he was banned from returning to South Africa) as soon as possible. 'Although you don't believe me, I love this country very much, and desire much happiness and much peace for all who live in it. I left Mozambique with tears in my eyes, and without any rancour.' She harboured some sympathy for her son's politics and wished him well on his chosen path. Her letter contained a bittersweet and all too accurate prophecy:

> Carlitos, I believe faithfully in your ideology because it is honest, and in others who are like you, but unfortunately you are few in number. Your struggle will be very tough. You will suffer immensely, indeed you are already suffering, but you don't give up. OK! You will be rewarded for all your strength, Carlitos, but not on this planet.

The two family houses in central Maputo were now in Cardoso's possession. In February 1976 came the government's nationalisation of all rented housing, and Samora Machel's ringing declaration 'Landlords? In our country? What do we want landlords for?' People who owned rented housing could keep two homes for themselves – one in the city, and a holiday home elsewhere. Everything else was to be handed over to the newly created state housing agency, Apie. This was mainly what changed the face of Mozambican cities, as black Mozambicans moved into houses and apartments that had once been rented out by Portuguese (and some Mozambican) landlords. Cardoso voluntarily handed over the house where his parents had lived to the state, although it had never been rented. Even in the second Cardoso house, which consisted of rented flats, he just kept the first-floor flat and gave the much larger second-floor one and the ground floor to the state.

Throughout the economy, experienced Portuguese managers were leaving; their places would be taken by young Mozambicans of all races who hoped their commitment would compensate for their lack of experience. Perhaps nowhere was this truer than in the media. Older journalists who had been mouthpieces for the colonial regime had mostly fled or been driven out before independence. Indeed, within days of the 25 April coup, the colonial censorship had been swept away. Journalists simply stopped submitting their copy to the censor. After the botched settler uprising of 7 September, any journalists ideologically committed to colonialism who had not been purged earlier, left. Before Frelimo leaders even set foot in Lourenço Marques, the media was solidly behind the liberation movement, and nothing embodied this spirit better than the weekly magazine *Tempo*.

Tempo and its parent company, Tempografica, were set up in 1970 by five journalists (José Mota Lopes, Ricardo Rangel, Ribeiro Pacheco, Areosa Pena and Rui Cartaxana) who had left the daily paper *Notícias*, then the main mouthpiece for colonial propaganda. They used Cartaxana's personal friendship with the last colonial governor-general of Mozambique, Baltazar Rebelo de Sousa, to obtain a licence to open a weekly magazine. They needed money, which they obtained from local businessmen, particularly Augusto de Sá Alves, a man with extensive interests in agriculture, trade and transport. This was an uneasy alliance between radical journalists and that faction of colonial capital that wanted to break free of restrictions imposed by the Salazarist regime. The journalists were minority shareholders – but they established an agreement with their financial backers under which the newsroom was entirely autonomous.

Tempo, though still shackled by colonial censorship, was the nearest thing to an opposition publication in Lourenço Marques. Some of the journalists, particularly Mota Lopes and Rangel, were already in contact with Frelimo. Mota Lopes was a clandestine member of Frelimo from 1971. There was an unwritten code of never writing about the colonial war. But editorial autonomy disappeared in 1972, when the magazine negotiated with Sá Alves for an increase in its capital. This generated a struggle between the journalists and the managers imposed by the majority shareholders. By early 1974, the magazine the five founders had dreamed of was virtually dead. What jolted it back to life was the 25 April coup in Lisbon. The pro-Frelimo journalists moved to reassert control. On the day of the coup itself, *Tempo* became the first publication to stop sending its articles to the censor's office. 'We were able to pressure the administration, which was still very strong, to accept this,' Mota Lopes recalls. It was in the pages of *Tempo* that the uncensored Frelimo was available for the first time to the public of Lourenço Marques, relying on material collected clandestinely by Mota Lopes. Leading *Tempo* journalists called for immediate independence, and in June 1974 *Tempo* became the first of the Mozambican media to visit Frelimo's liberated areas in the north of the country, and the first to publish an interview with Samora Machel.

After independence, when Mota Lopes was moved into the newly established ministry of information, the magazine was run by a troika of its most experienced reporters: Albino Magaia, Calane da Silva, and the country's top photo-journalist, Ricardo Rangel. This collective management was not part of the Frelimo style, and *Tempo* soon clashed with orthodox figures in the leadership, notably with the information minister, Jorge Rebelo. Rebelo was much admired for his integrity and utter incorruptibility. This went hand in hand with single-minded devotion to Frelimo. While he was willing to change his mind on many issues, these did not include his belief that the media must serve the objectives of the party. In mid-1975, *Tempo* was running several paces ahead of Frelimo. It was openly anti-capitalist, although Frelimo did not formally adopt Marxism-Leninism as its ideology until 1977. 'We were way to the left of Frelimo,' recalls Albino Magaia. And when journalists took positions to the left of the party, they would be labelled 'ultra-leftists'.

Carlos Cardoso applied to join *Tempo* immediately on his return to Maputo in September 1975. He left South Africa on 1 September, spent 11 days in Lisbon, waiting for his ticket back to Maputo, and started work at *Tempo* on 4 October. He was thus unemployed for less than a month. There were no great formalities. It was Mota Lopes who suggested that Cardoso work as a journalist. Immediately on meeting him, 'I was highly impressed by his culture, personality and intellectual honesty and I pushed him into *Tempo*,' Mota Lopes says. For the next three and a half years Cardoso was at the heart of *Tempo*, enduring the exuberant ups and depressing downs of revolutionary journalism.

❖

No revolutionary movement can have come to power in a more favourable climate of public opinion than Frelimo did in 1975. Organised opposition had disappeared after the collapse of the 7 September coup. Frelimo did not have to take over or purge the press. By the time the transitional government was sworn in on 20 September 1974, the media were entirely in the hands of fervent supporters of full independence under Frelimo. Many of the leading journalists had no difficulty in describing themselves as Marxists, although Frelimo's formal definition of itself as a Marxist-Leninist party still lay in the future. Nowadays we are so used to western ideologues denouncing Marxism as 'discredited' that we forget that in the mid-1970s it was capitalism which looked discredited. Capitalism and colonialism seemed inseparable, and it was Portuguese capitalists who were scurrying out of the country, taking whatever they could with them, and sabotaging their companies.

Furthermore, the world's leading capitalist power had just been humiliated in Indo-China. Mozambican independence was declared less than two months after the client regime in Saigon collapsed and Vietnam was united. Imperialism, it seemed, was on the run. The fall of the Portuguese colonial empire was not an isolated event but part of a worldwide trend. The Soviet bloc and China were regarded as natural allies. They had provided much of the military hardware and training for Frelimo's guerrilla war. Internationally, they were the bulwark to which radical third-world regimes could look for alternative sources of aid and, in extreme circumstances, for protection.

So in 1975 there was nothing strange or exotic about being a Marxist – Marxism had become the revolutionary mainstream. This was not something imposed on reluctant journalists from outside; instead it was eagerly embraced as a theory and methodology that helped make sense of the world. No leading journalist queried the one-party state. Nobody disagreed with the assertion that the one-party state was not only compatible with democracy, but that the 'people's democracy' it bought was a qualitative improvement over 'bourgeois democracy'. In the Mozambican landscape of those days it was impossible to find intellectuals who would admit to holding liberal or social democratic (let alone right-wing) views. Indeed, 'social democrat' became a term of abuse.

The Mozambican journalists of 1975 were not concerned with 'freedom of the press' as that phrase is understood today. The 1975 constitution said nothing about press freedom, and it was not until a decade and a half later that the country's journalists commented on its absence and did something about it. Indeed, press freedom was initially regarded as a bourgeois concept and as a smokescreen behind which monopoly capital manipulated the western media. In Mozambique it was openly recognised that journalists were not free agents: they were at the service of the revolution. They took sides – with the revolution and against reaction. And being with the revolution meant accepting the 'leading role' of the revolutionary party.

Frelimo enjoyed enormous prestige. It had defeated a Nato army and led the country to independence. It spoke out not only against colonial rule but against all the backwardness of Mozambican 'tradition', usually written off as 'feudal'. It was the sole modernising force in the country. In Samora Machel it possessed a leader of extraordinary charisma, a spellbinding orator, a man driven by a passion for justice for his people. Most Mozambican journalists would have followed Samora wherever he led. On 29 August 1975, Machel himself met with media professionals and made a series of off-the-cuff recommendations. His concern was to turn the Mozambican media into 'a revolutionary press at the service of the people, a press that portrays our revolutionary struggle'. Machel noted, and criticised, the failure of some of the media to break with the colonial style of writing. He saw nothing revolutionary in papers that thought they could adapt to the new situation by writing 'Love live Samora!' where they had once written 'Long live Salazar!'

The key points in Machel's speech concerned the relationship between Frelimo and the media. Who guides the work of the press? 'The party, only the party. It is the party that represents the totality of the struggle of the working classes ... There is a confusion among our journalists: freedom or anarchy. There is a confusion between liberty and liberalism.' Machel defined liberalism as 'lack of respect for structures, lack of respect for the political line that guides our work ... Lack of respect for discipline: where there is liberalism, there is no sense of responsibility.' We can't live with people who practise liberalism, warned Machel. 'Installing reactionary ideas means setting up a base, a camp of the enemy in our midst ... We cannot tolerate this ... Many speak in the name of the people in order to spread reactionary ideas against the people. These are forms of liberalism.'

Nobody objected: many of Machel's 'guidelines' were broad enough to bear considerable interpretation, and a discussion with the president did not sound like a set of rigid orders. Surely any future problems could be solved through dialogue? After all, were they not all – the leadership and the journalists – on the same side? There was a remarkable absence of cynicism towards power. Journalists might have reservations about this or that government policy, but nobody assumed that Machel and his comrades were driven by a lust for power, much less simple greed. On the contrary, Frelimo adopted a spartan style. There was no sign that the treasury was being looted to fill ministerial pockets. Apart from the usual transport and accommodation perks, the leadership did not enjoy many privileges. The government's austere behaviour was a source of pride: the country might be poor, but its leaders were honest. So any differences that might exist were viewed as differences among people who had the same basic objective, that of building socialism under the leadership of a vanguard party.

Has any other revolutionary movement in history ever walked into the capital city to find that all the journalists are already on its side? Much of the history of the press in independent Mozambique is the story of how Frelimo frittered away this priceless asset. For, rather than welcoming such a friendly press, Frelimo displayed, after the initial euphoria of victory, considerable suspicion. Much of the Frelimo leadership inhabited a different cultural universe from the young urban intellectuals running the newsrooms. As Machado da Graça put it: 'Right from the start, there was almost no dialogue. The government distrusted those newsrooms made up of young people, with a relatively high academic level, who lacked the military discipline that prevailed in combat zones, and who wanted an active and critical media. And, apart from all this, with a high percentage of whites.'[1]

Frelimo had developed its own media during the independence war, and it looked at the press in Lourenço Marques through the prism of its own experience. Its magazines and radio stations (in Tanzania and Zambia) were unashamedly agitational – they were part of a determined drive to defeat colonialism and secure Mozambican independence. When it took power, Frelimo tended to regard the Mozambican media as just a larger version of the media of the liberation war. Although the journalists all professed their support for Frelimo, Frelimo did not trust them. 'We knew nothing of Maputo,' says Jorge Rebelo. 'We were facing a completely new situation. Maputo was enemy territory. The enemy had left its seeds and its agents there ... Only with time and work did we get to know the journalists, and trust could be established.'

Most of the journalists had not gone through the guerrilla struggle: their experience of politics was largely of student struggles. Their Marxism was not monolithic – they came from various schools of thought, some influenced by the Portuguese Communist Party (PCP), one of the most pro-Soviet of western European parties, and some by Maoism. Exotic battles on the Portuguese left were to some extent mirrored among Mozambican intellectuals. One thing was very clear: the journalists were not used to taking orders. They had broken free of the colonial censor and had no intention of submitting to a revolutionary censor instead. They did not equate supporting the Frelimo line with obeying diktats from the ministry of information. The idea of instituting any regime of formal censorship was also repugnant to Frelimo. So there was never anybody with a blue pencil sitting at a ministry of information desk deleting paragraphs from the following day's copy of *Notícias*.

It soon became clear, however, that journalists were expected to censor themselves. The party had set down 'guidelines', and they were told to follow them. But the guidelines often proved vague, sometimes contradictory, and certainly did not provide instant answers to every problem that cropped up in day-to-day reporting. The most outspoken journalists fought, not for 'freedom of the press' but for the right to criticise. The major debate in the mid-1970s over what the press should write hinged on the terms 'criticism' and 'denunciation'. The difference between the two words was made clear in one of the working groups that prepared the 1977 First Information Seminar: 'The vanguard party distinguishes between criticism, the purpose of which is to consolidate the ranks of the working classes, and denunciation, which is part of destroying the internal and external class enemy, and its objective expression among ourselves.' Exposing economic sabotage by a fleeing capitalist was denunciation, but investigating problems inside the new state apparatus was criticism. Frelimo had few problems with denunciation, but criticism was a headache; for by reporting what was going wrong in government departments, the media risked treading on the toes of Frelimo leaders. To what extent could journalists report on incompetence, or even corruption, among state officials?

This question was far from resolved when Carlos Cardoso first sat at a typewriter at *Tempo*. For Frelimo, Cardoso was something of an unknown quantity. He had no background in the Mozambican student movement, he had no history of clandestine links with Frelimo. He had lived in South Africa for 10 years. Could he be trusted? Furthermore, his appearance set him apart from other journalists. At this stage Frelimo was strongly in support of neat personal appearance, particularly for anyone attending official functions. A suit and tie, and a crisply ironed shirt, or at least a safari suit, were *de rigueur*. Dress standards among radicals at the University of the Witwatersrand were quite different, and colleagues remember the Cardoso of late 1975 as a heavily bearded man with hair flowing over his shoulders, wearing a pair of dirty blue jeans and what appeared to be a rugby jersey. In short, he looked a bit like a hippie – at a time when Samora Machel had just declared, 'We would not like to see hippies here in Mozambique. Hippies bring negative values, they destroy the society we want to build in Mozambique.' Eventually Cardoso would come round to the Frelimo dress code, but in those early months, in the eyes of purists, he was condemned before he even opened his mouth.

Cardoso experienced the self-management of the *Tempo* newsroom for only a short period. In February 1976 Frelimo moved to exert some control over the wayward weekly: Muradali Mamadhussen was appointed interim director. This was one of the results of the Macomia conference of the Frelimo information and propaganda department in November 1975, which concluded that the media, though strongly pro-Frelimo, were not actually under party control. It called for an 'internal restructuring of the press' and restated 'the principle that it is up to Frelimo to direct the entire Mozambican media'. So there was to be no more rotating editorship. Rebelo asked the *Tempo* newsroom to propose someone for the post of director. When the journalists could not agree, the ministry simply imposed Muradali. He already had a job: he was national director of information (the number two in the ministry), and was expected to combine this with the post of interim director of *Tempo*.

Muradali was a charming, urbane man, but in Lisbon he had been close to the PCP and he was regarded as spokesman for a pro-Soviet line. He and Cardoso soon clashed. 'Muradali and Cardoso could not stand each other,' recalled Albino Magaia. 'For Cardoso, Muradali was a foreign body in *Tempo*. For Muradali, Cardoso was somebody who had infiltrated. They just couldn't get on together.' In an interview shortly before his death, Cardoso recalled: 'When we used to write articles heavily critical of the government or of a policy, no matter what it was, he tried to cut us. And we opposed this kind of censorship. So the relationship with Muradali was very tense ... he gave himself editorial powers and we denied them to him.' The tension would degenerate into shouting matches. 'There were incredible newsroom meetings ... We were screaming at each other ... There was a profound defence of the right to say what we believed in.'[2]

The newsroom walls were decorated with posters of revolutionary heroes: Lenin, Che Guevara and Mao Tse-tung. When a Soviet delegation was visiting the magazine, Muradali demanded that the poster of Mao come down. The newsroom refused: all the journalists, regardless of their attitude towards Maoism, united in defending the poster. It was a question of dignity. 'We were neither pro-Soviet nor pro-Chinese, we favoured a path of our own, a socialism made in Mozambique,' Cardoso recalled decades later.

Within the newsroom Cardoso was already gaining a reputation as the man who knew about South Africa and regional politics. Nobody else on the magazine had been educated in South Africa, and few Mozambicans spoke English with his ease and fluency. 'He was the person who contributed most to us understanding what was going on in South Africa and Rhodesia,' said Albino Magaia. 'He could discuss apartheid from personal experience. It was from Cardoso that I learnt what apartheid was doing to South Africans.' Cardoso was one of the few Mozambican journalists who understood the historic significance of the school students' revolt that broke out in Soweto in June 1976. He had no hesitation in going to Radio Mozambique to argue that the radio should interrupt its normal programming and devote all its resources to covering the unfolding drama in South Africa. 'There's going to be a revolution in South Africa!' he told the sceptical radio newsroom. 'He was much more excited about Soweto than anyone else,' recalled Sol de Carvalho, who was then a radio journalist. 'And he had a point.' But Cardoso's enthusiasm was not enough to persuade the radio to break from its routine: the Soweto uprising was just another international news item, albeit an important one. It was *Tempo* that put Soweto on its front cover, with some of the photos of the revolt that were to become internationally famous.

The article 'Soweto: the revolt which shook apartheid' is one of the first lengthy pieces that can be confidently attributed to Cardoso. This was a turning point, he argued: for 30 years or so, black South Africans had used peaceful methods of struggle, but these had met ever more savage repression from the apartheid state. 'Some 12 years after the imprisonment of Mandela and other ANC leaders, a qualitative change in the struggle is under way: pacifism has been abandoned, and the South African people are finally making use of the only remaining alternative, the mass violence of the people.'

Cardoso believed that the uprising shook the myth of 'racial superiority that is intimately linked to the myth that blacks are unable to struggle. Put simply, the myth says "The blacks can do nothing: they are peaceful and will be that way for ever."' This myth was now in tatters, as was that of the invincibility of the South African police. Nor was the uprising an isolated phenomenon – it was linked, albeit indirectly, to the armed struggles that had overthrown Portuguese colonialism. 'The Soweto revolt is the result of capitalist exploitation and of the humiliation imposed by racist ideology in all its details: it is also the inevitable result of years of armed struggle beyond South Africa's borders, which culminated in the independence of Mozambique and Angola. It necessarily points towards new revolts.'

This article is unmistakably Cardoso's on stylistic grounds, though it is not signed by him. Indeed, at this stage no articles in *Tempo* were signed, and the same trend can be seen in *Notícias*. For the younger journalists this anonymity was politically correct. 'Not signing our articles had to do with the idea that Frelimo was a collective voice,' recalls Mia Couto. 'The word "I" was suspect.' This was certainly the view of the party itself. Rebelo recalled that during the liberation war nothing was signed, not even poems: 'What was important was Frelimo, not the individual.' But there were other perspectives on anonymity. Older journalists took a practical view.

For Albino Magaia, anonymity was a defence mechanism. 'We thought it better not to put our names to articles, because *Tempo* was well to the left of Frelimo,' he said. Only in late 1977 did articles begin to appear under bylines.

The immediate crisis facing Mozambique was not with South Africa but with Rhodesia. Indeed, Machel had no doubt that southern Africa had to be liberated in stages: Ian Smith was the immediate enemy – Pretoria could wait. Frelimo had longstanding links with the Zimbabwean liberation movements, and in 1971 fighters of Zanla (Zimbabwean African National Liberation Army, the armed wing of Zanu, the Zimbabwe African National Union) were able to enter northern Zimbabwe via areas that Frelimo had liberated from Portuguese rule in Tete province. After Mozambican independence, the whole eastern Zimbabwean border became vulnerable to the guerrillas.

Attempts to persuade Smith to negotiate seriously failed; and so, on 3 March 1976, Machel announced that Mozambique was implementing UN sanctions against the Smith regime. That same night a radio station, Voice of Zimbabwe, operating with Radio Mozambique equipment, began its nightly broadcasts in English in support of the Zimbabwean liberation movement. The borders were closed, and Rhodesia lost its shortest and cheapest outlets to the sea. From now on, all Rhodesia's trade would have to pass through South Africa. Given the sharp divisions inside the Zimbabwean liberation movement, Mozambique sponsored a new force, the Zimbabwe People's Army (Zipa), which claimed, untruthfully, to be a merger of the guerrilla forces of the two established movements.[3]

Tempo covered the Zimbabwean struggle in great detail. The magazine's experts on Rhodesia were António Alves Gomes and Carlos Cardoso. Gomes described the division of labour as 'I did the reporting and Cardoso put in the analysis' (though this summary was rather unfair to both of them). Gomes and Cardoso were enthusiastic about Zipa, and for a time really did envisage it replacing the traditional liberation movements. Briefly, *Tempo* denounced both Nkomo and Mugabe as opportunists whose time had passed. A Cardoso article declared confidently, 'Nobody can rule Zimbabwe without Zipa or against Zipa.' In fact, key Zipa commanders supported Mugabe's wing of Zanu, and once Mugabe and Nkomo patched up their differences enough to form the Patriotic Front in late 1976, Mozambique no longer had any use for Zipa. Cardoso and Gomes performed a volte-face, accepting that any Zimbabwean armed struggle launched from Mozambican soil would be led by Mugabe and his followers.

Rhodesian incursions, which began even before the borders were closed, now became much vaster. On 9 August 1976, Rhodesian troops massacred about 670 Zimbabwean refugees at the Nyazonia camp in Manica province. This set the pattern for the next three years. The Rhodesians would announce operations in 'hot pursuit' of 'terrorists' – but most of the real targets were Mozambican civilian infrastructure or Zimbabwean refugee camps. Alongside this went the creation of what were once called 'pseudo-terrorists' – a Rhodesian fifth column within Mozambique. Under the guidance of the head of the Rhodesian Central Intelligence Organization, Ken Flower, units were formed out of former Pide agents and one-time members of Portuguese special units, defectors from the Mozambican army, and peasants who were simply pressganged in areas near the border.[4]

Thus was nurtured an 'opposition' to Frelimo. At first, neither the Mozambican government nor the press paid much attention to this phenomenon. It seemed little more than a propaganda radio station, Voz da África Livre (Voice of Free Africa), which gave its address quite openly as a Salisbury PO box. The radio spoke of a shadowy organisation supposedly called 'Magaia', but no more was heard of this name after December 1976. As from 1977, the name 'Resistência Nacional Moçambicana' was used. From the English translation, Mozambique National Resistance, derived the acronym MNR. Initially, the members of this hastily created opposition did not seem to know what they were called. RNM, Resistência, África Livre – all were used. The Portuguese abbreviation, Renamo, was not invented until 1983.

❖

From the vantage point of the early twenty-first century, the *Tempo* of 1976–77 belongs to a vanished world. The magazine had no hesitation in publishing verbatim every major speech (and quite a few minor ones) of Samora Machel. On the one hand, Frelimo expected no less – but then neither did *Tempo*'s public. In the politicised atmosphere immediately following independence, Machel speeches were a selling point. People wanted to read them. And *Tempo* could never have been accused of disguising its politics. When Mao Tse-tung died, his portrait occupied the entire cover (issue of 19 September 1976). For May Day 1976, *Tempo*'s cover was just the yellow star of internationalism against an all-red background. Inside, a photograph of Lenin occupied over half a page. The issue of 26 May 1976 carried a Portuguese translation of Engels's essay on the role of labour in the transition from ape to man. Short biographies of Marx, Engels and Lenin were published on 3 October 1976 on the pretext that Maputo streets had just been named after them. A famous chunk of *Das Kapital* on commodities, price and profit appeared in Portuguese translation on 17 October 1976. As the Frelimo Third Congress approached, so *Tempo*'s stance became ever more strident. On 9 January 1977 the cover was the new Frelimo emblem (a crossed hammer and hoe – the Mozambican hammer and sickle variant), with the slogan 'Long live the worker–peasant alliance!' The issue of 23 January had a picture of Marx on the front cover and Engels on the back cover, while page 1 declared: 'Long live the dictatorship of the proletariat, the highest form of democracy!'

Albino Magaia thought Cardoso was important in the developing politics of *Tempo*. 'He taught us Marxism,' he said. 'He could speak openly about Marxism. He was the first to speak coherently about Marxist philosophy.' *Tempo* used to have 'open meetings' of the newsroom for a couple of hours every Friday and Saturday, in which people were invited to say whatever they liked. Magaia recalled Cardoso's role in those meetings as that of a 'political commissar' who could dominate the discussion because he was better versed in Marxist theory than anyone else on the magazine. Later in his life, Cardoso scorned those who claimed that journalists were obliged to follow a Marxist line: '"Oh, poor wretches, we were under pressure!" What a lie! I was not forced to believe in socialism. I believed in socialism, and if Frelimo had not been socialist I would still have fought for socialism … In the most active part of the press, there was a consensus around socialist ideas.'

Of course, Cardoso's knowledge of Marxism came from his university course (the 'locked room' in Wits library), mediated through the anti-apartheid struggle in South Africa. This was rather different from the Marxisms flourishing elsewhere in the media, which were deeply coloured by the Sino-Soviet split. *Notícias* in particular was supposedly a hotbed of Maoists and other 'ultra-leftists'. A string of critical articles in *Notícias* led Rebelo to fire the paper's director in September 1976, following which 21 of the paper's journalists left. The new director, the young journalist Arlindo Lopes, had to produce the country's main daily without most of its experienced staff. The intervention in *Notícias* cast a shadow over the media. For Cardoso these events were symbolic of a blind devotion to orders from above which 'began to penetrate the entire Mozambican media', and of which the appointment of Muradali in *Tempo* had been a foretaste.

❖

Cardoso received letters regularly from his parents. Jaime and Maria Luísa were worried about his health: was he taking anti-malaria pills? his mother asked. They wanted to meet him in Swaziland (impossible, since he had no intention of using a Portuguese passport and had not yet acquired a Mozambican one). And in one unfortunate phrase, they suggested he should give up politics. This provoked a lengthy reply, the draft of which has survived among Cardoso's papers. (At least, the erasures make it look like a draft – but possibly it was the final letter, and Cardoso changed his mind and did not send it. In any case, it throws some light on his relations with his parents.)

> You ask me to abandon politics, that I should choose a mode of life essentially similar to yours. What you have learnt in life, the socialisation you have gone through, and which makes your awareness what it is today, has taught you that history is a repetition of cycles, identical in their definition: rich and poor, exploitation and exploiters, oppressors and oppressed, etc. etc. This

form of socialisation was characteristic of a particular phase of human development in which bourgeois ideology, the series of ideas and actions of which bourgeois ideology consists, ruled. You were taught that you should despise political thought.

'You were taught the first step to despise humanity, which is contempt for yourselves as political beings who can potentially transform society,' he admonished his parents. Each generation throws out something from the baggage of its predecessors, Cardoso said. But he had gone further than that: he had made a structural break with the past. 'I have denied, rejected, liquidated and I continue to liquidate in me your ideology,' he wrote. 'Knowing you as I do, I am perfectly aware that you want a new world of equality and peace. But your ideology teaches you that this is impossible because "there will always be rich and poor" etc. etc.' This was what Cardoso did not accept. He was certain 'that the new world is not only possible, but is already being built. I work for it consciously.'

'I cannot abandon politics because I, like anybody else, am a political being,' he declared. 'Do not ask me to commit suicide, or to die every day a little more.' He did not blame his parents for anything, he added, and he would willingly give them anything material he possessed – but they could not have his spirit. 'I have not written this letter to depress you, but to tell you once again what I have already told you so many times, and which has only been half understood,' he said. What must have particularly pained him was that he had in his hand his mother's birth certificate: at her request, he was dealing with Maria Luísa's rejection of Mozambican citizenship.

Friends from Wits contacted him. Frequently they complained that they knew nothing of what was happening in Mozambique. Although Mozambique was next door, disinformation in the apartheid media, plus the language barrier, meant that the revolution might as well have been taking place on the moon for all that the average white South African knew about it. 'We remain terribly uninformed here, and I would appreciate any news, comment, analysis of the Mozambican situation that you may have time to send me,' begged Sean Moroney. He was on the editorial board of a new publication, *The National Student*, and wanted Cardoso to write articles for it. Oliver Duke had left South Africa for London. He joined the semi-Trotskyist group, the International Socialists, and asked Cardoso to supply a 2000-word article for its magazine. Cardoso had difficulty in meeting such demands. He told Duke to contact the Mozambican support group in London 'since journalism here is a full time job, which means more than 10 hours work every day'.

But in February 1976 he did reply to a couple who signed themselves Richard and Liz, with his own analysis of the first months of Mozambican independence – quite at odds with the orthodox line of linear progress. The initial nationalisations of July 1975 (of land, education, medicine and law) 'blew the colonial bourgeoisie to pieces. Economic sabotage was the only option left open to them.' But the 'national petty bourgeoisie' tried to step into their shoes, and grew in strength 'through better salaries, purchase of houses, places in the government and party etc. That petty bourgeois rise was naturally accompanied by an equivalent rightism inside the party: misuse and abuse of power, corruption and organised disorganisation,' Cardoso argued. 'An African petty bourgeoisie, save some exceptions, is hardly a democratic force; on the contrary, its intention, its ambition as a rising class make it fully repressive. It is precisely this that we are fighting against.' Cardoso read the February 1976 nationalisation of rented housing as a blow against the petty bourgeoisie, who had seen 'their great opportunity for class growth and consolidation of their ideological objectives being abruptly taken from under their feet'. (He was certainly thinking not just of the apartment blocks vacated by the Portuguese, but of the Mozambican slum landlords in the suburbs, who were equally hard hit by the nationalisation.)

He had no doubt that an ideological struggle within Frelimo was under way. 'The struggle inside the party is permanent just as the class struggle is permanent,' he wrote. 'The left can come to power and in no time lose it through bureaucratisation and statization of the party ... Each crisis brings to the surface the contradictions lying beneath the false climate of cooperation, and use of the same terminology.' In this letter, for the only time that I have found in his writings, Cardoso used the term 'revisionist' to describe the Soviet Union – an indication that in early '76 he had at least some sympathy with the Maoist position.

Many of Cardoso's immediate friends were those who, like himself, were of European origin but who considered themselves Mozambicans and threw in their lot with the revolution. Several of them, such as Fernando Lima and Miguéis Lopes Junior, were among the *Notícias* 'ultra-leftists'. With Lima, Cardoso was to have a long, sometimes collaborative, sometimes conflictual, relationship. Like Cardoso's parents, Lima's had left the country, but they had gone to Portugal rather than South Africa. But Cardoso also moved in other circles. Revolutionary purists such as Lima and Miguéis criticised him for his friendship with 'revisionists' and 'centrists' including Leite Vasconcelos, now a senior figure on Radio Mozambique. In early 1976, Lima recalls, 'the left' in the media consisted of the core reporters on *Tempo* and many on *Notícias*, while leading figures on the radio were 'centrists'. After the upheavals in *Notícias* of September 1976, *Notícias* came to be seen as 'the right', the Radio was still 'the centre', while *Tempo* and the Mozambique News Agency (AIM – where Lima had moved) were 'the left'.

Now, three decades later, such labelling looks bizarre: it is part of a political landscape that has entirely disappeared. But in 1976, 'right', 'centre' and 'left' had nothing to do with whether you supported capitalism, the free market, neo-liberal economic theory and so on. It was assumed that capitalism was coming to the end of its life. Nobody was about to denounce Marxism (not publicly, at any rate). Rather, the clashes were on the terrain of Marxism and concerned attitudes towards the 'revisionist' Soviet Union and towards the role of the revolutionary party. Nobody doubted that there could only be one party, Frelimo – that was part of the shared Leninist heritage. But how Frelimo should interact with society (and particularly with the press) was a source of sometimes bitter disagreement.

❖

Cardoso was a frequent visitor to Vasconcelos's house, as were other radio journalists such as Orlanda Mendes, Sol de Carvalho and his sister Odete. Cardoso would frequently entertain these gatherings with his guitar. 'It was fun,' recalls Odete nostalgically. 'Cardoso was always welcome. In those days, he was always amusing and happy.' Orlanda Mendes recalls that 'Cardoso would always find something to argue about, even when people were eating or dancing.' Right from the start, she found Cardoso 'an intellectually honest and generous person. He was never able to stab anybody in the back.' Shortages began to plague Maputo in the late 1970s: friends would stick closely together to share the food and drink they had obtained, and to swap information about where prized items were to be found. Despite the shortages and the huge queues for desirable commodities, there were frequent parties, notably at Vasconcelos's house. 'For Vasconcelos, any commemorative date was an excuse for a party,' recalls Odete.

Odete's husband, Rui Pereira, had played bridge when he was studying in Lisbon. Now he introduced the game to Cardoso's circle: Cardoso, Vasconcelos and Abdul Magid Osman (later to be finance minister) were among those to whom he taught the game. As from 1977, they were playing regularly. Cardoso 'wasn't a good player, but he amused everyone,' said Pereira. Sol de Carvalho delicately described Cardoso's bidding as 'creative'. 'He wasn't a safe partner,' he said. Bridge was also one of the things that brought Cardoso into contact with South African exiles who were devotees of the game – notably the laywer Albie Sachs (now a member of the South African constitutional court), the former Robben Island prisoner Indres Naidoo, and Joe Slovo, chief of staff of the ANC's armed wing, Umkhonto weSizwe. At its height, this informal club was playing three times a week, often at Vasconcelos's house. 'They talked politics all the time at the bridge table,' recalled Sol de Carvalho. But according to Pereira, more of the chatter came from the Mozambicans – the South Africans, Slovo in particular, were not about to let down their guard and give ANC secrets away. The journalists assumed the apartheid regime had got it wrong – this affable, bridge-playing, middle-aged white man could not possibly be running an armed struggle! 'He looked nothing like the image of a tough military guy,' said Lima. Doubtless Slovo would have regarded that as a tribute to his effectiveness.

CHAPTER 4

Ultra-leftist!

The tensions of the 1976 newsroom battles dissipated with the First Information Seminar. The idea for such a seminar had been raised by Samora Machel at his meeting with the media in August 1975. It was taken up again by several of the most active journalists in 1977, and received the blessing of the leadership. For months the newsrooms throbbed with discussion. Everything was, in theory, open to debate. Problems of journalists' training, of how to distribute the written press, of advertising, of the use of Mozambican languages in the media, were all discussed.

But politics was becoming more structured and monolithic. The dynamising groups, the grass-roots bodies in neighbourhoods and workplaces that had been key to mobilising support for the revolution, were beginning to atrophy. And at its Third Congress in February 1977, Frelimo officially adopted Marxism-Leninism, and set out to structure itself throughout the country as a vanguard party built on orthodox Leninist lines. Even so, most journalists did not bother to apply for party membership: they were quite happy to support the revolution in a freelance way, despite Machel's strictures against 'Marxists without a party'. Machado da Graça recalls that in the *Notícias* newsroom of 1976 Arlindo Lopes was the only Frelimo member. Rebelo once asked Machado if he was a party member – he replied he had not asked to join 'because I don't like other people thinking for me'. Fernando Lima didn't join because he regarded Frelimo as going soft and social-democratic. Cardoso was out of step – he did apply, but never got beyond candidate membership.

Preparations for the seminar took place precisely when Frelimo was attempting to impose its version of Leninism – which entailed ensuring that the media worked as an arm of the revolution, under party guidance. Everybody had to be geared to the same goal, and steered towards it by Frelimo. The implications of this for the seminar were not clear at first, and the debate took off enthusiastically. Journalists were encouraged to analyse each of the media, looking at their strong and weak points. *Notícias* was in the firing line. This was not just a case of sour grapes from the journalists who had left *Notícias* in 1976 – one of the harshest critiques of *Notícias* came from Cardoso, who had never worked on the paper.

Cardoso's broadside began with an attack on the curse of protocol journalism, as in talking about the president.

> When the people talk of our president, they don't say 'Samora Moises Machel, president of Frelimo, president of the People's Republic of Mozambique'. The people say 'Samora', or 'Comrade President', and without that tone of severity that we, and many people nowadays, give to the word comrade … The people say Comrade President with joy, because they feel, they know, that he is their comrade … We should think very seriously about what this means, about the cultural distortion involved … Instead of looking for the popular feeling about the president, and taking this feeling into the media, we go straight to the fascist past of much of the Mozambican press, and from it we extract, mechanically, stereotypical formulae about how to inform people of events.

For the same reason, Cardoso objected to the constant photos in the press of Machel receiving ambassadors. 'The link between President Samora and the people is revolutionary, intimate,' he wrote. 'The relationship between President Samora and the people through our press is bureaucratic, it creates the idea of distance, and is thus counter-revolutionary. It is a way for the enemy to separate Comrade President from the working masses.'

What have journalists done to Frelimo slogans? Cardoso asked. They have sucked the life out of them. 'We have bureaucratised this entire language, bit by bit we have destroyed its mobilising and organising strength, its revolutionary content.' The classic case was 'A Luta Continua!' (The Struggle Continues!), repeated as mechanically and unthinkingly as 'amen' at the end of a prayer. But what does the struggle continue against? asked Cardoso. 'Against hunger, misery, obscurantism (the highest expression of human submission), but little of this struggle appears in the pages of our press.' He attacked the dull and grey nature of much *Notícias* writing. 'Our people are joyful. Our press is sombre. Our people laugh, sing, dance. Our press is the opposite of laughter.'

In a further series of notes for a debate on *Notícias*, Cardoso attacked the paper's foreign coverage, which he regarded as 'irresponsible'. An interview with the Zipa leader, Rex Nhongo, for instance, was 'all upside down, giving the impression that Comrade Nhongo is politically illiterate. It is not through this sort of transcription that we can mobilise the Mozambican people to support the struggle of the Zimbabwean people.'

Another case of serious irresponsibility was 'the news item on the jubilee of Queen Elizabeth of England with photographs and all, without comment, without any criticism' – in 1977 the British monarch celebrated 25 years on her throne, and *Notícias* succumbed to the frenzy of royalist sycophancy. 'When we attack the Smith regime, we are also implicitly attacking British colonialism, which is the historic cause of the Smith regime.' Cardoso pointed out that all British governments after UDI had collaborated directly or indirectly with Smith and 'with the oppression of the Zimbabwean people. And at this very moment, the British government is organising a series of manoeuvres to keep Smith in power until imperialism has set up its neo-colonial alternative.' This made the British government complicit in Rhodesian attacks against Mozambique. 'Because of all this, I think it irresponsible for a Mozambican journalist to publish news items without comment on British royal events; without even the minimum perspective of saying that all that is opposed to the interests of the working classes of Great Britain.'

But Cardoso went much further when he turned to the paper's coverage of industrial disputes, and accused it of becoming a mouthpiece of the internal bourgeoisie. When *Notícias* wrote of workers accused of disciplinary offences,

> there is not the slightest respect for those accused, for their human dignity. There is not the slightest investigation … You cannot treat an undisciplined worker in the same way you treat a bourgeois conscious of his class strength … As a whole, *Notícias* reflects the basic position of the internal bourgeoisie. It has no critique, it has no opinion. Every day it applies the bourgeois principle that the leaders make history … Failure to speak to the workers about their problems is to demobilise them, disarm them ideologically.

Notícias, Cardoso added, 'represents the type of journalism I would hate to see institutionalised in Mozambique'.

António Souto, then chief news editor of *Notícias*, recalls heated arguments with Cardoso on some of these matters. The urban elite, which was the main readership for *Notícias*, 'had to be shown that we had a state of our own, and a head of state. It was my mission to say "now we have a state."' So the constant references to Machel by his official titles was a deliberate choice, as was front-page treatment of Machel meeting ambassadors.

Cardoso also joined in criticising *Tempo* and Muradali's management of the magazine. There were 'incorrect work methods', including 'lack of theoretical discussion of the Frelimo political line, and of any kind of consistent ideological debate among the journalists'. It was wrong that staffers refused to sign articles, 'as if they were written by the people for the people'. *Tempo* had become characterised by 'mechanical repetition of Frelimo slogans, and a complete lack of critical sense in the articles. These do not transmit the social reality of the sharpening class struggle in the country.' State pressures were targeted too: 'When an article appears criticising a particular detail in a sector of state activity, immediately this or that official appears in the newsroom (or on the telephone) asking who wrote the article. This is a form of pressure that inhibits journalists.'

A dozen working groups were set up to prepare the seminar, and journalists were at liberty to take part in all of them. Minutes from the key group, on 'Criticism and Denunciation', indicate that the group was grappling with such questions as: Who undertakes critiques? Criticise whom (definition of the enemy and of priorities)? How to do it? What methods to use? How did the enemy react to criticism? And how did the people react? What about 'the bad interpretations' of criticism? These minutes ended with the ringing proclamation: 'The meeting also agreed that the final document will not be a compromise document, but a revolutionary document, that is, in agreement with the Frelimo political line.' Of course, everyone could declare themselves supporters of the party line as long as Frelimo had not made it clear what that line was.

As part of the preparations, leading figures were invited to give lectures at the journalists' club. This was an opportunity for some heresy from within Samora Machel's inner circle. Machel made a point of surrounding himself with intellectuals: he chose as advisers people who might very well disagree with him. The first director of Machel's office was the abrasive Marxist, Sérgio Vieira, and his deputy, Luís Bernardo Honwana, was one of the country's leading writers, whose collection of short stories, *We Killed Mangy-Dog*, is widely regarded as a masterpiece of Mozambican literature. Another Machel adviser, Aquino de Bragança, was the director of the African Studies Centre at Maputo's Eduardo Mondlane University. Aquino and Honwana were open, inquisitive figures, who actually enjoyed the company of journalists. Aquino, speaking at the journalists' club on 13 August 1977, remarked that 'bourgeois' journalism could often be much better, from a professional standpoint, than journalism of the left. He recalled that when he was in Moscow, since he was unable to read Russian, he looked for papers in French or English, and found that *L'Humanité*, the daily paper of the French Communist Party, was the only one readily available. 'After reading it, I was convinced they were going to take the Bastille,' he remarked drily. He had to find someone with a subscription to *Le Monde* if he wanted to know what was going on in the world.

But the most famous of these talks was delivered by Luís Bernardo Honwana. Some of what he had to say was music to the ears of the *Tempo* revolutionaries.

> The repression of individualism has led to the disappearance from articles of the names of their authors ... But also, since it has been misinterpreted, it has led to the disappearance of editorials, of regular features, of the search for news, of investigative journalism, of the liveliness of a media that ought to be young, flexible, dynamic, mobilising ... The journalist has become a media official. His work consists of taking the official photograph, publishing an entire speech, putting slogans into the headline ...

These words clearly resembled the complaints that Cardoso and others had been making against *Notícias*. Like Cardoso, Honwana thought the media had forgotten how to smile. 'Humour has been expelled from the Mozambican media. Maybe they think that in order to be revolutionary, you must be austere, grey and sombre,' he said. 'Optimism, joy, laughter – maybe these things all belong to the bourgeoisie, to the reactionaries.'

But Honwana's lecture coincided with the return of Jorge Rebelo from a trip abroad. His first intervention took place immediately after Honwana had finished speaking. According to Machado da Graça, 'When the talk was over, the then minister of information brought the question of criticism to the debate, and heard some interventions on this theme. His response was so violent that everybody understood that the work was undergoing a 180-degree change of direction.'[1] After 25 years, nobody (including Rebelo himself) can remember exactly what the minister said. But the general feeling among participants is that Machado da Graça was right: a promising experiment in free thinking was being whipped into line. Cardoso assumed that Rebelo had been briefed 'by his yes-men', and said what he witnessed that night 'was a wipe-out'. 'Rebelo felt that a group of experienced intellectuals was trying to impress on the media a line that was independent of Frelimo,' said Arlindo Lopes. 'Rebelo felt marginalised. He made his intervention in order to regain control.' Orlanda Mendes recalled: 'I felt Rebelo was treating us as enemies of this country, as if we were an undisciplined and chaotic bunch of liberals.' It was then that it became clear to her that 'Frelimo did not trust journalists'.

The immediate result of Rebelo's intervention was that a drafting commission was set up to rewrite the documents for the seminar. Sol de Carvalho, who had chaired some of the meetings on 'Criticism and Denunciation', found that the document from the group was 'unrecognisable' after the commission had worked on it. The key paragraphs insisted on party guidance of the media: 'In their work, journalists come across mistakes and deviations within, or practised by, party and state structures ... Immediate publication as public criticism would have no other effect than contributing, in practice, to an attack against power and the state.' The right thing to do was for the reporter 'to communicate the mistakes or deviations noted to the relevant party or state bodies.' The facts could then be published alongside 'measures taken by the party or state to solve the problem'. The document was silent as to what journalists should do if the 'relevant bodies' ignored warnings of deviations.

The dilemma facing Mozambican journalists who wished to criticise anomalies was summarised thus by Albino Magaia:

> You made a denunciation or even a simple criticism, and you were accused of serving 'the enemy', and of destroying 'the people's gains'; you kept quiet, and people stopped believing you; you had a meeting with the president of the Republic, with Samora, and he urged you to denounce anomalies. When you found and denounced the first one, you were immediately accused (but not by the president) of criticising 'outside of the structures'.[2]

Cardoso was not happy with the outcome of the seminar. 'For me it was a disappointment,' he recalled in the last interview he ever gave. 'I hoped that the Seminar would expand journalists' freedom a little further. And it did not expand it – quite the reverse ... Those who were prepared to take orders by telephone ... consolidated their position by the end of the seminar. The left in the media was defeated at this seminar.'

❖

Within a fortnight of the seminar, *Tempo* had a proper full-time director. At Muradali's suggestion, Rebelo appointed Luís David – a decision that Gomes said took everybody else in the newsroom by surprise. It should not have done – after all, Luís David had been interim news editor since November 1976, when the journalists had been unable to agree who should do the job. Rebelo held a meeting with the *Tempo* staff in late September 1977, and towards the end announced the appointment of Luís David as director. 'Is anybody opposed?' he asked. One hand shot up, that of Carlos Cardoso. He later recalled, 'I was frozen and felt myself weakening. But a moment later I summoned up my strength and asked to speak.' But Rebelo would not accept opposition. He told Cardoso to sit down and said that the appointment was in the name of the Frelimo standing political committee. Again Cardoso asked to speak, and again Rebelo refused. When he tried for a third time, Rebelo lost his temper and called Cardoso 'an ultra-leftist and a *nitista*.'

Ultra-leftist was a standard Leninist insult – but to be called a *nitista* was more serious. This term, entirely forgotten nowadays, derived from the Angolan minister of the interior, Nito Alves, who led a coup attempt against the government of Agostinho Neto on 27 May 1977. Some of the best cadres of the MPLA, notably the finance minister Saidi Mingas, were killed by the *nitistas* before the coup was crushed. Nito Alves was usually described as an ultra-leftist, and so the implication was all too clear: Beware of these ultra-leftists! Their politics are a threat to the state and might lead to murder.

What Cardoso wanted to say, he wrote later, was that Luís David 'in none of the regular *Tempo* meetings took any political positions. He kept quiet like someone afraid to say something wrong.' But he had also heard reports that David 'had belonged to the shadow office of the last colonial governor, Pimentel dos Santos. I only wanted this to be cleared up by those who knew him.' And prior to independence David had indeed played a minor role in a colonial 'analysis office'. Cardoso's main objection to David was not political but professional: he thought David did not possess 'the slightest dynamism to head a magazine'.[3]

After this meeting Cardoso fell into depression. He was so disheartened, he thought of resuming his academic studies. He went to the Lesotho Embassy to ask about the possibility of enrolling at

Roma University in Maseru. There he might be able to finish the course he had begun at Wits. Work at *Tempo* became 'a mechanical gesture' as the magazine slipped into 'the most bureaucratic mediocrity so far experienced'. But Cardoso also recognised that David 'was a tough organiser and forced everyone to meet deadlines'. Also, under David the old principle of anonymity was jettisoned, and signed articles began to appear sporadically. The first one to bear Cardoso's name appeared on 30 October 1977, under the title 'South Africa: Vorster bans'. It dealt with the regime's closure of the papers *The World* and *The Weekly World*, and a fresh round of detentions and bannings. This was when the government outlawed Saso (the South African Students Organisation, for black students weary of what they saw as weak white liberalism in Nusas), the Black People's Convention (the political wing of the Black Consciousness Movement, which drew on the thinking of murdered activist Steve Biko) and 16 other organisations.

Luís David did not last long as director. In a few weeks Rebelo changed his mind, and accepted that Cardoso had been right. He said as much in another meeting with the *Tempo* staff, in February 1978, at which he announced the removal of David. This was an altogether livelier event than the meeting of September 1977. At one point, according to Alves Gomes, Cardoso declared he could only think of one person who could run the magazine. 'Who?' asked Rebelo. 'Me,' came the confident reply. Rebelo and everyone else in the room burst out laughing. In fact (as Cardoso must have known), the party had already decided to appoint Alves Gomes. He was called to a prior meeting in the ministry of information and asked if he wanted the job, and he accepted.

Under Gomes, the magazine became more daring – some would say outrageous. Twice *Tempo* so annoyed Frelimo officials that it was pulled off the streets. The first of these incidents occurred with the issue of 2 April 1978. The magazine decided to break taboos on sex and reproduction by printing photographs of a woman giving birth (the woman in question had consented, and the women workers at *Tempo* decided which of the pictures should be published) – and the Mozambican Women's Organisation, a body set up by Frelimo, 'was completely scandalised', Calane da Silva recalled. The order went out from the ministry of information to seize all the copies. But Frelimo failed to understand the dynamics of *Tempo*: the magazine went on sale at about 07.00 on the streets of Maputo (and copies for the provinces were dispatched on early morning planes). By the time the party had digested the contents, most of the copies had already been sold. Gomes recalled that only 100 copies of the offending issue were brought back. The magazine put out a second issue for that week, with the same number of copies, and sold out again. Gomes regarded the party interference as a blessing in disguise – a licence to print more magazines and make more money. Cardoso thought the birth pictures had been a mistake and had given genuine offence to women who felt their privacy had been invaded. Gomes was not so sure: he noted that many of the letters of protest *Tempo* received came from the same place and seemed to have been orchestrated. Nonetheless, he issued an apology two weeks later. 'We had a very puritanical attitude,' Rebelo admits. But seizing the paper was a serious mistake. 'It just meant that more people wanted to read it.'

The magazine functioned perfectly well even though its mother company had been deserted by the shareholders. In legal terms it was a mess – but it was making a profit, and never paid its workers late. 'We were highly organised,' Cardoso recalled, 'much more organised than the Council of Ministers (the Cabinet), which worked on Monday and rested on Tuesday, Wednesday and Thursday. We worked from morning to night, sometimes until midnight. We worked and we put that magazine onto the streets without fail. Clearly we weren't yes-men,' he added. But they found themselves under purist fire 'because somebody had long hair, somebody wore jeans, somebody hadn't polished his shoes'.

❖

April 1978 saw the founding conference of the National Journalists Organisation (ONJ). There was substantial mobilisation and debate prior to the conference – but not on the scale of the seminar. Journalists were becoming sceptical. Rebelo opened the conference and could not have been clearer on the role Frelimo envisaged for the ONJ: 'The organisations created by Frelimo are extensions of itself, arms to carry out its policies.' Mozambican cities, said Rebelo, had been enemy fortresses, and not merely in the military sense. 'They were also fortresses of enemy ideology, the nurseries where colonial capitalism nurtured and permanently developed its ideology of oppression and exploitation … In this phase ideological struggle becomes increasingly important,' stressed Rebelo, 'because the battle we wage for mentalities is ever more decisive … Our journalist must be the journalist of the transition to socialism … he must fight the tendency to become a media bureaucrat, passive and indifferent to the acute class struggle that characterises this phase of transition.'

Commitment to the revolution was the key, he declared. 'For the journalist, there is no neutral ground: he is either with us or against us. He is either with the people, living and suffering their problems, sharing their joys and victory, or he is against the people; he is either with the party, accepting its leadership and guidelines, or he is against the party.' The media were to speak for the vanguard party. As Rebelo put it: 'Journalists are propagandists for the values of the new society we wish to build.'

Cardoso wrote the *Tempo* summary of the conference that appeared in the issue of 23 April 1978. He was optimistic. 'With the creation of the ONJ, the journalist is not dying: what is dying is his isolation from other journalists, it is the ineffectiveness of isolated action that is dying,' he wrote. The conference had stressed the need for 'people's correspondents' – people who could collect news but were not trained journalists. Cardoso was enthusiastic about this: indeed, throughout his life he believed that the best journalists would come from where the stories were happening, and not necessarily from faculties or schools of journalism. He called for the 'demystification of journalism' by expanding the network of 'people's correspondents'. The quality of what they wrote could be improved through 'basic journalism courses'.

> In ending the monopoly on the practice of journalism, many working men and women will acquire the theoretical data allowing them to make new, more correct analyses of their own lives, and of the society surrounding them … A society that does not examine itself – in

the factories, in the *bairros*, in the schools, everywhere
– can never be a socialist society.

But Frelimo's determination to control the organisations it set up
proved highly damaging. It was the party which chose the ONJ leadership and presented a list to the conference, which simply approved
it. Machado da Graça later wrote: 'Clearly this way of appointing the
organisation's leaders transformed it from the start into what it in
fact became: an amorphous body that was inoperational for many
years.'[4] And it wasn't just the method of election that was problem-
atic – it was the candidates chosen by Frelimo. The ONJ leadership
was filled with people who were already directors or editors, because
these were the people whom the party knew and trusted. They were
precisely the people who could never have time to devote to the
ONJ. There was no full-time general secretary: the man chosen for
the job, Rafael Maguni, was already running Radio Mozambique. In
practice, the ONJ was left to drift. Its premises, once the Lourenço
Marques English Club, had been given to the journalists by Machel
himself. But the place was allowed to get run down and soon became
little more than a bar, a cheap restaurant and a handy spot to hold
press conferences. The once excellent sports facilities fell into dis-
repair. With a passive membership and an absent leadership, equipment deteriorated or disappeared.

Tempo continued to cover the Zimbabwean war blow by blow. The
word Zipa dropped out of sight. The reality was that Zanla was operating out of Mozambique, Zipra out of Zambia, and Mugabe and
Nkomo put on a diplomatic show of unity via the Patriotic Front.
The British and American governments made a series of proposals
which looked like a trap that, it was imagined, the Zimbabwean
nationalists would reject. But instead, the Patriotic Front and the
Front Line States accepted the proposals as a basis for negotiation,
and Smith produced his own 'internal accord' with a handful of black
politicians (Bishop Abel Muzorewa, Sithole, and a tribal chief named
Chirau) who had little or no credibility. As the year wore on, Zanla's
war spread across all of eastern and central Zimbabwe. Attacks were
increasingly daring, and, on 11 December 1978, 25 per cent of

Rhodesia's fuel reserves went up in smoke in a Zanla attack on the fuel tank farm on the outskirts of Salisbury. Such a raid, wrote Cardoso, imposed 'on the regime, on the settlers and on the world the image of a guerrilla force able to reach the heart of the enemy fortress'.

The tanks belonged to prominent western oil companies – Shell, BP and Caltex, all openly violating UN sanctions against Rhodesia. 'It is public knowledge that the British and US governments have downgraded their intentions of fighting the oil companies who break the sanctions against Rhodesia through the regular supply of fuel to the Salisbury regime,' Cardoso's article continued. Hypocritically, the Bingham Commission was set up to investigate the sanctions-busting – when everybody knew it was happening. 'With or without the commission, it is certain that the fuel that went up in flames in Salisbury came from the west … But this attack has reaffirmed the obvious: the Smith regime has one foot in the grave.'

Cardoso's last signed article as a *Tempo* reporter, in the issue of 11 February 1979, also dealt with Zimbabwe. He spoke with four white prisoners whom Zanla had captured inside Rhodesia, marched over the border, and released into the hands of Amnesty International at a press conference in a Maputo hotel. The four – Johannes Martins, Thomas Wigglesworth, John Kennerley and James Black – said they had been well treated throughout. Wigglesworth, who was a retired major in the British army, told Cardoso, 'I was isolated for about a month, but I was always treated courteously. The guerrillas have a tough life, but what little they had, they shared with me.' Asked to comment on Zanla's behaviour, he replied, 'As a professional soldier, I was surprised at their efficiency on the ground, their discipline, and particularly their high morale.' Johannes Martins had a heart condition, so the Zanla guards always let him rest. 'President Mugabe came to see me twice in the bush,' he said. 'He asked me if I was well, and if the guerrillas were treating me decently. So I'd like to express publicly my thanks for the fact that they never treated me badly.'

❖

Cardoso's job in *Tempo* suddenly ended when a second issue under Gomes's management was withdrawn by order of the ministry. In the 4 February 1979 issue an article by Miguéis Lopes Junior described an extraordinary meeting of the coordination bureau of the Non-aligned Movement held in Maputo. The story clearly showed that the movement's unity was a myth, and attacked one of Mozambique's allies, Yugoslavia. Gomes stood by the article and told Rebelo that, if Frelimo was not happy with his performance as director, then he would resign. Rebelo immediately accepted Gomes's resignation, and a shake-up in the staff followed. Mia Couto was appointed director. Gomes went on holiday but eventually returned as *Tempo*'s resident expert on Zimbabwe. Miguéis was transferred back to *Notícias*, Mendes de Oliveira went to the experimental television station that was being born, and Cardoso was dispatched to the cultural section of Radio Mozambique. 'They separated us,' remarked Gomes.

Although many years later Cardoso remarked that he was dumped 'on the shelf', his colleagues recall him throwing himself into his work at the Radio with enthusiasm, as a challenge that he readily embraced. As an amateur musician and poet, Cardoso was no stranger to cultural matters, and had written several cultural pieces in *Tempo*, including an obituary of Charlie Chaplin. He worked with Manuela Soares under the direction of Santana Afonso, who became well known for his children's programmes and songs. 'We increased musical production and theatrical production,' said Soares. 'Cardoso was involved in all of this. Sometimes he was both director and actor in the radio plays.[5] There was a strong artistic bent in Cardoso. He was versatile. He was passionate about life. And he never did anything he didn't enjoy doing.'

But by now, Cardoso had come to the attention of Samora Machel. Probably the first time Machel met Cardoso was when he covered a presidential visit to Nampula province in 1977. As happened frequently on such visits, Machel gave the reporters the occasional off-record briefing – and was impressed at the questions coming from the young *Tempo* reporter. Too often reporters assumed that, if the president wanted to talk to them, it was to 'transmit guidelines'. But Cardoso assumed that a discussion goes both ways, and that Machel wanted to hear from them too. Lima, who was also on the Nampula trip, recalls Machel's surprise at running into a journalist who was not afraid to make critical comments. Cardoso told

President Samora Machel makes a point to Cardoso over a cup of coffee, 1983.

Machel that the Nampula provincial officials were showing the president only what they wanted him to see. It was at this time that Machel told government protocol officers to treat the press with some respect. 'The journalists don't eat in the kitchen,' he ordered. The reporters, he said, were as important as anyone else on a presidential delegation, and in order to report accurately they had to be close to him and to other government leaders.

Machel also came to appreciate the work undertaken at *Tempo* by Cardoso and Gomes on the unfolding dramas in Rhodesia and South Africa. According to Sérgio Vieira, 'Samora liked Cardoso a lot – which doesn't mean he always agreed with him. He respected the quality of his analysis. But he didn't like his tendency to jump to conclusions before all the pieces of the puzzle were available.' Rebelo recalled, 'Samora appreciated people who spoke openly of problems and were not afraid of criticism. He liked people who were not cowards and opportunists, and who said what they thought.' Samora's widow, Graça Machel, agrees: 'The people who challenged Samora the most were Cardoso and Aquino,' she said. 'They were bolder, and prepared to criticise. The kind of questions Cardoso would raise were unusual. That aroused Samora's interest. So they had a strong intellectual relationship – even when they disagreed.'

She could see a certain similarity between the two. 'When Cardoso embraced a cause, he did so with passion, almost with obsession. He pursued it to the end, he wouldn't let go. Samora was like that too. They had the capacity to look to the long term, and so they were both misunderstood.' But perhaps the strongest resemblance Graça could see was that both Machel and Cardoso were utterly fearless. 'Samora wasn't afraid of anyone. Neither was Cardoso – he wasn't even afraid of Samora.'

❖

Meanwhile, negotiations had opened in London to solve the Zimbabwean crisis. Mozambican journalists (notably Gomes and Iain Christie, the Scottish-born journalist who was training the Zimbabweans on the 'Voice of Zimbabwe') went to London to follow the talks that produced the Lancaster House constitution. Cardoso followed from afar. This was his route back into political journalism: once a week, Gomes did a lengthy programme on the state of the Lancaster House talks for Radio Mozambique, and Cardoso was on the other end of the line, following up with a detailed interview. Eventually, Lancaster House produced a constitution for an independent Zimbabwe, and a blueprint for elections to be held in February 1980. The final stages of the negotiations saw a strong input from Mozambican diplomacy, with Machel himself leaning heavily on Zanu. Machel recognised the Lancaster House constitution, despite obvious flaws such as the racial franchise, with 20 seats reserved for the whites, as the best deal the nationalists were likely to obtain. He saw no reason why Mozambique should be sacrificed any further for marginal improvements here or there in the text. So Zanu was free to continue the war if it liked – but without Mozambican support. Mugabe signed.

Machel had one enormous advantage over his Front Line colleagues, who were mostly still backing Nkomo. He had troops inside Zimbabwe: Mozambican units had been fighting alongside Zanla since 1978. The Mozambican government kept quiet about this and so, oddly enough, did the Smith regime. Mozambican military intelligence was extremely well informed about the situation on the ground. And the message they sent back was: Don't worry, in any free election Zanu will score a massive victory.

The Rhodesians dreamed of marginalising Zanu: they pinned their hopes on a reasonable electoral showing by those former nationalists who had defected to Smith (notably Muzorewa). After the vote, a coalition between Muzorewa, Smith and Nkomo, it was imagined, would keep the 'Marxist' Zanu in the cold. The Rhodesians wanted to detach Nkomo from Mugabe. So they must have been as surprised as many observers in the Front Line States (but not in Mozambique) when the Patriotic Front simply broke up. The alliance had always been uneasy, and now Zanu announced that it was standing alone. Nkomo was shocked: he had assumed that the two movements would fight the election together, and that, as the elder statesman, the father of Zimbabwean nationalism, he would get the top job after independence. But Mugabe knew that internecine struggles within Zimbabwean nationalism, and the course of the war, had reduced Nkomo to ethnically based support in Matabeleland. He calculated that he could win the election without Nkomo. Mugabe's decision made political sense, but it was to leave a legacy of bitterness. Both nationalist movements swiftly appropriated the name of the Patriotic Front, becoming Zanu-PF and PF-Zapu.

Just two Mozambican journalists, Alves Gomes and Carlos Cardoso, covered the Zimbabwe elections from start to finish. Gomes believes they were handpicked by Samora Machel, though it is unlikely that Machel would have taken this decision without at least consulting Rebelo and Mota Lopes. Gomes planned to travel overland, accompanying Zanla commander Josiah Tongogara. But Tongogara's death in a traffic accident delayed Gomes's arrival – and so Carlos Cardoso became the first journalist of independent Mozambique to set foot in a country now in transition from Rhodesia to Zimbabwe. When Gomes arrived, the two reporters divided the work: in principle, Cardoso would file pieces for the radio, while Gomes wrote articles for *Tempo* and *Notícias*. In practice, Cardoso was at heart a print journalist, and much of the coverage of the elections in *Notícias* was from his pen.

Mugabe returned from Maputo on 27 January 1980 to a huge welcome at Zimbabwe Grounds, just outside Salisbury. The *Notícias* reporter Joaquim Salvador accompanied Mugabe in the plane, and asked him to comment on a forecast by a right-wing British paper, the *Daily Telegraph*, that Zanu would get only 30 seats. Mugabe scoffed and made the uncannily accurate prediction that his party would win between 55 and 60 seats. Salvador and Cardoso wrote the *Notícias* front-page story on Mugabe's triumphant return. Cardoso remarked,

> Paradoxically, the British authorities as well as Muzorewa himself and his Rhodesian allies, thanks to all the obstacles that they raised to Robert Mugabe's return, which delayed it for a fortnight, have helped increase expectations around his return still further. The distorted image of the Zanu-PF president, produced by the racist propaganda machine, thus ended up producing no negative impact on the mass of the people. On the contrary, they have tended towards increased identification with the person whom the racists and their allies define as the main enemy.

Cardoso was now convinced that Mugabe was right, and that Zanu would indeed win a crushing electoral victory. The Rhodesian propaganda had been counterproductive, as was the entire campaign waged by Muzorewa. 'Whenever Muzorewa speaks to the country he seems to have nothing more interesting to say than repeating his previous attacks against Robert Mugabe and Joshua Nkomo, thus leaving open for them the national arena of political debate.'

Cardoso was writing prolifically during these weeks, supplying the radio and *Notícias* with thousands of words, day after day. He followed closely the violence waged by Muzorewa's 'auxiliaries', the accusations of intimidation against Zanu, the Rhodesian harassment of returning refugees, and, worst of all, the attempts to assassinate Mugabe. One of these attempts was almost successful. This led to a strategic decision by the Zanu leadership to evacuate Mugabe to Maputo immediately after he had cast his vote. The high regard in which Zanu held the young Mozambican journalists was shown in their choice of Gomes to secure Mugabe a place on the Mozambique Airlines flight to Maputo that day.

When the votes were counted, Cardoso was on the spot at the counting centre in Salisbury, while Gomes followed from live radio and TV coverage. Gomes phoned Maputo and just kept the line open as the count went on. 'So we had a live broadcast from Salisbury,' he said. Gomes could update the figures, while Cardoso provided the atmosphere at the count, and regular interviews. The following day, virtually the entire Radio Mozambique lunchtime news broadcast was occupied by Cardoso's summary of the election results. The Mozambican government, and the media, felt triumphantly vindicated: they had backed someone once regarded as a no-hoper, and he had swept to power. Zanu-PF took an absolute majority of votes and of seats. With 57 seats for Zanu, Mugabe's prophecy was confirmed. Zapu was confined to just 20 seats in Ndebele areas, while Smith's main black ally, Muzorewa, picked up just three. The 20 white seats were won by Smith's Rhodesian Front, but they were, to all intents and purposes, irrelevant.

During the election campaign, Salisbury was full of foreign journalists, many of whom were only too willing to accept anti-Zanu propaganda. Few had followed the war closely or had any sympathy for African liberation struggles. One exception was Julie Frederikse, the correspondent of US National Public Radio. She struck up a friendship with Cardoso, and the two of them found a house in Salisbury that would serve as both an office and a flat, thus freeing Cardoso from the expense of the Monomotapa Hotel. Cardoso, Gomes and Frederikse were among a small minority of reporters who became convinced that in a free election Mugabe would win. 'Carlos was the one doing the hard work of reporting, and agonising over the analysis,' Frederikse adds. 'He really was enjoying greatly being back in the fray and writing on such a cutting edge story.'

She noted that initially much of the cynical western press corps dismissed Cardoso 'as a far-left white Frelimo sycophant'. They regarded themselves as the real professionals, with their flattering portraits of the British governor, Lord Soames, and their disdain for the politics of nationalism. But in the end, Frederikse says, 'Carlos did win grudging respect in the face of great prejudice because he worked hard as a journalist, wrote well, and ultimately produced excellent analysis, and predictions that were borne out.'

CHAPTER 5

Small Agency, Big Ambitions

Immediately after the Zimbabwean elections, Cardoso was transferred from Radio Mozambique to the Mozambique News Agency (AIM), where he officially started work on 8 March 1980. The agency was crammed into the second floor of what was then the ministry of information, with just a handful of journalists, minimal administration, and two telex machines for putting out its stories. AIM was set up immediately after independence. Unlike the rest of the print media, it was entirely new and had to start from scratch. The colonial authorities had never bothered with a news agency. Setting up AIM was a genuinely strategic move by the ministry of information: it was to transmit the image of Mozambique to the outside world.

The initial core of journalists for AIM was recruited from *A Tribuna*, a paper that Frelimo closed down. Not that the party had anything against *A Tribuna* – the decision was taken largely to economise on scarce human resources. Frelimo reasoned that Maputo did not need two daily papers, but the country did need a politically reliable news agency, and the staunchly pro-Frelimo staff of *A Tribuna* would provide the seeds for that. The party dreamed of creating a Mozambican equivalent of Tass or of the East German agency ADN. Fortunately this proved impossible. The ex-*Tribuna* journalists saw no reason why loyalty to Frelimo should be in contradiction with a critical attitude towards Mozambican society.

From *A Tribuna* came Fernando Magalhães, appointed the first director of AIM until he left Mozambique in 1977, and two people who were to make names for themselves in literature, Mia Couto and

Luís Carlos Patraquim. The political activist Teresa Sá Nogueira, who had been in exile in Brazil, joined the staff. So, for a brief period, did Muradali, fresh from his studies in Portugal. 'Everybody was young, working out of enthusiasm, out of militancy,' recalled Magalhães. As the medium that would communicate Mozambique to the outside world, AIM could not simply write in Portuguese. An AIM English service was set up, run initially by Iain Christie. At Rebelo's insistence, the agency also worked in French; but the economics of this were never thought through properly, and the French service just became a drain on its meagre resources.

Iain's wife, Frances Christie, came to AIM in April 1977, just at the time Benjamim Faduco took over as director from Magalhães. Some of the 'ultra-leftists' who had left *Notícias* the previous year – notably Fernando Lima and Miguéis Lopes Junior – were now at AIM. Frances was not impressed. 'There were about 14 journalists and output was minimal,' she recalled. As for the politics of the newsroom, Christie was scathing. She said she was 'absolutely amazed to find this absurd student politics going on. It didn't seem to have anything to do with Mozambique.' She was referring to hangovers from the days of Lema, the Maoist-inclined League of Anti-Imperialist Mozambican Students, which Miguéis and others had joined as students. They still harped on doctrinal disputes rooted in the Sino-Soviet split. (For her, one of Cardoso's refreshing attributes was that he was much more interested in Zimbabwe than in rows over Soviet revisionism.) By 1977 Iain had been transferred to Radio Mozambique, where he was in charge of the 'Voice of Zimbabwe', helping to train Zimbabwean journalists. Frances took over the AIM English service and became responsible for the monthly magazine in English. Directors changed rapidly: Mia Couto took over from Faduco, but in early 1979 he was transferred to *Tempo*, and AIM was left to drift. For one reason or another, most of the experienced staff left.

Cardoso was put in charge of AIM as part of a major reshuffle in the ministry of information and the media in early 1980. Rebelo left the government in changes announced on 3 April. He had disagreed with Machel over the feasibility of setting up a Mozambican television station. The huge costs involved persuaded Rebelo that the major priority should remain ensuring that Radio Mozambique's signal could reach the entire country, and in languages that could be understood. One of Rebelo's last decisions as minister was to appoint Cardoso as AIM chief news editor – which showed that, no matter how irritated he might occasionally have been with Cardoso, he recognised his capabilities.

Rebelo remained a key figure in the party hierarchy: in the new position of Central Committee secretary for ideological work, he would still be in overall charge of the media. But the man who became minister of information was José Luís Cabaço, an urbane intellectual trained in Italy, whose relaxed style contrasted with the austere image that Rebelo had cultivated. He shared Machel's enthusiasm for television, and his contacts in western Europe meant he could raise funds for it. Cabaço reads his own appointment as part of Machel's attempt to shift strategic gear. With the end of the Zimbabwean war, the immediate threat seemed over, and the country could now concentrate on development tasks. In his 1980 New Year message, Machel declared, 'This is the decade when we shall definitively eliminate from our country hunger, ignorance and misery. This is the decade of the building of a socialist society ... By 1999, we want the People's Republic of Mozambique to be a country in full development towards advanced socialism.' Competence was prioritised. Politics might still be in command, but at one remove. Thus, in the media, Rebelo's approach may have looked a bit dated, so he was shifted upwards to keep an overall eye on the ideological content.

Cabaço and Mota Lopes, who as national director of information was now number two in the ministry, wanted to give fresh impetus to AIM, and believed that Cardoso could do that. Cabaço had great respect for Cardoso's abilities and for his detailed knowledge of South Africa – something that was to become ever more important as Mozambique moved inexorably into deeper confrontation with Pretoria. When Cardoso arrived at AIM, 'the Portuguese service was at rock bottom,' Frances recalls. Just two people were doing most of the writing: Lima, and Gustavo Mavie, who had started work at

AIM as a telex operator but whose writing ability had led Mia Couto to transfer him to the newsroom. Cardoso replaced José Branquinho, who had been trying to resign as editor for months. Fernando Lima became the deputy editor. Nobody was appointed director. Mia Couto assumes that Rebelo vetoed giving a directorship to Cardoso. In practice, it did not matter: Cardoso was running the show, and so everybody referred to him as 'Mr Director'. Lima was informally upgraded to chief news editor.

There was an infectious enthusiasm to Cardoso which pushed production up. He and Lima began to sign cooperation agreements with other news agencies, and to recruit more staff. One man who would later become a key agency figure, Fernando Gonçalves, simply walked in and asked for a job. Lima interviewed him and he was recruited on the spot. In those days, such matters were very informal. The English service had to be stiffened; via the Canadian NGO Cuso/Suco, a Canadian journalist, Lois Browne, was recruited. And so was I, from London.

Gonçalves recalls Cardoso treating his subordinates with respect. 'He was not someone who pushed you around to get things done,' he said. 'He was open to consultation, and he edited the copy of young reporters in a straightforward and helpful way. He was an editor who would explain your mistakes, and in a way that you would not feel humiliated.' Cardoso's openness towards his staff built up their confidence, easily compensating for their lack of formal academic qualifications.

Relations between Cardoso and Lima were key to the entire operation. The two men were very different: Cardoso the dreamer, the visionary; and Lima the administrator, the organiser. The editorial line came from Cardoso, while Lima worried about the agency's money and equipment, and saw it as his duty to put the brakes on those ideas of Cardoso he regarded as impractical or simply 'crazy'. Both were committed to the revolution but took different attitudes towards Frelimo. Cardoso regarded Frelimo as his party and attempted, unsuccessfully, to join it. He never got beyond candidate membership. But Lima, while admiring Machel and others in the leadership, took a more sceptical view and never applied for Frelimo membership. AIM needed both faces – Lima the realist, and Cardoso the utopian – and the two worked remarkably well together.

❖

In the early 1980s Unesco tried to help set up national news agencies so that countries emerging out of colonialism would be heard. Why should the international media be entirely dominated by the rich north? The United States wrecked Unesco's plan for a 'New International Information Order', but in 1980 that was not foreseen, and Cardoso pushed ahead with a strategy of linking AIM up with other news agencies in southern Africa, with the pool of non-aligned news agencies (which in truth never functioned well) and eventually with the Pan-African News Agency (Pana). Pana was supposed to be a means for Africans to talk to each other without going through the western agencies. Starting in 1983, Pana initially distributed its stories by radio teletype – an inefficient method, vulnerable to climatic interference, and often arriving at their destinations garbled. For the national agencies, sending material to Pana was simply another cost – from most African countries, sending a telex to Pana HQ in Senegal was just as expensive as sending it to Europe. But AIM was one of the agencies truly enthusiastic about Pana. We thought that, on balance, the risks of political interference were worth taking, and the money worth spending.

Despite the huge telecommunications costs involved, under Cardoso AIM made a point too of sending all its English stories to national news agencies (and, where these did not exist, to government information departments) in southern Africa and in other former Portuguese colonies. Cardoso also cultivated relations with the South African press. This was enemy territory – but there were anti-apartheid journalists and honest professionals working on some of the papers. We took the attitude that every time the *Rand Daily Mail* or the Johannesburg *Star* published material from AIM, that was a small victory for the anti-apartheid movement and for the Front Line States. We even offered stories to the main Afrikaans paper, *Beeld* – challenging the paper of the apartheid establishment to carry a Front Line view. In this way AIM became a much greater thorn in the flesh of Pretoria than if we had just dismissed the South African media as untouchable racists. As the years wore on, so AIM attained an aura of credibility. The South African editors who dealt with Cardoso knew that AIM was not just a government mouthpiece, that it was usually accurate, and that it never consciously lied.

Cabaço admits that the government never got round to deciding how it wanted the national news agency to function. On the one hand this gave Cardoso considerable room to manoeuvre, but on the other there was always a feeling that AIM was semi-abandoned, left to drift. 'All the work done to improve the agency was exclusively due to the journalists, led by Cardoso, and not to the ministry,' says Cabaço. 'We were always waiting to define a profile for the agency, and that never happened.'

❖

Cardoso was not going to be an armchair editor. Scarcely had he arrived than he was off to Zimbabwe to cover the independence celebrations. A couple of months later he was with Machel in Sierra Leone for the OAU (Organisation for African Unity) Freetown summit. This was a high point in Mozambican diplomacy, as Machel led the drive for the admission of the Saharan Arab Democratic Republic into the OAU. The question had not been on the summit's agenda: Machel's speech put it there.

At this time Cardoso was regularly accompanying the president. Thus a month later, he was back in Harare for Machel's first state visit to Zimbabwe. Huge crowds, emotional scenes, symbolic moments – such as renaming a thoroughfare in central Harare Samora Machel Avenue. And throughout, a consistent thread of anti-racism and anti-tribalism from Machel. He knew full well the deep divisions in Zimbabwean society and urged his audiences to overcome them. 'To ensure national unity, there must be no Shonas in Zimbabwe, there must be no Ndebeles. In Zimbabwe, there must be Zimbabweans,' he told a Bulawayo rally. 'Some people are proud of their tribalism. But we call tribalists reactionary agents of the enemy.' In Harare, on 7 August, Machel took a Zimbabwean flag and declared: 'This flag covers everyone. Today there are no blacks in Zimbabwe, there are no whites, there are no mulattos and Indians, today there are just Zimbabweans.' Cardoso noted that this militant anti-racism wounded some Zimbabwean susceptibilities, but Machel commented: 'The truth hurts, the truth punishes, but it is the truth and thus contains purity.'

In September 1980, Cardoso was in Beirut, where he signed an agreement between AIM and the Palestinian news agency, Wafa. The signing was merely symbolic, since the Palestinians were in no condition to send material to AIM. Cardoso had won the PLO's trust, and they took him deep into Lebanon. He believed he was 'the first journalist in the last six years to visit the most advanced Palestinian bases along the frontier of occupied Palestine'. He spent one night in a 'forward base' six kilometres from the border, 'almost on top of the buffer zone' occupied by the forces of Israel's ally, Faad Haddad. Cardoso found this position held by 12 PLO guerrillas, the youngest of whom was 15 and the oldest 27. Their commander was a 22-year-old who had fled the West Bank after spending time in an Israeli jail. Cardoso admired the determination of this young man, who told him:

> The will to fight, to return to Palestine, comes from generation to generation. Since we were children, we have heard our parents and grandparents speak of Palestine. Those not born there learn of it. And there's a second important factor. Outside, in or out of the struggle, we are always reminded that we are Palestinians. In any Arab country we are repressed or barely tolerated. This helps push us back towards Palestine.

Cardoso could hear the dull thumping of artillery in the distance. 'They told me repeatedly that here bombardment happens at any time of day or night. The state of alert is permanent.' In the town of Nabutiye, Cardoso's host was a young Palestinian named Asmaan, deputy commander of the South-East. They discussed Israeli and American strategy. On his last day in Lebanon Cardoso found a 12-year-old boy named Hassan in charge of a machine-gun mounted on a jeep. 'His toys are AK-47s, and his talk, his drawings, his dreams are full of images of war ... 12 years is enough to see a lot of death and destruction.'

January 1981 saw Cardoso covering the Geneva conference on Namibia. The conference was a fiasco: Pretoria had no intention of releasing its grip on Namibia, believing, accurately enough, that there would be no meaningful pressure to do so from the main western powers. Cardoso wrote prolifically in both Portuguese and English. He sent instructions that his material should also be transmitted to the president's office and the foreign ministry, since he doubted that they had any other means of knowing what was happening in Geneva. He was irritated to find that *Notícias* showed no great interest in the conference. 'I learnt that *Notícias* didn't publish the first piece from yesterday,' he telexed Lima. 'Please speak with the national director to see what can be arranged. AIM has neither the authority nor the desire to tell *Notícias* what it should publish, but the money spent on my presence here justifies the broadest possible coverage of Geneva in all the media.'

At the time, there was great optimism that Geneva might succeed. Indeed, as Cardoso watched, with increasing scepticism, the South African manoeuvres in Geneva, Jorge Rebelo was confidently telling a visiting Swapo (South West African People's Organization) trade union delegation that 1981 would be the year of Namibian independence. Swapo bent as far as it could. It said it was ready for an immediate cease-fire, it accepted the UN plan for Namibia in its entirety, and it was even prepared to drop its UN-bestowed title of 'sole legitimate representative of the Namibian people' – but only after a cease-fire was in place. The UN secretary-general, Kurt Waldheim, tried to appease South Africa, which merely confirmed Pretoria in its belief that it need make no concessions. Cardoso attacked the UN's spinelessness:

> The UN's tactic has been to appear flexible; the South Africans demand, and the UN yields, retreats. The claim is that in this way the UN is removing all of the South Africans' arguments. This tactic is, to say the least, dangerous. The more Waldheim yields, the more the South Africans demand ... The UN cannot go on using the tactic of flexibility much longer, since it is already becoming a sign of weakness.

The South Africans demanded that their local puppets, the 'internal' Namibian parties, be treated on an equal footing with Swapo. But this demand had nothing to do with implementing Security Council Resolution 435, which was about South African decolonisation of Namibia. With the South Africans refusing to budge, the conference collapsed.

❖

Geneva was a clear sign that the South African position towards the entire region was hardening. Prime Minister John Vorster, once an open fan of Nazi Germany, had been as ruthless as any of his predecessors in cracking down on opposition within South Africa, but abroad he had followed a policy of 'détente', seeking to expand Pretoria's relations with independent Africa. He had disapproved of the 1975 invasion of Angola; he had vetoed any attempt to prevent Mozambican independence; and had been prepared to sacrifice Ian Smith. But in 1979 Vorster was pushed out of power: the man who had ordered the Angolan invasion, PW Botha, was now prime minister, and the former head of the SADF, Magnus Malan, had been promoted to defence minister. In dealing with their neighbours, the first instinct of these men was to use the stick, not the carrot.

Cardoso had seen child soldiers in Lebanon. Now Mozambique was to produce many child soldiers of its own as it slipped into a wave of death and destruction unparalleled in previous southern African history. For the MNR/Renamo was far from a spent force: with the connivance of the British, the entire operation was shifted bodily from Rhodesia to South Africa in 1980, and South African military intelligence took over from the Rhodesian Central Intelligence Organisation, which under Ken Flower had created it. Failure to appreciate the significance of this shift was an enormous political and security blunder. With the independence of Zimbabwe, Machel's government let down its guard. So 1980 was the year of relaxation, a year of relative peace, a year in which it was possible to hold a census (in August) over virtually the entire country without the census brigades risking their lives. And it was a year in which the apartheid military were planning to tear Mozambique to shreds.

CHAPTER 6

'Let Them Come!'

The first shots of the new war came on 30 January 1981. That was when South African commandos infiltrated the city of Matola and murdered 12 South African exiles, all members of the ANC, plus a Portuguese electricity worker who got in the way. Naturally, Pretoria claimed this was an attack against 'terrorist bases'. Although the 12 dead men were almost certainly members of Umkhonto weSizwe (MK), the ANC did not site sensitive military bases in densely populated areas such as Matola. The Mozambican government had no difficulty showing diplomats that there was nothing remotely military about the three houses attacked by the commandos. What Pretoria had done was to redefine the concept of 'terrorist base' – it now meant anywhere that ANC or MK members happened to be living.

Cardoso's response was an editorial in English entitled simply 'Who's afraid?' He argued that the South African war machine was far from invincible. The regime's military might had been challenged by the youth of Soweto, the liberation war in Namibia had forced the regime to the negotiating table in Geneva, and the South African backing for Smith or for the Portuguese colonial rulers of Mozambique had not saved them. The purpose of the Matola raid, Cardoso argued, was 'to frighten the people of Mozambique into accepting the "natural" regional supremacy of the apartheid regime'. But instead of submitting, the people would fight, he predicted.

> The argument that the people of Mozambique cannot withstand another war is yet another myth, an argument that was repeated over and over again when the

Mozambican government gave efficacy to sanctions against Rhodesia by closing its borders with the then rebel colony. Anti-guerrilla war, sabotage by reactionary movements, air raids, napalm, tanks, massacres, the people of Mozambique have gone through it all in their struggle for independence and in their contribution to internationalism.

Apartheid did not understand the nature of 'people's war', argued Cardoso. 'Freedom fighters are not uniformed soldiers to be singled out from among the masses. They are the masses themselves, and in Mozambique and South Africa there are 35 million soldiers. So, who is afraid?'

This confident approach was not something dreamed up by Cardoso – its source was Samora Machel. A fortnight after the Matola raid, Machel threw down the gauntlet to Pretoria. At a mass rally in Maputo's Independence Square, he embraced ANC leader Oliver Tambo and warned the South African government that if it wanted a war it could have one. Mozambicans would not allow themselves to be dominated, he declared, and must prepare themselves 'so that no aggressor will leave the country alive'. 'We don't want war. We are peacemakers because we are socialists,' said Machel. 'One side wants peace, and the other wants war. What to do? We shall let South Africa choose. We are not afraid of war. Let South Africa choose whether we should live in peace or at war. And we don't want cold war either. We prefer open war.' He added:

> They want to come here and commit murder. So we say: Let them come! Let all the racists come … Let them come! Let us liquidate war once and for all. Then there will be true peace in the region, not the false peace we are now experiencing. Let the South Africans come, but let them be clear that the war will end in Pretoria! The war will certainly end in Pretoria, for the majority will take power in Pretoria.

Let them come. And they did.

❖

In hindsight, Machel's speech and Cardoso's editorial might look like foolish bravado. But at the time they seemed perfectly rational responses to apartheid aggression. Nobody yet appreciated how much the international scene was changing: the revolutionary tide of the 1970s was on the ebb, and the left was internationally on the defensive (though it often failed to realise this). In Europe, outside its Nordic strongholds, social democracy was in retreat, and a resurgent right, best represented by Britain's Margaret Thatcher, was advancing. Much worse, a B-movie actor named Ronald Reagan had won the US presidential election. Reagan, Thatcher and their acolytes elsewhere were qualitatively different from earlier right-wing leaders. They were ideologues rather than pragmatists. They broke the postwar consensus, most obviously in their embrace of neo-liberal economics and their onslaught against the welfare state.

This had serious implications for foreign policy. For the Reagan administration, South Africa was not a polecat state but an ally in the global crusade against communism and 'Soviet expansionism'. Often this would mean subordinating American economic interests to ideology. Nowhere was this clearer than in Angola: the US oil corporation Chevron had excellent relations with Angola's Marxist government and was happily expanding its business. It had not the slightest desire to see a revival in the fortunes of Unita (the National Union for the Total Independence of Angola). But for Reagan, Jonas Savimbi was a heroic fighter against the 'evil empire'. So, after a period in which Unita had come close to destruction, it was to be revived (and even given Stinger missiles).

As for South Africa itself, when the assistant secretary of state for African affairs, Chester Crocker, visited Pretoria in early 1981, he told President Botha and Magnus Malan that the top US priority was – not economic development, not ending apartheid – but 'to stop Soviet encroachment in Africa'. A memo Crocker sent to his boss, Alexander Haig, suggested that he assure the South African government that 'a Russian flag in Windhoek is as unacceptable to us as it is to you'.[1] In this case, 'a Russian flag' was just another way of referring to a Swapo government.

Had the Mozambican government been fully aware of the momentous changes in US policy, it might have hesitated before publicly unmasking CIA operatives in Maputo. On 4 March 1981 six US citizens were expelled – four embassy officials and two of their wives. There is no good reason to doubt that these people were indeed spies, nor that the Mozambicans arrested (including the head of personnel in the foreign ministry, José Massinga) had been recruited as informers. Information on the CIA network had been obtained by a white Mozambican air force officer, Carneiro Gonçalves. He was approached by the CIA and informed the Mozambican security service, Snasp, who told him to work as a double agent. The tables were turned: Snasp had penetrated the CIA.

The humiliation of the CIA in Maputo was a morale booster for the left across the world, but it came with a price tag. At the press conference announcing the unmasking of the spy network, a journalist asked Cabaço if he expected the US government to retaliate. Cabaço gave a spirited reply. 'Retaliation for what? Retaliation because we defended our sovereignty? Because we want to be free? Retaliation because of the impertinence of becoming independent without authorisation? We haven't hit anybody – we just raised our arm so that they shouldn't hit us.' But of course there was retaliation. Even under Jimmy Carter, Washington had been hostile towards the Mozambican government. In 1977 the US Congress prohibited any provision of development aid to Mozambique without a presidential certification that such aid would be in the foreign policy interest of the US. Nonetheless, plans to supply development aid were drawn up – only to be thrust into cold storage when the CIA ring was exposed. The post of US ambassador to Mozambique, already vacant at the time of the expulsions, was not to be filled for another four years. Crocker was in Maputo the following month, and demanded an apology for the expulsions. He did not get one, Machel refused to meet him, and Crocker left Maputo with a scowl on his face.

The Matola raid led to a serious strategic miscalculation. The government imagined that a conventional war was on the cards, talked about air raid shelters, and started training citizens to defend Maputo from a conventional onslaught. In fact, throughout the war, direct South African strikes were to be the exception rather than the rule. Instead, Pretoria chose to wage surrogate war through the MNR.

But in late 1981, Machel felt confident enough to launch an offensive within the defence and security forces. He held a rally on 5 November, at which the target was not the South Africans or the MNR, but abuses within the armed forces and police. Of all Machel's speeches this was perhaps the most daring. Here was a head of state publicly denouncing the behaviour of his own armed forces. He told the crowd he had come to discuss 'systematic violations of legality', and 'a particularly serious aspect of this situation is that many of these violations are committed by members of the defence and security forces. In other words, legality is violated by members of the very forces who have received from the people and the party the glorious task of defending the constitution of the People's Republic of Mozambique.' Someone who abused the people, committed arbitrary arrests, or used torture to extract confessions might wear 'the glorious uniform of the FPLM [the Frelimo guerrilla army], but he is not a soldier, he is someone who has infiltrated our ranks. He may wear the uniform of our people's police, but he is not one of our policemen, he is an enemy who has infiltrated.' Such people 'consciously or unconsciously, are at the service of reaction, they serve the counter-revolution'.

Machel pledged to wage a 'legality offensive' which would 'dislodge the traitors and kidnappers, the corrupt, the arrogant, the power-hungry, the negligent, the incompetent, the abusers, the thieves, the rapists, the murderers, those who want to ride on the backs of the people'. He promised: 'All cases of beatings, physical aggression, corporal punishment, torture, rape, abuse of power, illicit appropriation of citizens' property that are denounced shall be rigorously investigated and those responsible shall be punished implacably.' Machel insisted that 'the laws on who makes arrests, and on time limits for detention, must be strictly complied with', and he declared: 'In the People's Republic of Mozambique, torture, beatings and corporal punishment are absolutely forbidden.'

Diplomats from Soviet bloc states were amazed. No leader of any other socialist country had ever castigated his own security forces in this way. Were such statements not the height of recklessness? Was Machel not inviting a coup d'état? But there was no coup. Cardoso, and the intelligentsia in general, were delighted at Machel's courage (though it may have earned him some resentment among the armed forces). Cardoso would later write an article for a Swedish publication describing Mozambique as 'A country without coups'. For Cardoso, Mozambique was 'a rare case in the history of nation forming. This remains perhaps the most stable regime in all of Africa, despite a tragically weak material base, and an extremely vulnerable geopolitical situation.'

❖

Frelimo did not believe that Mozambique should stand alone against apartheid. Machel and Botswana's first president, Seretse Khama, were the leading spirits behind a new regional organisation, the Southern African Development Coordination Conference (or SADCC). This economic offshoot of the Front Line States was set up in the wake of Zimbabwean independence: it was broader than the Front Line, since it attempted to draw in Pretoria's satellites Lesotho, Swaziland and even Malawi, the only independent African state to establish full diplomatic relations with Pretoria. SADCC was a direct challenge to the 'Constellation of Southern African States' that Pretoria strategists dreamed of. Its purpose was to reduce the dependence of other southern African states on Pretoria – and to achieve this, Mozambique's ports and railways were of key importance. They were the alternative to the logistical stranglehold that South Africa tried to impose on regional trade.

Cardoso was always an enthusiast for regional integration. But he knew it would not be easy, since there were forces in the SADCC countries that were quite happy with dependence on South Africa. Even in Botswana, which housed the SADCC headquarters, Cardoso found members of the local elite whose lifestyle depended utterly on imported South African goods and on regular trips over the border. They were psychologically locked into South Africa. So, if taken seriously, SADCC would affect the class struggle both in member states and in South Africa. 'Whether we like it or not, the class struggle does not have the same borders as geography,' wrote Cardoso. 'It crosses those borders like a thief in the night, or a clandestine migrant.'

Cardoso compared the economy of southern Africa to an eight-headed cow. The creature had 'one head in Mozambique, another in Swaziland, two more in Zimbabwe and Zambia, one in Malawi, another in Botswana, and another in Namibia. But the cow's milk, that goes to South Africa.' He went on:

> It will be extremely tough for us to cut off the heads of this cow. For on the day when the teats of the cow begin to give less milk, the architects of apartheid are not simply going to say that their poor beast is sick. Instead they will try to cut off the hands of those who go about chopping off the cow's heads.

In the ensuing years this prophecy would be brutally fulfilled.

❖

Gradually the intensity of the war revived. As in all irregular wars, this was incremental – an ambush here, landmines planted there, a raid on a village somewhere else, an insidious build-up punctuated by the occasional spectacular piece of sabotage. The FPLM concentrated on knocking out large MNR bases near the Zimbabwean border (in the Sitatonga mountains in 1980, at Garagua in late 1981) – but the MNR was quietly re-establishing itself in Gorongosa, and the war was gradually spreading all across Sofala province.

Reporters had difficulties even at the most basic level. What should we call this phenomenon? When the MNR was just an irregular extension of the Smith regime's forces, the question scarcely arose. But now South African military intelligence was promoting it as something autonomous, as an organisation with its own leadership and spokesmen (and not just a PO box in Salisbury). Frelimo decided this was not a real organisation, much less a real counter-revolution. It was just 'armed bands'. And so the official terminology for the MNR became 'armed bandits'.

This line was imposed on the media; but Frelimo did not have to push very hard, since nobody was arguing that they were anything else. The nature of their activities – grisly mutilations, attacks on buses full of unarmed passengers, stealing food from defenceless villagers – surely meant that banditry was an accurate description. Ordinary Mozambicans had another word for them: they were

'Matsangas', a term derived from the name of the first MNR leader, André Matsangaíssa. Over two decades later, Jorge Rebelo has no doubt that the term 'bandits' was correct. This was an organisation set up by foreign intelligence agencies, he argues, so it would have been wrong to call them 'rebels'. Rebelo accepts that later on Renamo did indeed gain some popular support, owing to blunders made by Frelimo, but that did not invalidate the 1981 arguments over what to call them. At AIM Cardoso insisted strongly that 'armed bandits' was the correct term to use. He genuinely believed that to describe the MNR as 'guerrillas' was to insult real guerrilla armies. In debates in the newsroom, I disagreed. I feared that use of the pejorative term 'bandits' would damage our credibility, while I believed the word 'rebel' was neutral, saying nothing about the nature of the organisation. I secured a compromise for the AIM English service – there we would at least refer to them by the English acronym of their name, MNR. So in the English service, they were 'MNR bandits', but in the Portuguese service just anonymous 'armed bandits'.

❖

In November 1981 AIM moved out of its cramped offices in the ministry to occupy the top two floors of Cedimo, a documentation centre run by the Bank of Mozambique. Cardoso and Cabaço dreamed of merging AIM and Cedimo so that in effect AIM would take over the whole building. Cedimo put out a daily bulletin to all ministries (essentially a compilation of press cuttings from the South African and western media, which was, ludicrously, stamped 'Confidential'). Cardoso thought this was something AIM should do; and rather than spend vast amounts of paper photocopying the bulletin to be distributed by messenger, it should be put on tape and sent out over AIM's telexes. But the merger never happened. Nobody sat down in 1981 to draw up the organisational and financial arrangements needed to absorb Cedimo into AIM. The window of opportunity slammed shut later in the decade when the ministry of state administration was set up, moved into the building, and absorbed Cedimo.

Covering the economy was sometimes almost as difficult as covering the war. With no freedom of information legislation, and no right of access to official sources, top-ranking officials could declare whole areas taboo to the press. Sérgio Vieira had now been appointed agriculture minister, and he sent a notorious memo round his ministry telling officials not to speak to the media without his authorisation. The memo was leaked to the press, of course, but journalists' complaints were to no avail. Vieira later became a strong proponent of press freedom – but to this day he still believes there was nothing wrong with his 1981 memo. He argues that untimely release of information might harm delicate negotiations. 'I gave instructions because what happened was that, if everybody spoke, that would endanger negotiations,' he says. 'You can't negotiate on the front page of the papers.' He feared that, if every agricultural official spoke to reporters, this might lead to 'contradictory information, or incorrect information, that would compromise our work'. But it was not just information on negotiations with foreign partners that became inaccessible. Even basic agricultural statistics were hard to come by. Regardless of Vieira's intentions, journalists believed that the whole of agriculture had been placed off limits.

By now Cardoso's personal circumstances had changed. He had fallen in love with Maria José ('Zé') Calheiras, a stewardess working at Mozambique Airlines. Finding his first-floor flat too small, he regretted his generous gesture of 1976 and tried to recover the Cardoso family home. It was too late: the state housing body, Apie, had no intention of returning the three-storey building he had given up. So Cardoso moved into Zé's flat. Zé worked wonders on Cardoso's appearance: he cut his hair, and the last vestiges of the dishevelled student disappeared. He would appear for work in an ironed shirt or sometimes in a smart safari suit. He was eating properly and appeared relaxed and at ease with the world. He was domesticated, suddenly living in something approximating to a nuclear family with Zé and her two young children from a previous relationship. But Cardoso was determined to keep his personal and professional lives separate. 'Cardoso was very discreet,' Lima recalls. 'He never commented about his love life.'

Even in a country at war, not everything is serious. In the immediate post-independence years Christmas was not a public holiday. People were expected to work – unless they were practising Christians, in which case they benefited from *tolerância de ponto* – that is, they could absent themselves and they would not lose any wages. It was the same for Muslims on the Islamic festivals of Eid-ul-Fita and Eid-ul-Adha. In other words, religious believers enjoyed more holidays than those who followed the materialist ideology proclaimed by Frelimo. So in December 1981 Cardoso jotted down a light-hearted demand for atheists (which unfortunately was never published):

> I, a Mozambican citizen, a communist and an atheist, hereby make, very respectfully, this claim. Christians and Moslems have, ever year, their days off work. But I, an atheist, an active militant for the lay nature of my state, I don't have that day off. Christians and Moslems have, every year, one day less at work than I do. But at the end of each month they earn the same as me. Conclusion: I am discriminated against …
>
> I, a Mozambican atheist, in the name of all Mozambican atheists, demand that the government initiates this year, National Atheists' Day …

Some people might want to get rid of this *tolerância de ponto* altogether. Not at all! declared Cardoso. In fact, the National Atheists Holiday should be three days off …

> And these three days would all be carnivals in the best tradition of pagan festivals … Furthermore, in our workplaces we know who the religious believers are, we know who, out of conviction or opportunism, take this day off work. OK, none of them can come to the National Atheists' Holiday. None! Or let them first look in the mirror and tell themselves that being religious is no good.

He was sure that, after one such National Atheists' Holiday, 'none of them would again want to face the mediocrity of the altars'.

❖

In 1982, the military situation deteriorated sharply. MNR units had filtered into Gaza and Inhambane provinces, and suddenly every bus that arrived in Maputo was full of terrifying stories of villages burnt, vehicles destroyed, young men pressganged into the rebel ranks. But these stories did not make it into the press. Media coverage of the war consisted of sporadic military communiqués, mostly about bandit bases captured and bandits killed. Almost never were any figures given for FPLM dead and wounded. Of course, had the military been so successful, then there would have been no need for Samora Machel to tour Inhambane and Gaza in February and March 1992, addressing rallies at which the people demanded guns so that they could protect themselves.

The military statements made less and less sense. The war was now approaching Maputo: plenty of Maputo residents had relatives in Gaza and Inhambane from whom they learnt the true state of affairs. In the absence of any official information, waves of rumour rippled through the city. The sense of uncertainty worsened when a key official in Snasp, the national security director, Jorge Costa, defected to South Africa on 7 June. At this time AIM was repeatedly contacted by South African journalists asking if Maputo really was under siege. From Europe (notably Lisbon) worried relatives and friends rang up Maputo residents to find out if they were in imminent danger.

Machel moved to stop the rumours at a rally on 22 June, at which he presided over the distribution of guns to former Frelimo guerrillas, local militias, and members of dynamising groups. The guns, he said, were to defend Maputo against banditry organised by the Pretoria regime, and all other crimes that disturbed the peace of Maputo citizens. His speech was a sharp attack on the revolution's 'class enemies', particularly 'the aspirants to the bourgeoisie'. When Frelimo arrived in Maputo in 1975, he said,

> The aspirants to the bourgeoisie looked at us with our uniforms and our pistols, and said: 'You know, Mr. President, the uniform doesn't suit you. It's not elegant. But you look very good in a suit and tie.' And we took off our pistols. We gained elegance, and they had the guns. We made a mistake. But we will not make it again … We shall use our pistols again. This is a liber-

ated city, we must defend it. We are going to stop making concessions to the bourgeoisie and to those who want to become bourgeois. In order to get rid of banditry, we must force the bourgeoisie completely onto the defensive.

Machel compared the bourgeoisie to a crocodile. 'When someone catches a crocodile that's just emerged from the egg, he thinks it's an interesting creature,' he remarked. But as it grows, so it needs ever larger amounts of fresh meat and blood. 'It's like the bourgeoisie. If we let it grow, it corrupts our institutions ... Our crocodiles are still little wrigglers, they're still aspirants to the bourgeoisie. But if we do not liquidate them when small, if we let them grow, they will become more dangerous.' The revolution had been 'too tolerant', he said. The *candongueiros* (racketeers profiting from chronic shortages) were representatives of the enemy within, and complemented the activities of the 'armed bandits'.

He had harsh words for people such as Jorge Costa, Adriano Bomba (a MiG pilot who defected to South Africa) and António Rocha, a diplomat in the Mozambican Embassy in Harare who defected. 'Since they can't find boots to lick in Mozambique, they run away to South Africa. They run away to clean the Boers' toilets.' But Machel predicted a tough time for traitors at the hands of the South Africans. 'When they don't need them any more, they won't be any use even to clean toilets.' Machel was right: Bomba and Rocha met early deaths, murdered in the internecine battles that characterised Renamo and its relations with the South African military, while Costa is believed to have slipped away to Portugal.

This was a magnetic performance by the president, aimed at restoring confidence in the capital and convincing its residents that they were in no immediate danger of being overrun, no matter how often MNR spokesmen in Lisbon might boast that Maputo was about to fall. It worked too: the atmosphere in Maputo was notably calmer after Machel's speech than before it – which seemed to prove that the enemy thrived not on news about the war but on silence.

Speaking in Beira, Machel made the pragmatic argument in favour of press freedom: 'If we do not tell the truth, then the enemy will tell the truth in his own way.' But the military did not follow this excellent advice (and, to be fair, Machel himself was inconsistent in applying it). Attempts were made to improve coverage of the war. In mid-1982, there was a series of meetings intended to organise regular liaison between the FPLM general staff and the media. Cardoso later wrote:

> In these contacts it was agreed that a small group of journalists, in which I would be included, would spend part of their working time in liaison with the General Staff. I received instructions to open a small operations room with a phone at AIM, which would ensure this liaison, and where the group would meet once a week, and would study and analyse events in South Africa and the region.

The link between the reporters and the general staff would be a small group of Snasp agents who would, straight away, 'ensure someone was on duty at the security ministry, until 20.00 every day'. Writing about this experience some months later, Cardoso recalled that he had confronted sceptics: some journalists believed that the military had no interest in releasing information. 'This won't go anywhere,' they said, while Cardoso replied, 'Let's work.'

Cardoso was wrong. He admitted as much in a lengthy letter to Rebelo. 'The first contacts were made with Snasp. Nothing. More phone calls. Nothing. Meanwhile, the enemy continued with his daily propaganda.' Cardoso then heard that the Snasp agents supposed to work with the media had been arrested in the crackdown following the defection of Costa. 'Once again discouragement,' wrote Cardoso. There was no longer anyone to liaise with. So Cardoso started personal contacts with senior figures in the military – Generals Pedro Juma, Tomé Eduardo and Sebastião Mabote (the chief of staff), and even a fleeting contact with the defence minister, Alberto Chipande. Verbally, they agreed: they all thought it important to establish an institutional link between the army and the media. Mabote promised all possible support – even helicopters and jeeps!

Cardoso's initiative produced a few effects. Several officers were told to work with him. He contacted a Lieutenant Givale two or three times a week, to be given a summary of FPLM actions. This did lead to a few AIM news items. And then Cardoso left Maputo on missions to Cabo Delgado and Berlin, and the scheme just fell apart. 'The news vacuum was my fault,' he admitted. But there was also a problem of credibility with war reporting that just gave FPLM claims about dead bandits and captured bases, and said nothing about rebel actions. In this private letter to Rebelo (which may never have been sent – Rebelo does not recall receiving it) Cardoso's main message was very simple: the media should tell the truth about the war. Why hide weaknesses and failures when Machel had publicly proclaimed the failings of the most sensitive parts of the state in the legality speech of November 1981? There was no need to hide enemy actions. Instead journalists could use them 'to educate the people in more detail as to how the enemy acts'. 'It was possible to build a journalism that abandoned once and for all the greyness and defensive spirit that characterises journalism in most of the socialist countries,' he declared. Possible – if only the party would just let journalists do their jobs. Cardoso delicately suggested that FPLM communiqués that only mentioned enemy dead just followed in the footsteps of the Portuguese colonial army, which had always trumpeted 'victories' of Portuguese commander Kaulza de Arriaga over Frelimo 'terrorists'.

In July 1982, Cardoso was offered a weekly column on the back page of *Notícias* as part of Mia Couto's drive to enliven the paper. Cardoso called it 'Moçambicanamente'. The first of these columns struck a typically optimistic note, regarding life in revolutionary Mozambique not as a hardship but a privilege. Mozambique's revolutionary theory, he wrote proudly, was not blindly copied from other people. 'Today we have our own substantial contribution to the innovative thinking of an epoch of people in rebellion of which we are, in our Mozambican fashion, co-authors.' Yes, it was true that this was the generation that had to spend much of its time in long queues,

> but we are also the generation that is making its children hold their heads up high, without the sores of race

and tribe. And while the revolution does have the goals of providing more bread, more houses, more clothing, more books, making the revolution is in itself a freedom, an act of liberation. It is the bread and water of the mind.

Several of Cardoso's columns of mid-1982 dealt with the Middle East – this was the period of the Israeli invasion of Lebanon and the siege of Beirut. Day after day the resistance of the Palestinians and their Lebanese allies to the Israeli invasion was splashed across the front page of *Notícias*, sometimes in articles written by Cardoso, who kept in close contact with the Palestinian representative in Maputo, Hani Shawa. Cardoso attacked not only the Israeli aggression but also 'the passivity of the Arab regimes ... Not even the shade of Nasser has inspired in them more decent gestures than late and hypocritical condemnations in the corridors of diplomacy.' The Arab states, in abandoning the PLO, had shown themselves 'as rich in oil as they are poor in vision'.

The comparison between the Middle East and southern Africa was inevitable. 'What if Maputo were Beirut?' was the title Cardoso gave to one of his columns. He argued that the violence of the Israeli onslaught was not specific to Zionism, much less to Judaism. It was 'one of the threats of the current offensive of imperialism in its attempt to recover part of what it was forced to lose in the last seven years' since the American defeat in Indo-China and the collapse of Portuguese colonial rule. Cardoso drew parallels between the Israeli and South African governments, between the far-right Lebanese Falangists and the MNR – and between the Camp David agreement between Egypt and Israel 'and the "non-aggression treaty" proposed by Pieter [PW] Botha as an attempt to persuade the countries of the region to abandon their support for the ANC'. On 11 August he wrote:

> Each centimetre of Beirut asphalt occupied by Israel is a violation of our own political space. But each day the Palestinians resist raises our own morale. Each Zionist tank destroyed makes our own flag fly a little higher ... We should have no doubt that right now the apartheid

generals are studying in detail the Israeli military tactics used in the invasion of Lebanon.

❖

On August 17, Pretoria struck in the heart of Maputo. The university's Centre for African Studies and the Mozambican National Commission for Unesco had just staged a highly successful 'Experts' Meeting on Problems and Priorities in Social Science Training in Southern Africa', largely organised by Ruth First, the centre's director and Joe Slovo's wife. After the discussions were over, several participants were chatting in Ruth First's office. A parcel had arrived for her in the mail, apparently containing a book. As she talked, Ruth opened the parcel. It exploded, killing her instantly and injuring Aquino de Bragança and two other colleagues, Pallo Jordan, head of the ANC research division, and American academic Bridget O'Laughlin. Cardoso was unaware of it at the time, but the bomb was sent by somebody he knew – Craig Williamson, one of the government spies who had been on the Wits SRC in 1974. He was in the security branch of the South African police; after the fall of apartheid he admitted to the Truth and Reconciliation Commission that he had organised the murder of Ruth First. He applied for, and received, amnesty, to the anger of Ruth's three daughters. Interviewed by the eldest daughter, Gillian, Williamson admitted the killing. Ruth had to die, he said, because the apartheid state was convinced she was 'a key player, one of the top ideological thinkers in the South African Communist Party' and was 'worried about her involvement in Mozambique'.[2]

The murder came as a shock to Cardoso, who had greatly respected Ruth and her work. In his AIM editorial, Cardoso wrote:

The apartheid regime has murdered an anti-apartheid militant who had no involvement of a military nature. She was a journalist, a writer and a researcher in the social sciences. But this was enough. At a time of a great upsurge in mass struggle and armed struggle inside South Africa, the regime finds it important to silence all its opponents. In the process, all that remains of the facade of scruples falls to the ground in blood

and pain. South African state terrorism knows no constraints on its activities.

Just three days after the murder the South African defence minister, Magnus Malan, threatened that Pretoria would not tolerate Mozambique placing 'sophisticated weapons' along the border. Machel replied at the end of a Frelimo Central Committee meeting on 22 August. Nobody in their right mind could imagine that an underdeveloped country such as Mozambique posed any military threat to South Africa. What really scared apartheid, he stressed, was 'the cultural alternative that Mozambican society already represents', with its 'coexistence of races, colours and tribes. This is what apartheid fears.' Yes, Mozambique did have a sophisticated weapon, Machel said: it was the 'alternative civilisation' represented by someone such as Ruth First.

South Africa's miserable press swallowed the regime's routine denial of any involvement in the murder – and even printed the foul suggestion that Joe Slovo had organised his wife's death. Since the Johannesburg *Star* was also distributed in London, Slovo was able to use the British libel laws. He sued the *Star* in a British court, and won.

CHAPTER 7

'Me? Arrested in Mozambique?'

On 15 November 1982, directors and editors were called to a meeting with Mota Lopes, at which new guidelines for reporting the war were supposed to be issued. But these guidelines were infuriatingly vague. Cardoso summarised them in his notebook. The first point was: 'Don't include any more scattered news items about FPLM actions against armed bandits.' But what exactly were 'scattered news items'? Much clearer was the second point: 'No statements from commanders.' In a later letter to Rebelo, Cardoso gave a somewhat different summary: 'The national director transmitted the presidential guidelines that all news items about the actions of our forces and about attacks by armed bandits of the pillaging, mutilation, destruction type should stop.' Allegedly, the president's rationale was: 'The bandits whom our forces kill are also Mozambicans operating in areas where tribalism is still very strong. Those killed have their families there. It was necessary to stop and think.' Cardoso left the meeting puzzled and frustrated. He felt he was being asked to 'eliminate seven years of a way of thinking'.

Unknown to Cardoso, the top leadership of Frelimo was beginning to rethink its strategy. According to Mota Lopes, for the first time 'a political solution to the military situation' was being considered. While this rethink was under way, Machel decided 'that there would be, over the coming days, a temporary suspension, and as brief as possible, of coverage of the war, and that discussion meetings, in the media and at Minfo, should take place about the problems we were facing in this coverage'.[1] Within the Frelimo ideology department other discussions were taking place, to which not even Mota

Lopes was invited. No longer in the ministry, Rebelo did not have the benefit of any regular, day-to-day input from journalists. Mota Lopes saw him as surrounded by party bureaucrats who turned the analysis of the media 'into an increasingly inquisitorial process of denial which basically called into question … the patriotism, the politics and the professionalism of the great majority of our best journalists'.

The 15 November guidelines did not appear to cover opinion pieces, and so Cardoso thought he was not violating any order by making a comparison between the kidnapping tactics used in Mozambique and in Angola in his weekly 'Moçambicanamente' column. The article appeared on 17 November and mentioned (as anybody who listened to foreign radio stations already knew) that the MNR had released Portuguese hostages on the border. The key paragraphs read:

> Last Wednesday it was reported that the six Bulgarians kidnapped last August in Zambezia by the armed gangs had been set free as a result of FPLM action.
>
> 24 hours earlier, in order to hit the headlines before the case of the Bulgarians, the armed gang who had abducted seven Portuguese citizens in Manica dropped them on the Zimbabwean side of the border.
>
> On the 14th there were two cases. The armed gang that had been holding the Chilean Moses Carril ever since he was kidnapped last year in Gorongosa took him to Muanza in Malawi, and released him there. At much the same time, Unita freed the Archbishop of Lubango, kidnapped some weeks earlier.

Cardoso's attack was aimed not so much at the MNR or Unita as at their South African paymasters: he thought it necessary to make the point that hostage-taking and -releasing were both commanded from Pretoria. 'Both Unita in Angola and the armed gangs in Mozambique take their orders from Pretoria. And they receive them daily by radio. Pretoria gave the order to abduct and later ordered the Archbishop of Lubango, Carril, and the Portuguese to be released.' Cardoso discussed the piece with Mia Couto and Miguéis, who was then *Notícias* news editor. They thought it was right to make the denunciation. Neither of them thought Cardoso was breaking the guidelines. Cardoso dashed off the article 'in less than 15 minutes'. He was not on form, and recognised 'it was a mediocre job, a banal article compared with others I had written'.

But there was another guideline, given by Rebelo to Mota Lopes the day before, on 16 November, and passed on promptly to the media directors. This was that 'also temporarily, no references should be made to Unita, particularly statements in which the Angolan movement was put on a footing of equality with Renamo'. Mota Lopes believes that Machel and his close advisers were discussing 'the structural and strategic difference between Unita, an Angolan nationalist movement that was being used by the South Africans as an instrument of regional destabilisation, and the so-called Resistance or Renamo which was historically the result of a military and security counter-insurgency operation, first of the Rhodesians and later of the South Africans'. In other words, Unita had some nationalist legitimacy but Renamo did not, and treating them equally might play into Pretoria's game of presenting Renamo as a legitimate, endogenous opposition movement.

Mota Lopes personally informed both Cardoso and Mia Couto on 16 November of this guideline. So did they both consciously violate it that same day? Clearly neither of them thought he was breaching any instruction: Cardoso's own notes on the following crisis do not even mention Unita. Both Mia and Fernando Lima believed that Cardoso's article embarrassed military intelligence, who had apparently told Machel that not only the Bulgarians but also the Portuguese hostages were released thanks to action by the armed forces. By stating that the MNR had just dumped their captives on the border, Cardoso had unwittingly exposed this as false.

But Mota Lopes thought it was the comparison between Renamo and Unita that lay behind the enraged phone call he received from Rebelo on the afternoon of 17 November. In his diary Mota Lopes wrote, 'I'd never heard JR so harsh, so severe: what were we doing, he asked, with the "guidelines" that we received, why were they not transmitted?' Mota Lopes assured him that they had been transmitted, and were discussed with the media directors 'so that they might be implemented as correctly as possible, and particularly so that we could understand them and the reasoning behind them'. But Rebelo would not be placated, accusing Cardoso of acting in a confrontational way and serving the enemy.

> I tried to say no, that it wasn't like that, but I didn't succeed. He was shouting down the other end of the line, and didn't let me speak. He talked of police: 'At the slightest thing of this sort,' he said, 'I will order security to open an inquiry, starting with you.' I told him I was not afraid of security and asked him if I could transmit to the media directors what he had said about police inquiries 'at the slightest thing'. He said yes. He hung up. I had never seen or heard JR so furious, so rude, with his usual calm completely lost.

This was not the Rebelo whom Mota Lopes knew and respected. Threatening police action was not his normal style at all. Quite possibly Rebelo was under pressure from others within the leadership.

Later that day, Cardoso was at a meeting in Mota Lopes's office. Shortly after 18.00, the phone rang. Mota Lopes told the meeting, 'Wait here 15 minutes. Cardoso, come with me.' A Snasp agent was waiting outside, and took Cardoso and Mota Lopes to the security headquarters on Ahmed Sekou Touré Avenue. 'There I began to feel that the case was more serious,' Cardoso wrote in his diary. The agent returned with an arrest warrant, accusing Cardoso of 'a crime against the security of the people and the people's state'. The amazed Cardoso could only exclaim 'Me? Arrested in Mozambique?' While a sombre Mota Lopes returned to the meeting, five Snasp agents accompanied Cardoso to the Machava maximum security jail. An agent named Macie asked Cardoso politely if he wanted anything for his family. He wrote a note to Zé, and asked that the news be broken gently to her.

Cardoso was put in cell 38. No one expected him to try to escape – the door was always left open, and 'there was no special security for me'. Cardoso slept in his clothes on a foam mattress, but was tormented by mosquitoes. He craved cigarettes. At 08.00 next morning he was brought a bed, sheets, a blanket, toothpaste, soap, toilet paper, and some cutlery and crockery. And a soldier brought him six cigarettes. 'To combat boredom, I asked for a broom and set about sweeping the cells and the corridor,' he wrote. Then Cardoso looked for scraps of paper to write on, and asked a soldier to bring him a pen. Throughout his stay in Machava, Cardoso was writing – writing on anything that came to hand, the backs of cigarette packets, a biscuit packet, scraps of old newspaper, whatever he could find.[2]

That morning he was taken out of the jail and back to the Snasp HQ. The hope arose that he would be told it was all a terrible mistake, and sent home. But nothing at all happened at the Snasp HQ, and he was eventually driven back to Machava. 'There is nothing more horrible than imagining you are about to be released, and then returning to your cell,' he wrote. 'What hurts me is what will be happening to her [Zé]. Poor thing, so many problems and now this. Longing for her sometimes breaches the calm I have managed to keep. Despair and anguish took hold of me. I made an effort to keep these feelings at bay.'

By now Cardoso had a splitting headache. He was taken to the prison clinic, but the nurse wasn't there. Hungry and sick, he lay on the bed. The guards brought him food, but he had difficulty eating it, despite the 'good meat'. When the nurse arrived, Cardoso was given aspirin and Resoquin (against malaria). A friendly soldier arranged 16 cigarettes for him, which lifted his spirits. Cardoso promised to pay as soon as he recovered the money he had left with the prison office, 'but he didn't want to hear anything of the sort. He was giving me the cigarettes and that was all.' The soldier told him he was from Beira, and that this wing of the prison had previously hosted the Snasp men interrogated for possible complicity with Costa. Cardoso knew several of them: 'Right now they are enjoying the beautiful things of life, such as walking in the street or simply entering their front door, things which take on an almost mystical quality when we don't have them.'

He was worried, not so much for himself as for what this might do to Mozambique's reputation.

> Sooner or later, the arrest of a journalist becomes an international matter. My detention may be used in the

most vile manner. This country's enemies will certainly fill their mouths with my name, using it as a contradiction between Mozambican journalists and my party. I hope all this will be settled before my name is used as a political plaything by the enemies of Frelimo.

I must get out of here as quickly as possible, and we must all reach, definitively, a strategy for the press. That's the real explanation for all this: we don't have a strategy. I feel there is no reason to be afraid. I have committed no crime against the people, the party or the government.

I have already been jailed by the enemy. It's tough. But it's tougher to be jailed by one's friends, particularly by a deeply popular regime for which I have given an important part of my life.

By now prison was leading him to break his resolution not to smoke more than one cigarette an hour. Despite the smoke, the mosquitoes were still attacking, and Cardoso struck back: 'Right, I'll kill some mosquitoes before lying down. One smack and he's gone. Once he was alive, and now he's dead. And once I was outside, and now I'm in jail.'

On the third day Cardoso ate breakfast ravenously and washed his socks, which were beginning to smell. So was his shirt. 'I need to receive clothes today,' he wrote. He was now looking more closely at his surroundings, discovering names, dates, drawings of naked women, scribbled on the walls. That morning Cardoso was interrogated 'politely' – but his improvised diary is silent on the questions and his replies. A prison guard gave him some clothes and two packs of cigarettes that someone had brought from home. He immediately offered some of the cigarettes to the soldier who had helped him. In the empty adjoining cell, he found the phrase: 'Friend, bear up, as I have borne up, for everything comes to an end.'

To kill time, Cardoso measured the length of the corridor outside the cell. It was 73 paces: so at 80 centimetres a pace, it was 58.4 metres long – 'much better' than the 11 paces outside his cell in Hillbrow in 1975. There was just one other prisoner in this block, a man named João Marcos, who was permanently handcuffed. He said he was arrested because somebody told the authorities he was with 'the Resistance'. 'When I get out of here, I must write everything down for the minister, or for the president,' wrote Cardoso.

> The president is thinking in one way, and we in another. I think this is what's happening. This can lead to more cases like mine, or then we enter a terrible phase of permanent self-censorship. We've been seven years seeking out our path, and finding it in some aspects. We cannot throw into the trashcan seven years of our fatigue and a few ulcers.

On Saturday, 20 November, Cardoso was feeling hungry for information. He had seen no newspaper, heard no radio broadcasts for over two days. 'Being jailed really is the best way of alienating us from the world.' He washed the floor of the cell with a pair of old trousers some earlier prisoner had left in the bathroom. The guards told him that they couldn't bring him the rest of his possessions (notably clothes) that arrived at the prison on a Friday 'because today is Saturday and tomorrow is Sunday. Even here, bureaucracy pursues us.' A prisoner passing by the cell door recognised him and exclaimed, 'Carlos Cardoso!' He identified himself as Adriano from *25 de Setembro*, the irregularly published army magazine. Adriano spoke to him at the cell door. This was in violation of prison regulations, 'but it's a regulation that the soldiers enforce in an elegantly relaxed manner'. Adriano said he had been in Machava for two years because he had tried to go to Zimbabwe to see his family and was accused of being a 'Matsanga'. He said the relationship between guards and prisoners used to be very bad, with soldiers beating up prisoners. But then the guards were detained and replaced as a result of Samora Machel's legality offensive in November 1981. Thus it was to Machel that the prisoners owed the relaxed regime Cardoso described.

That day's lunch, to Cardoso's pleasure, was chicken. He now realised that he was receiving VIP treatment. He felt anxious about his friends and colleagues, particularly at AIM. 'It must be horrible for them ... And I don't doubt there will be those who right now are saying, "Well, that guy spent 10 years in South Africa, who knows what he's up to?"' Indeed, this was precisely the suspicion within some circles of Frelimo, expressed even by Rebelo at a meeting requested by foreign journalists working in the state media to discuss Cardoso's arrest. Iain and Frances Christie, the Portuguese AIM journalist Bruno da Ponte, the Canadian Ole Gjerstadt and the Briton Tim Cook (both working with Iain on the radio's English service) and I sent a letter to Rebelo asking for a meeting. He responded at once and the meeting was held on the third day of Cardoso's incarceration. In other countries, such a group of foreign journalists might have been ignored. But the Frelimo leadership still acknowledged the role played by international solidarity during the liberation war – and these journalists had mostly been active on the information front then, particularly Iain as the first western journalist to visit Frelimo-liberated areas. So they were respected, and felt Rebelo might listen to what they had to say.

Rebelo, dressed in military uniform, did indeed express suspicion about Cardoso's origins. Where had he come from? He suddenly appeared from South Africa, full of fervour, acting as if he were more revolutionary than Frelimo. Whose side was he really on? The foreign journalists insisted that Cardoso was no enemy of the people. They knew him as a patriot and convinced supporter of the revolution. One short article on the back page of *Notícias*, even if it did break a party guideline, was not sufficient reason to send him to jail. Rebelo insisted that the guideline had been perfectly clear. But it was not clear to anyone else in the room. There had been a meeting between Mota Lopes and editors; what had he said? Iain gave his recollections of that meeting, from which Rebelo concluded that Mota Lopes had not said what he was supposed to say. At this meeting I assumed Rebelo was talking about the guideline to suspend articles on the war; I did not even know there was a guideline about Unita, and Unita was certainly not mentioned during the discussion.

I can speak of this meeting from personal recollection. But there were other, and doubtless more important, initiatives afoot. Aquino de Bragança, for instance, was upset at the detention. He told me that he would speak to Samora about it, since 'Cardoso is not an enemy of the revolution'. A worried Manuel Tomé, a senior journalist on

Notícias, contacted the minister of the interior, Mariano Matsinha, who assured him he wanted Cardoso's speedy release. AIM journalists were called to the Central Committee building and asked whether Cardoso was a spy. Gustavo Mavie says his reply was: 'Everything Cardoso did was for the benefit of his people and his country. Yes, of course he talked on the phone with South African journalists. We all knew about it because he left his office door open and we could all hear. A spy wouldn't leave the door open.' Mia Couto had gone to Beira on the day of Cardoso's arrest, but on his return he immediately asked Rebelo why he too hadn't been thrown in jail. After all, he was the director of *Notícias*, he had read Cardoso's article, and he had authorised its publication. Rebelo told him: 'Don't be so nervous.'

By now Cardoso was quite determined to write to the president, and on Sunday morning he acquired a few scraps of paper for this purpose. 'It's not much, but in small handwriting it will do for a letter to the president.' He spent much of the day composing the letter. When it was finished in 'tiny writing', there was still a quarter of a page left. He planned to ask his interrogator to type the letter out neatly.[3] On Monday morning came more VIP treatment – an omelette for breakfast. 'I note down the smallest things, because here everything has meaning, each small human act is a heart brimming with life,' he wrote. 'Nothing that is truly beautiful has been built without fatigue, without mistakes and without some injustice. What we are trying to build is beautiful, and we will reach the point where even those who now despise us will encourage us to continue. We must not give up.'

He wondered if his detention was an omen of worse to come, perhaps a brusque shake-up in the management of the media.

> I sincerely hope not, because this process, with all its confusions was, for example, leading several journalists to want to join the party. We inherited a journalism infected with oppositionism, with a certain infantile form of critique, which is only useful and necessary under an oppressive and anti-popular regime. But we have grown, and in the last 12 months another attitude has clearly begun to take shape in many of us, bound

more to a journalism of construction, of defending gains, but without abandoning the core of critique and denunciation … I am afraid of a setback such that only many years from now will we manage to start creative journalism anew.

That day his interrogator said he could send a letter to Machel, and offered to type it up the following day. But he refused to hand over the clothes that were brought: Cardoso would soon have to abandon even the few personal clothes he did have, and switch to prison clothing. The same Monday, 22 November, Mota Lopes met with Machel, and inevitably the two discussed Cardoso's detention. Machel remarked. 'He [Cardoso] must understand our guidelines. The media is a very sensitive sector.' Mota Lopes wrote in his diary:

I replied that I agreed, but that detentions don't solve anything … It's not right: maybe it would be preferable to speak to the journalists, to have more trust and consideration for them … In reply, and before changing the subject, he told me that the case of CC would soon be solved. And that Aquino had broached the same subject with him yesterday.

But at the end of the meeting Machel returned to Cardoso, and how the media should deal with the war. He was worried that, in their offensive against Mozambique, the country's enemies were using all the ills that colonialism had left behind – 'decadence, ambition, individualism. And also tribalism, racism and regionalism.' If they were not careful, journalists might unwittingly help the enemy. So it was necessary to rethink coverage of the war. Machel said he did not want any return to censorship, and wanted journalists themselves to contribute to drawing up 'guidelines'. He told Mota Lopes:

When we reply to the attacks of South African propaganda, when we wage counter-propaganda, we are taking up a defensive position: we must transmit our own image to the outside, and not just a reply to the South Africans … Cardoso did not understand this, he has still not been able to understand these points.

On Tuesday morning, Cardoso's thoughts turned to his family. 'I would like to see my parents,' he wrote. 'In the last seven years I've scarcely seen them – just twice when they visited Maputo.' Before that he had been 10 years in South Africa, only seeing his family on brief holiday trips back home. This reminded him that he had not taken a proper holiday for five years. His pen was beginning to run out as he started to write on his hundredth scrap of paper. He asked for another pen and was told that a superior officer would have to authorise it. And if the request was refused, what could he write with? he asked himself. But when his interrogator arrived, all thoughts of pens and paper disappeared. 'You don't need anything. Pick up your things from the cell. Let's go.' He packed up his precious scraps of paper in a red tin that had once held cigarettes, and said his farewells to Marcos – who, much to Cardoso's surprise, began to weep. As he left the prison, other prisoners asked him for cigarettes and wished him well.

He was driven to the Snasp HQ, and after an hour and a half of formalities and hanging around, he was free. Mota Lopes greeted him with a warm embrace, and Cardoso held back the tears.

> I told him I had been well treated, but I didn't understand the point of that useless detention. I almost wept with sadness and a little rage when I said that all my work for seven years on behalf of the revolution had counted for absolutely nothing in the thoughts of those who ordered my arrest.

The release was as unexplained as the arrest. But, according to Mia Couto, the Portuguese hostages whom Renamo had dumped on the Malawian border were now staying in a Maputo hotel. They were interviewed, and their account corroborated Cardoso's article. Their captors had simply released them and there was no sign of FPLM intervention. This tape reached the Frelimo leadership. Mota Lopes, however, believed this had little or nothing to do with the decision.

That afternoon, the workers at AIM were drafting a petition to be sent to the party and the minister requesting Cardoso's release. It was to be respectful but firm: we did not believe our director had done anything criminal. It was never sent – perhaps an hour into the meeting Lima left, and returned with Cardoso a few minutes later. That week Cabaço came to the agency to reinstate Cardoso formally as its head. Cabaço had been on holiday in Nampula province when Cardoso was arrested; on receiving the news he hurried back to Maputo. He had full confidence in Cardoso and took the risk of reinstating him without contacting the party leadership first. He informed Rebelo afterwards, who told him he had acted 'very well'. Cabaço recalls that nobody in the Frelimo leadership had any hesitation about reinstating Cardoso. But equally, nobody actually apologised to Cardoso – and in the ensuing months this weighed heavily on his mind.

Cabaço says that on his return from Nampula, 'I was told that Cardoso had published information that endangered national security, and it was necessary to see whether this was deliberate or not.' There were even comments in some quarters such as 'He's very insolent, he needs a lesson'. 'I thought you couldn't throw someone in jail just to teach them a lesson,' Cabaço remarked. He blamed the whole thing on 'a certain sector in the military which was very irritated by the persistent questioning from Cardoso'. Those sectors were not satisfied when Cardoso kept his job – but Cabaço in retrospect regards Cardoso's reinstatement as of crucial importance. 'If he had been sacked, that would have been a great defeat for the media,' he said.

The lid had been kept on the story, and it never became an international scandal. For most foreign journalists in Maputo, it was more important to get Cardoso out of prison than to publicise the case across the world. The correspondent of the Portuguese news agency Anop had written briefly about the detention and interviewed Cardoso shortly after his release. Cardoso was determined not to provide Frelimo's enemies with ammunition, and replied,

> I was held for investigations, and released after the investigations were complete. I was detained by the security of my party, my country and my people. In Mozambique, no one is privileged. When security thinks there are grounds for investigations, even into leaders, it would be senseless to believe that a journalist, or any other citizen, could be above this.

He politely refused to reveal the content of the interrogations. 'The reason for the investigations concerns only the relevant party and state bodies and my comrades in the profession.' Even in Portugal the story was relegated to a couple of paragraphs on inside pages. The rest of the world did not know about it. When the Angolan agency Angop sent a telex asking about the original Anop story, Lima simply bluffed and denied there had been any detention.

But the experience shook Cardoso. The day after his release he received a call from José Caetano, a sympathetic journalist on the *Rand Daily Mail*. Caetano had been stuck in Maputo airport for the previous two days waiting for a visa. He was understandably annoyed, not to mention hungry (in those days conditions at Maputo airport could have been politely described as spartan). Cardoso tried to find out what had gone wrong: Mota Lopes brushed him off: Caetano had not followed the visa application rules, he claimed. But he had, and AIM could prove it – I had received the telex from Caetano with his visa application giving all the relevant details, and had promptly passed it on to the ministry of information. Cardoso was about to set off for the airport on a mercy mission, carrying food for José Caetano, when a paranoid thought struck him. Was he being set up? Was the idea to keep a South African journalist in miserable conditions for several days in the airport, precisely so that he would go back, write a virulently anti-Mozambican article, and include in it something along the lines of 'and the only person who helped me was the director of AIM, Carlos Cardoso'? So Cardoso changed his mind, and sent somebody else to the airport with Caetano's meal.

He revealed his suspicions in a lengthy letter to Rebelo, the manuscript of which has survived. 'I feel that over these years there have been people building a picture of me, which is something like this – Cardoso is undisciplined, Cardoso is rude, he has no idea of hierarchy, and that's why he speaks as he does etc. etc.' But the truth, he told Rebelo, was that he spoke the way he did because he had nothing to hide: when people asked him for his opinion, he gave it 'without hidden agendas, without the slightest machiavellianism in my heart'. Indeed, if he had committed any 'mistakes in perspective', it was

> not to have seriously analysed or discussed certain
> injustices committed by the very men and women who

sowed the grand justice of our independence. And when people discussed, pessimistically, the problems of the queues, of the prisons full of people who have no reason to be there, and other major problems, it was always Cardoso who did not despair, who was the chronic optimist, who said 'Everything will be solved, bit by bit. With Frelimo an injustice will not last long. We need strength.' So far the revolution has given me an inexhaustible source of enthusiasm that some people reduce to the word 'romanticism'.

The question posed is always: why did I misunderstand the presidential guideline? It was seven years of one way of thinking and acting that we were brusquely ordered to stop. These seven years have created their own inertia and perhaps this inertia had led me to understand as partial a stoppage which was supposed to be total.

Cardoso was not someone who boasted in public about his political credentials. But in this private letter to Rebelo he outlined them clearly:

I am aware that over the last 10 years of my life, I have given my youth and some of my health to the struggle for human dignity, initially in South Africa. There I fought against apartheid through the peculiar forms of university student radicalism. I then fought to publicise Frelimo in Johannesburg, Soweto, Durban, Cape Town, contributing modestly to the struggle of the South African people, and to the wave of popular glee that swept across South Africa after Frelimo's victory in Mozambique.

Back in Mozambique, he continued, he found himself in the 'inferno' of *Tempo* in 1976–77:

I battled for 16 to 18 hours a day, Sundays included, so that the magazine never missed an issue … And in the past two years, I have done something which for me was the most precious moment in my political definition: I have written dozens of articles against the bandit gangs, without any ambiguity of style, clearly, frontally against them and their South African command. And I signed all of them.

He was not presenting the party with any demand:

There's no invoice to present, because this is also my revolution, my country, my daily life of struggle as culture. And because this is also my party, and these are my leaders, and this is my newborn motherland. And because without all of this, I would be nothing of what I am.

So what arrested me was the process from which I have drunk my inspiration. It was as if one part of me was jailing the other part.

This letter ran to over 60 pages in Cardoso's handwriting. Since Rebelo cannot recall ever receiving it, perhaps it was written more as a form of therapy, and never sent.

Despite his detention, Cardoso was a member of a commission set up by Cabaço to prepare for a meeting between journalists and Machel (a meeting which never took place). The commission, whose other members were Mia Couto and Albino Magaia, held a series of meetings with reporters in Maputo and Beira. Their reports contained the main points made in discussion, not attributed by name. As a commission they refrained from giving their own views. The atmosphere at all the meetings was one of frustration at the obstacles put in the way of journalism. 'It's a disgrace that the best coverage of Mozambique is done by the BBC correspondent,' somebody remarked in Maputo, while another pointedly quoted Samora Machel's remark: 'If we don't tell our truth, the enemy will tell his.'

In Beira, the commission was told, 'A province in a state of war has a newspaper [*Diário de Moçambique*] of a province at peace. Silence is no answer. It's not the news that causes the climate of war. The war has entered people's homes through rumours and the constant cuts of water and power supplies.' Somebody recalled Sérgio Vieira's instruction to ministry of agriculture staff not to speak to the press. 'The agriculture minister forbade the transmission of information. What if all ministers did the same? Do we close down? Why doesn't the ministry of information take measures to unblock the situation?'

But Cardoso's heart did not seem to be in this work. His detention had shaken him and, to make matters worse, his relationship with Zé snapped. She dropped Cardoso – and started an affair with Mia Couto. Cardoso felt no resentment towards Mia; indeed, Mia recalls that, on the very day of his release, Cardoso went round to his office and said he knew of the affair. Instead of remonstrating with Mia, he suggested that the two of them should work together 'so that she can be happy'.

His immediate problem was somewhere to stay: he could not remain at Zé's house, and did not want to return at once to his own flat. Depressed and lonely, he spent a week with his loyal friends Rui Pereira and Odete de Carvalho. 'He came to us for comfort and moral support,' Odete recalled. 'He didn't understand why he had been detained. He was anguished that his loyalty had been called into question. The government never explained what he had done wrong,' she said. 'His depression came after prison, when they didn't call him, didn't explain anything to him. He was very, very low.'

Who authorised the detention? Cardoso suspected that it could only have been Machel, which made matters worse, given the enormous respect in which he held the president. Interviewed for this book, Rebelo emphatically denied ordering the detention. However, his phone conversations of the time with Mota Lopes give a different picture, with Rebelo prepared to take responsibility for what was a party decision. Mota Lopes's diary contains an entry for 15 January 1983: on that day Rebelo phoned and during their conversation said, 'When what happened with Cardoso happened, I took the decision to punish him – but afterwards I felt bad, because it's not the Party that should take these decisions, but you [the ministry of information]. But you don't do anything.'

For several months Cardoso was depressed and subdued. He decided to go to see his parents, who had left South Africa: his father was building up a new business in the northern Portuguese town of Guimarães. Wisely, he took several weeks' holiday in Portugal; but he only finally broke out of his depression with the Frelimo Fourth Congress in April 1983.

CHAPTER 8

Best of Times, Worst of Times?

The year 1983 brought out the best and the worst in Frelimo. As the apartheid regime stepped up the war, Frelimo reiterated its solidarity with the ANC, and the party's Fourth Congress was the high-water mark of Mozambican Marxism. But in the same year measures were taken that had nothing to do with Marxism, and seemed a retreat from reason in the face of mounting social problems. The first of these was the *lei de chicotada* (law on lashing), which introduced corporal punishment as an additional penalty for a wide range of offences. Convicted criminals could now expect to be lashed as well as jailed. Between three and 90 strokes were to be applied in cases of major theft, armed robbery, child molesting, and all forms of black marketeering and racketeering, now covered by the generic term *candonga*.[1]

The measure was deeply disturbing, first because it seemed to hark back to colonial methods (the lash and similar instruments were associated with Portuguese rule), and secondly because it was in such stark contradiction to Samora Machel's legality speech of 5 November 1981. Furthermore, the law was not even passed by the full parliament: it was rushed through by the Standing Commission of the People's Assembly on 1 April, just days after the full Assembly had ended a meeting. Since the leadership had been thinking about this for at least a few weeks, there was a clear decision not to put it before the full Assembly, presumably for fear that some deputies would speak against it. The constitution outlawed torture, and Machel had spoken out vigorously against torture in 1981 – but did this new law not bring back a form of torture? One member of the government did speak up. Shortly before it became law the minister of justice, Teodato Hunguana, wrote to Machel outlining his objections to the proposal. The result was that a few months later Hunguana was sacked.

Even worse, the use of the death penalty was extended. The 1979 law on state security introduced capital punishment for such offences as high treason, armed rebellion and terrorism. The death penalty had been used sparingly, against Rhodesian agents and MNR members in cases where civilians were killed. But in March 1983, the Assembly made serious forms of racketeering, as well as armed robbery and rape, punishable by death. So on 2 April, Goolam Nabi, accused of large-scale smuggling of prawns, one of Mozambique's main foreign exchange earners, was executed (despite pleas for clemency from some Islamic embassies), along with a train driver who had organised the robbery of his own train, two thieves who had robbed a bakery and killed its owner, and two MNR members found guilty of terrorism. The executions were semi-public. A large number of party members and state officials were summoned to witness the deaths by firing squad. This ensured a grotesque form of transparency.

There had already been public executions of several MNR members captured near the scenes of their crimes. These were in response to public anger, and in one case Joaquim Chissano, who was then acting governor of Maputo province, later said he intervened to save several others who would otherwise have been lynched. But the death of Goolam Nabi for defrauding the country of a certain amount of foreign exchange was a chilling new development. It aroused such revulsion that the leadership backtracked: nothing like it ever happened again. There were no more public executions of black marketeers.

Cardoso, unlike António Souto and a few other leading journalists, was spared the need to attend the executions – partly because he was not a Frelimo member, and anyway he was on holiday in Portugal. He returned in time for the Fourth Congress. Initially he was sceptical. 'Do you think anything will come of this congress?' he asked Lima. But by the end, his old fervour had returned – for the congress, though highly regimented, also showed Frelimo at its most attractive, hurling defiance at apartheid and at the United States, and standing shoulder to shoulder with liberation movements around the globe.

Machel's magnetic presence dominated the congress, and perhaps never more so than in an entirely unscripted exchange with a veteran of the liberation war, José Paulo Nchumali, who was infuriated at the lack of medical assistance for wounded soldiers. Nchumali turned to face Machel and declared, 'We have been infiltrated. Some of our enemies are sitting on the Central Committee. Some of our enemies are on the Council of Ministers.' A day later, Machel returned to Nchumali's remarks. 'It's not that the state apparatus is infiltrated. It's corrupted!' he declared. 'It's not that it's directly linked to the enemy. The problem is one of comfort.' The easy life of Maputo, the trappings of office, could corrupt leaders and distance them from the people. Ministers ran the risk of becoming 'slaves to their furniture, slaves to their residence'. He recalled: 'When we began the war of national liberation, a minority had to accept sacrifices for the majority. They had to break with comfort.'

That spirit was required to carry out the congress directives, said Machel. Those who found sacrifices too difficult should say so at once.

> The desertions can start now. We encourage this, we encourage people to give up now, instead of holding us back on our march. Whether you're a minister, a director, a secretary of state, if you can't do it, then you'd better say 'Look, congress delegates, in my ministry I am not able to do this' ... Better a few but good, than many but bad.

He suggested that ministers could leave the government and be sent to do other jobs for which their professional experience qualified them. Some might be better employed running major development projects. But the ministers might not react well to this. They might think they would lose their right to ride in a white Volvo, with a little flag of the Republic fluttering from the bonnet. 'Power corrupts, doesn't it?' remarked Machel wryly. 'This name of minister, secretary, governor also corrupts. They've become used to it.' Cardoso later recalled this as an example of Machel acting to 'deconsecrate the symbols of state'. This was 'the most difficult of liberations, not to be enslaved by the symbols that he had helped build. It breaks all the rules of the normal behaviour of power.' Machel, in Cardoso's vision, 'has taken the Socratic position of the gadfly of the state, a gadfly fighting against the trends to enclose men of state in their own symbols, and against the consequent theory of the need to reproduce this enclosure'. This improvised speech at the Fourth Congress was one of the pivotal pieces of evidence for Cardoso's claim that Frelimo was practising a qualitatively different sort of politics, what he called a 'mutation' in politics, and Machel was 'the first mutant'. He even wrote an unpublished book, entitled *The Mutants*, taking the form of a series of dialogues on Frelimo politics. 'The basic thing', he wrote, 'is not to allow a revolutionary power to be enclosed in a sphere of dogma so that that theory does not have to use binoculars in order to understand reality.' But what would happen if a gulf grew between the revolutionaries and the people? What would happen if the revolutionary gadflies were buried under a mountain of paper work? He answered with a grim prophecy: 'Reduced to a heap of marvellous memories, the revolution would finally wear the clothing of the executive or of dogma, and despair would reign supreme.'

❖

AIM was proud of its work during the congress. It had never produced so much material so fast before.

But a more important test for AIM came three weeks later. On 23 May, the South African airforce bombed Matola, killing six people and wounding a further 39. The South Africans claimed they were attacking military targets, 'ANC bases'. In fact, the main target hit was the Somopal jam factory, where three workers were killed. Anti-aircraft fire kept the planes away from the bridge over the Matola River, and from the oil refinery. They did, however, cause extensive damage to several large Matola houses owned by well-off Mozambicans, including Francisco Morgadinho, head of the state advertising company. The apartheid propaganda machine claimed that journalists only saw what the Mozambican government wanted them to see. In reality, what happened was that we got into whatever cars were available and drove to Matola without anybody stopping or directing us. Lima, Anders Nilsson (a Swedish photographer recruited to train up the AIM photo department), Joe Hanlon of the BBC, and Manuela Ferreira of the Portuguese agency NP were at Somopal within an hour of the strike, reaching the factory before Mozambican security did.

So AIM had the story and the photos – but we had no connection with the rest of the world. In a knee-jerk military reaction, the government had cut all telecommunications. We had the evidence of our own eyes, we had dramatic photographs, and we had no means of transmitting them, no phones, no telexes, no means of countering the South African propaganda which was by now all over the world. Cardoso contacted Cabaço and informed him that we couldn't do our job unless telecommunications links were restored. An agonising couple of hours followed, but shortly after lunchtime we were back in business. It's not clear whether this delay made much difference: Pretoria had a head start anyway, since the South African government issued its version as soon as the planes hit Matola. And since the main western media had offices in Johannesburg but not in Maputo, it was this version that was on the wires first.

But the AIM counter-attack was successful in that the English-language South African press did timidly report the Mozambican version. And the government was smart enough to invite South African journalists in. They could hear, from the tapes kept at the Maputo airport control tower, that the 'warning' broadcast by the South African planes, telling the government not to interfere because they were conducting 'operations against the ANC', had been broadcast not before the raid but after it, and so was just a propaganda ploy intended to soothe South African white opinion. They could also visit the site of the raid and see for themselves that neither the Somopal factory, nor Morgadinho's house looked much like a military base. Despite this access, South African press coverage was mostly disgraceful. Apartheid papers such as the *Citizen* and liberal ones such as the *Rand Daily Mail* by and large endorsed the official

Pretoria version. The Johannesburg *Star* would include AIM reports, but giving greater credence to the official Pretoria line. Idiotic declarations by the apartheid ambassador in London were printed before the report of the *Star*'s own journalist, Brendan Nicholson, who had bothered to go to Matola and admitted that 'Mozambican civilians were well-pounded'. One exception was the *Sunday Tribune*, which printed a long piece by Hanlon giving an accurate account of the strike. This called forth an angry response from the defence minister, Magnus Malan, who warned the South African press not to use 'foreign communists' as sources.

A week after the Matola raid, enemy aircraft were in the skies over southern Mozambique again. This time the FPLM exacted some revenge, and an unmanned spy plane of Israeli manufacture, with a powerful camera in its fuselage, was shot down over the bay of Maputo. The government did not repeat its earlier mistake. The story was on the wires immediately, and AIM was on hand when the wreckage of the spy plane was fished out of the bay the following day. The South African air force put out a denial. But we had the photos, we had the wreckage, and we had the plane's engine number. Eventually South African military intelligence admitted to the *Rand Daily Mail* that the Mozambican version was true. And AIM's credibility took another step forward.

Cardoso was also writing for the Portuguese press, attempting to show the true nature of Renamo in Lisbon, then the rebels' propaganda headquarters. For the weekly paper *O Jornal* he wrote of the grisly mutilations through which Renamo imposed its rule. There were the cases of Christina Menos and her mother Rosa Andrade, who lived in a Sofala village – after a Renamo raid, Cristina said, 'one of the bandits took a knife and sliced off my right ear. He began to laugh, and said I could call on Frelimo. My mother began to scream, and tried to flee. The same man grabbed her, cut off both her ears and threw them on the ground.' Then there was Joaquim Mapinda, a Sofala teacher, whose nose was cut off and who was forced to watch Renamo fighters raping the women of his village. Cardoso wrote,

> This kind of terror has been one of the most outstanding characteristics of the armed banditry phenomenon.

> Since it is so generalised, it cannot be blamed merely
> on the sadistic behaviour of this or that bandit. It is an
> attempt to provoke peasants to flee to the cities, where
> they will expand the ranks of the unemployed and
> worsen an already difficult food situation. It is the use
> of terror as an integral part of destabilisation.

Cardoso was shocked to find that even a centre-left paper such as *O Jornal* would uncritically publish statements put out by the Renamo Lisbon office. He wrote to one of the paper's editors, Caceres Monteiro: 'I've been shocked by the articles you've been publishing on the MNR. It saddens me to learn that *O Jornal* is not immune to the penetration of the South African lobby in Lisbon. It is hard to believe that you decided to give the benefit of the doubt to people whose lack of scruples is so painfully experienced in the bush.' *O Jornal* could not claim ignorance, since plenty of information on Renamo was available from Mozambican sources. 'I cannot dissociate journalism from the atrocities that the MNR has committed in my country,' Cardoso declared. After this, his collaboration with *O Jornal* came to an end.

❖

The Fourth Congress had stressed decentralisation, and Cabaço took this seriously. He argued that the media was heavily concentrated in Maputo, which was more comfortable than provincial capitals, let alone district capitals. Adapting Machel's speech on comfort and corruption, Cabaço, in a meeting in May 1983, asked how many journalists were prepared to leave the capital and work in the provinces. The result may not have been what he expected – many of the volunteers were senior journalists, still fired with the enthusiasm of the Fourth Congress. Among them was almost every senior journalist at AIM, including Cardoso and Lima. Younger journalists, by and large, did not volunteer. The photographs of the volunteers were placed on a roll of honour. And there the matter died. There was no follow-up, and none of the volunteers were dispatched to the provinces. In retrospect it is easy to see why. The wrong people had volunteered. Cabaço needed people like Cardoso and Lima in Maputo: dispatching them to the provinces would have beheaded

AIM. Furthermore, stiffening the media's presence in the provinces would have meant finding houses for these reporters, and ensuring reasonable communications. It would also have entailed overriding any reservations that provincial governments might have had: in the end the ministry of information was not powerful enough to pull this off.

In any case, within a few weeks the country was plunged into a new crisis, this time entirely of Frelimo's making. During the congress Machel had, in an apparently throwaway remark, suggested that people without work cards proving that they were in regular employment should be expelled from the cities and sent to the countryside to produce food. At a rally on 21 May he declared, 'Only those who work can stay in the cities', and threatened 'the unemployed, the under-employed, the parasites and the marginal elements' with forced evacuation to the countryside. This won a thoughtless round of applause, since nobody had really thought out what 'work' and 'unemployment' meant in a Mozambican city. Was the Frelimo leadership saying that nobody except workers in the formal sector could live in cities? Were they really unaware of the size of the informal sector?

But a month later the government pushed ahead with the grotesquely misnamed 'Operation Production', under which 'the unproductive' would be moved from a life of supposed idleness in the cities to productive work in the countryside. Interior minister Armando Guebuza was put in charge of the operation. The initial phase was voluntary: the unemployed were asked to register, and thus express willingness to work outside the cities. A fortnight later, in early July, the coercive phase began. 'Unproductive' people were rounded up and deported from the cities – usually by air to Niassa. Thus the country's meagre reserves of jet fuel were used to move the 'unproductive' from one end of the country to the other, rather than for anything economically or militarily useful. Nobody has ever provided figures for the enormous costs involved. Who were the 'unproductive'? Basically anyone who was not carrying any of three documents: an identity card, a resident's card, or a work card. Safeguards were supposed to be in place to ensure that people who were employed but, for whatever reason, did not possess a work card, were not expelled. But it was a bureaucrat's paradise and a nightmare for the honest poor. (The dishonest ones could look after themselves without much difficulty.)

Faced with abuse of human rights on this scale, what could reporters do? The dilemma was acute: frontally denouncing a government that was under attack from apartheid was out of the question. Most leading journalists were ideologically committed to Frelimo, and they would do nothing to betray Samora Machel. So the media opted for a strategy of mitigation. It denounced instances where the guidelines were violated, and where people who had every right to be in the cities were under threat of removal. Journalists denounced arrogant policemen who demanded documents that had nothing to do with Operation Production (such as marriage certificates). They looked for, and found, the settling of old scores, or cases where single mothers were accused of prostitution. There were cases when people without documents were rounded up and taken to evacuation centres even though it was obvious they could not be deported – they were too old, or they were pregnant, for instance. Guebuza himself had to intervene in some such cases. Occasionally teenagers were detained, so the government belatedly had to issue instructions that nobody under the age of 16 was covered by Operation Production (legally nobody under that age should work anyway). No doubt this sort of vigilance softened the impact of Operation Production. But the main problem was not isolated abuses – it was that the whole concept, from beginning to end, was one enormous abuse of power. And this the media, under the dominant paradigm for journalism, could not begin to tackle.

Operation Production hit AIM very directly. Fernando Gonçalves had been on a trip to Cape Verde. The day he returned he found that his 19-year-old sister had been detained as an 'unproductive' on the orders of the local dynamising group. She was a student, or at least was trying to be one. Because of the shortage of places in secondary schools, she had failed to enrol in eighth grade. The family regarded her as a student, the dynamising group as an 'unproductive'. Gonçalves went straight to the dynamising group office. He recalls starting to argue rationally with the officials, saying that Operation Production was not intended to round up teenagers who had been unable to enrol in school. When they paid no attention, he lost his temper and told the officials they were acting incompetently. Unknown to Gonçalves, there was a magistrate in the room, who promptly ordered his arrest, charging him with the crime of 'insulting the magistracy'. He was hauled before a Maputo court the following morning.

Gonçalves' family informed AIM, and Cardoso and Lima attempted to rescue him. They went to see the judge before the trial, to argue that this was all a misunderstanding. Unfortunately the judge, Albano Maiopuè, was a cold and arrogant figure, full of his own importance and deeply hostile to journalists, even though he was married to one (Margarida Guitunga, who later, ironically enough, went to work at AIM). The meeting was disastrous. When Cardoso extended his hand, Maiopuè declined to shake it. He said that in greeting a magistrate, it is the judge who extends his hand first, not the commoner. He listened impatiently to what the two had to say – and then threatened to have Cardoso arrested for contempt of court. Gonçalves was just one on a list of cases to be dealt with by Maiopuè that day. One by one, petty thieves and vagrants appeared before the judge for trials that were summary in the extreme. None of them had lawyers: they were represented by an 'official defender' – a young woman who said virtually nothing the whole morning. Cardoso remarked that she seemed to be there for merely decorative purposes.

Maiopuè passed sentence, mostly short terms of imprisonment, and then when Fernando Gonçalves was brought before him, to our surprise he pleaded guilty. I imagined he had wrongly assumed that a guilty plea would win him a lesser sentence. But he later he said he had no idea what he was doing. 'I wasn't told I had the right to a lawyer. I never even met the official defender.' The judge refused to allow Gonçalves to call family members as witnesses, and then launched into a lecture about Operation Production. This was a key policy of the Frelimo government, he declared, and it was incumbent on all citizens to support it.[2] Gonçalves's guilt was all the greater precisely because he was a journalist, and therefore should know better. The official defender was as useless and mute in Gonçalves's case as in all her previous ones that morning, making no attempt to indicate mitigating circumstances. To our dismay, Maiopuè proceeded to sentence Gonçalves to 12 months' imprisonment. Within 48 hours, he was on a plane heading for a re-education camp in Niassa. Gonçalves found the conditions on the plane broke elementary air traffic rules: there were more passengers than seats, and the surplus passengers sat in the aisle.

Cardoso was amazed at Maiopuè's behaviour: he had not witnessed this sort of trial before. Although the court called itself a 'people's tribunal', it seemed just a shoddy parody of a colonial court. Cardoso described the proceedings as a farce, and set about trying to get Gonçalves released. AIM sent a request to the new justice minister, José Oscar Monteiro. Lima recalls him as being sympathetic but pointing out the difficulty of a minister intervening to overturn a court decision.

Gonçalves was not released until he had served eight months of his sentence.

CHAPTER 9

Nkomati: Hope and Disillusion

Operation Production came to an abrupt end in August 1983. Reports of abuses had reached Machel from various sources, and he could see that, far from bolstering Frelimo's support, the bungled evacuations were ruining the party's prestige. In hindsight, Operation Production can be seen as a disastrous diversion. Government efforts were channelled into dumping planeloads of 'unproductives' in Niassa while the military situation deteriorated and the country was on the brink of famine.

A return to reality kicked in when Machel visited Zambezia in August and saw that the war, launched into this province from Malawi, was bringing the Zambezia economy to a standstill. The provincial capital, Quelimane, was virtually cut off from the rest of the province. The country's largest industrial project, a huge textile factory at Mocuba being built with help from the GDR, was years behind schedule, largely because equipment could not be moved to Mocuba from Quelimane port. Machel could see that the war itself was going very badly. He was angered to find that young officers sent from Maputo several months earlier to head operations and train local soldiers were avoiding combat. At the barracks in Mocuba he asked, 'How many actions have you participated in since arriving here?' Several officers replied, 'None.' So Machel demoted them, and drafted in eight veterans of the independence war, headed by José Ajape, who had commanded the Mozambican force in Zimbabwe, to launch a counter-offensive against Renamo. The Mozambican army could claim success in one area. Under the dynamic leadership of General Domingos Fondo, the FPLM restored order to much of

Inhambane province, driving Renamo out of its main base at Mambuili. But this was the only area where the military situation was markedly improving.

Military success revealed the extent of a hidden crisis. In 1983 the rains failed everywhere south of the Save River; in areas severely affected by Renamo's insurgency, drought turned into famine. Where Mozambican troops reasserted government control, they found tens of thousands of near-destitute people whose livestock and meagre food reserves had been plundered by Renamo. With the assistance of international NGOs, the government established relief centres. Hungry people flocked there, with many dying en route. Suddenly scenes that conjured up earlier famines in Ethiopia or the Sahel were recorded in southern Mozambique. Cardoso dispatched Anders Nilsson to Inhambane, and he brought back stark images of malnourished children with their matchstick limbs and swollen bellies. 'I never thought I'd see pictures like these from my country' was Lima's immediate reaction to the first photos.

Nobody knows how many people died in the 1983–84 famine in Gaza and Inhambane, though a round figure of 100 000 is often given. Droughts are cyclical in southern Mozambique, and this one had begun in 1981. The government appealed to international donors in January 1983; by then it was clear that in the southern provinces the main 1983 harvest would be a near-total write-off. The government appealed again to embassies and NGOs in June. But the famine had given the enemies of the revolution great leverage and, despite Machel's European tour of October, total foreign aid to Mozambique in 1983 was lower than it had been in 1982. The donors, as Joe Hanlon remarked, had gone on strike.[1] That was the background to the negotiations with South Africa that began in late 1983. The donors had made it clear that they would help Mozambique out of its plight, but only if it reached a deal with South Africa.

Then the rhetoric changed. When Machel announced that Mozambican and South African delegations were meeting in Swaziland on 20 December, he said this was crucial for 'finding a modus vivendi in the region'. Neighbours were not a matter of choice, said Machel, and 'we cannot change geography'. The announcement was an example of Machel outflanking his government. The Mozambican and South African governments had decided to keep the Swaziland talks secret. Clearly Machel thought this was a bad idea: when the talks opened, he was at a summit in Bissau, and broke the news to reporters there. This was one of the few occasions on which the Mozambican version of events hit the world press before the South African one. No doubt Machel broke the informal agreement with the South Africans because he knew that otherwise Pretoria would leak its own slanted account, painting the talks as a triumph for apartheid. Machel wanted Mozambique to be seen as an actor in the talks, not just as a victim.

Sol de Carvalho was reporting for AIM from the Bissau summit. On the long journey back (Machel called in at Benin and Angola en route), the president repeatedly briefed Carvalho on the plane, and Carvalho relayed it all back by telex from Cotonou and Luanda to Cardoso. Machel insisted that the talks signified no change in Mozambique's position towards apartheid: he stressed that South Africa had been given advance notice that Mozambique was not going to the talks to recognise apartheid or the bantustans, or to destroy the ANC. After further talks in Pretoria and Maputo in January, the outline of a deal was fairly clear: South Africa was to stop destabilising Mozambique in exchange for an end to support for the ANC's military wing. For most foreign analysts, this was a straight swap: Renamo for the ANC.

Cardoso did not accept this analysis, sticking to the line that there was no comparison, since there were no ANC bases in Mozambique. In a January 1984 editorial he wrote:

> The ANC is not the creation of Mozambique. Long before the first stirrings of Mozambican nationalism, the ANC was leading the struggle of South Africa's people against racial discrimination. The ANC is in South Africa. Its bases are there. Its militants are there. And that is where the idea of a non-racial South African nation grows day by day.
>
> For Mozambique and the whole of southern Africa, the underlying issue to be discussed is South Africa's

attempt to destabilise its neighbours. For the South African government, the real internal issue is how to keep the people of South Africa from continuing their fight against apartheid. Sooner or later, the Pretoria authorities will have to talk to the real leaders of the South African people.

Those who insist on spurious comparisons between the ANC and the bandits of the MNR, while trying to forget the growing struggle inside South Africa, are in for a short, sharp shock when they find that reality does not match up to their view of the world.

Spurious or not, the comparison was perfectly clear in a joint communiqué issued by the Mozambican and South African negotiators on 16 January, which said the two sides had 'considered measures to be taken in order that the territory of neither state should serve as a springboard for aggression and violent actions against the other'. Gone was all the defiant 'Let them come!' rhetoric. Instead the head of the Mozambican delegation, minister in the presidency Jacinto Veloso, was talking about establishing 'the principles of our relationship as two sovereign states, equal to equal' and of developing 'viable and long-range economic relations' with South Africa.

Two months later the pact was signed. But a couple of days before, there was an expanded meeting of the Frelimo leadership to which senior journalists, including Cardoso, were invited. Luís Bernardo Honwana recalls Samora Machel vigorously defending the impending Accord he was to sign with PW Botha at Nkomati, on the border. Honwana recalls Machel declaring, 'We have obliged the enemy to sign,' but it was clear that many in the room found that hard to believe. Machel tackled that latent tension with the rhetorical question: 'Is there anyone who doubts that the Nkomati Accord is a triumph for the Mozambican revolution?' This was met with almost total silence, except that one hand at the back of the room shot up and Cardoso replied, 'Me, Comrade President.' Honwana says he knew that plenty of people in the leadership had their doubts about the strategy outlined by Machel, but only Cardoso had the courage to say so. Unfortunately, the meeting just carried on, and

Machel did not ask Cardoso to explain his objections.

Certainly Cardoso had no objection to the principle of signing an agreement with Pretoria: indeed, in the media he was the foremost advocate of the agreement. What must have worried him was the triumphalist tone used by Machel: yes, Mozambican diplomacy had scored some points in the negotiations, but this did not mean that apartheid was about to collapse. Honwana says the image of Cardoso querying the president has remained vivid in his mind. Far from leading to any hostile reaction, he thought it increased Machel's respect for Cardoso.

❖

On 16 March 1984, South Africa got what it said it wanted from Mozambique: a non-aggression pact. At Nkomati, Samora Machel and PW Botha signed the 'Agreement on Non-Aggression and Good Neighbourliness'.[2] This very short treaty outlawed any use of force in the relations between the two countries. Its key clause stated:

> the High Contracting Parties shall not allow their respective territories, territorial waters or air space to be used as a base, thoroughfare, or in any other way by another state, government, foreign military forces, organisations or individuals which plan or prepare to commit acts of violence, terrorism or aggression against the territorial integrity or political independence of the other, or may threaten the security of its inhabitants.

To achieve this, each side pledged 'to forbid and prevent in their respective territories the organisation of irregular forces or armed bands' who intended to carry out such acts of violence. This was a simple quid pro quo: South Africa would stop its military support for the MNR if Mozambique stopped its support for the ANC. Contrary to what was believed in some quarters, there was no economic component to the Accord, and Mozambique offered no diplomatic recognition to South Africa. The South African side had hoped to extract further concessions when the preliminary discussions began. But in the end what they got was a simple pledge: if you don't hit me, I won't hit you.

Óscar Monteiro, who was then justice minister and on the negotiating team, points out that the South Africans (and the United States) were also obsessed that Mozambique might offer naval bases to the Soviet Union (indeed, entirely false claims about alleged Soviet naval facilities in the port of Nacala occasionally surfaced in right-wing papers). The Nkomati Accord thus denied support to any other state that might threaten the territory of either of the signatories. This cost Mozambique nothing: the government had never offered the USSR bases, and the USSR had never asked for them. But the clause made Mozambique look good in the eyes of the Reagan administration. 'The west really was afraid that Mozambique might became a base for the Soviets,' Monteiro recalls. 'This was an important point for them. We kept the US and Britain informed of the Nkomati talks, and we gave them guarantees that our territory would not be used by the eastern bloc. This was part of breaking out of our isolation.'

Cardoso attended the signing and was euphoric about it – despite an ugly piece of censorship. AIM had produced a dossier on the Mozambican viewpoint which we intended to distribute to the South African press, certain to be present at Nkomati in large numbers. We ran together a series of articles on South African support for Renamo, and the Mozambican rationale for a non-aggression pact, and duplicated a couple of hundred copies for distribution. But when Cardoso got off the train at Nkomati, it was all confiscated – not by South African but by Mozambican security. As a result, there was nothing to counterbalance the insidious spin put on the Nkomati Accord by the apartheid media-minders in South Africa. AIM was prevented from putting across a Mozambican view by agents of the Mozambican state itself.

In some quarters, the non-aggression pact was viewed as betrayal: the ANC itself came close to saying this in a statement signed by Alfred Nzo (later to become the first foreign minister of a democratic South Africa), and a savage editorial in the French radical magazine *AfriqueAsie* described Mozambique as 'la conquête de Pretoria'. Frelimo, however, hailed Nkomati as a victory for peace; and, whatever his reservations at the meeting with Machel may have been, the main person pushing this line in the press was Cardoso. He was not kowtowing to the party. He agreed on this issue, and what he wrote reflected a genuine, considered opinion. It was not one shared by the rest of AIM. Lima and I could not regard signing a non-aggression agreement with PW Botha as anything but a colossal retreat. After all, it was only three years since Samora had thrown down the gauntlet to Botha. Could there be a sharper contrast between the 'Let them come!' speech of February 1981 and the Nkomati signing of March 1984?

But Cardoso's argument was sophisticated, and is worth repeating in some detail. In an article entitled 'The painful return to Vorster' written shortly after the Accord, Cardoso argued that Nkomati showed that the militarist strategy followed by Botha and Malan had failed, and the apartheid regime was returning to a variant of the 'détente' policy followed by Botha's disgraced predecessor, John Vorster, in the 1970s:

> What the regime told its public – namely that it always wanted to draw up pacts of non-aggression with the countries of the region – is one thing. But what it actually tried to do through its destabilisation strategy is something completely different. No regime in the world spends a billion dollars a year in order to cobble together non-aggression pacts. This sort of money is spent in order to overthrow governments, or force them to change direction. This was what the South African regime desired in the region.

Botha and Malan's strategy towards Mozambique had been 'to force Frelimo to change its political direction – either to negotiate with the bandits, or to abandon its socialist programme'. At the same time, in Angola it tried to force the MPLA government to negotiate with Unita.

Cardoso argued that the regime failed on both fronts, while the costs of the military, and of keeping the colonial administration functioning in Namibia, soared. Furthermore, there was a real threat of the loss of many white troops if Pretoria maintained a military presence in southern Angola. The Soviet Union had made it clear that it would not abandon Angola; and, despite its anti-communist rhetoric, Reagan was not about to rush to Pretoria's rescue. So the regime performed a volte-face. South African soldiers began pulling out of Angola, the Namibian nationalist Herman Toivo ya Toivo was freed, and, Cardoso claimed, 'Journalists who are close to government leaders have been given the go-ahead to write articles on the military and administrative costs of holding on to Namibia, in order to prepare white public opinion for the eventual independence of the territory.' And on the border with Mozambique, Pretoria signed an agreement which, Cardoso confidently predicted, 'means the end of its support for the MNR'.

He suggested that 'with all this, Pretoria may be trying to gain international credibility, persuade the international community to shrug its shoulders at the violence of apartheid, win time – ten years, perhaps – to consolidate the bantustans, and thus retain the rule of the white minority in a future federal, balkanised South Africa'. The regime might also be moving 'from a position of military retreat to a position of economic offensive, trying to use its economy as the lever for regaining regional hegemony'. Thus Botha and Malan had wasted eight years in hard-line military antics before returning to Vorster's foreign policy. Botha and Malan believed that, because they were white, and because they had at their disposal a military apparatus of considerable proportions, they could make history run backwards. All that followed from this was a gigantic error. Made aware of their mistake, 'Botha and Malan have now disinterred what was the accumulated – albeit small – experience of the regime to which they once belonged: they have disinterred Balthazar Johannes Vorster who, perhaps due to his contacts with African presidents, had begun to have some inkling of how absurd were preconceptions of racial superiority.'

An AIM editorial from Cardoso's pen claimed, in April 1984, that the Accord 'is a success for Mozambican diplomacy, and a stage in a process where the goal is to create a climate of peace, stability and progress in southern Africa, free of racial discrimination and oppression'. Destabilisation had boomeranged against western interests, and the Reagan administration had moderated its initial support for Pretoria. Diplomatic efforts by Mozambique and other

African states 'helped clarify for the west, and for the United States in particular, what the true nature of the conflict in this region is, drawing attention to the importance and urgency of establishing a climate of peace and tranquillity in southern Africa'.

There were two major problems with Cardoso's analysis. It assumed that the regime was fairly monolithic, and that when Botha gave the signal everyone would change course. More seriously, it did not even consider that apartheid might regard Nkomati as a step, not towards a Vorster-style détente, but towards weakening Frelimo and the SADCC. True, a military offensive had not led Frelimo to deal with the MNR or abandon its Marxist ideology – but maybe the regime was quite capable of talking peace while resupplying the MNR at the same time. Which is exactly what happened. The war did not wind down – and Pretoria could play the innocent, claiming that, since it was not supporting the MNR, the rebellion must be endogenous.

Mozambique kept its side of the bargain. While there were never any ANC bases in Mozambique in the sense of fixed military installations, it was certainly true that ANC military operatives passed through Mozambique, and Joe Slovo did not merely play bridge in his Maputo flat. With Nkomati, the ANC presence in Maputo was downgraded. Mozambican security even went to the zealous extreme of searching the homes of about two dozen ANC members, including Joe Slovo, as if to say to Pretoria, 'Look! No weapons!'

Perhaps Nzo's statement was issued without Oliver Tambo's knowledge, or possibly he backtracked; for, a few days later, at a press conference in London, Tambo took quite a different line. He expressed an understanding for the Mozambican government's dilemma. 'I'm not sure that in their position I'd have gone quite so far,' he said, 'but it must be accepted that the South African regime had decided to destroy Mozambique, to kill it as a state, and the leadership was forced to choose between life and death. So if it meant hugging the hyena, they had to do it.' And a few weeks after Nkomati, Thabo Mbeki of the ANC executive was in Maputo to restore a working relationship. 'It's perfectly clear that the South African regime would like Mozambique and the ANC to quarrel,' he said. But they were still jointly committed to the destruction of apartheid 'whatever problems, differences or misunderstandings' might have arisen over Nkomati. This did not stop Slovo moving hurriedly to Lusaka. But ANC civilians could stay and carry on their normal jobs. Albie Sachs continued his legal work, and the ANC journalist Dan Moyana remained Christie's right-hand man on the radio's External Service. At AIM, Nkomati was no hindrance to recruiting a prominent ANC member, David Rabkin, who, under the pseudonym John Khumalo, wrote a stream of articles analysing events in South Africa.

❖

The partial unfreezing of relations between Maputo and Pretoria meant that Mozambican journalists could visit South Africa. Cardoso returned after a nine years' absence. He discovered that the militarisation of South African society in those nine years had led to enormous changes. He revisited Wits – to find that the university entrance had been redesigned 'as a sort of mini-labyrinth. That design had nothing to do with architectural aesthetics. In my time it had been relatively easy to escape from the truncheons of the police by running across the lawn. I wondered what today's students did.' On a door beside the Wits Great Hall, he found a notice bearing the words 'security information'. There had been nothing of the sort in the early 1970s. There was a security room, and uniformed men from a private security company strolled past. 'Nine years ago, it was the police who forced their way into the university to beat us up,' wrote Cardoso. 'Now, I am told, they don't need to make such a fuss. A university security apparatus, hired in order "to defend persons and property from possible terrorist actions," now intervenes from within to repress the students.'

Everywhere he went in Johannesburg he saw security systems, surveillance cameras, and uniformed men. 'The scenery is completed by an astonishing proliferation of walls. High walls,' Cardoso wrote. 'Walls round houses, walls round security premises. Walls everywhere.' For someone returning after almost a decade, the change was something of a shock. In fact much of the security was against violent crime, which had surged, but the walls reminded Cardoso of how Salisbury had looked on the eve of the 1980 Zimbabwean elections. To him, the apartheid regime was going down the Rhodesian road of increased repression and increased security.

There was a climate of fear among whites now, and it was not just fear that one day the ANC might seize power. When Cardoso visited earlier, on 16 January, accompanying a pre-Nkomati meeting of ministerial delegations, his first feeling was that South African journalists were careful to distance themselves from the handful of Mozambican journalists. There was none of the effusive atmosphere that characterised occasional meetings with those same journalists elsewhere in the region.

> A week spent in Johannesburg confirmed this feeling. I did not manage to speak to a single white intellectual (even among the supporters of PW Botha and his reforms) who failed to warn me of the need to take the greatest of care in anything connected with politics. Some of my old anti-apartheid comrades from my student days have survived a harsh process of prison and banning orders, and today they are still active in the legal opposition. Others have taken up a secluded, family life. But all seem wrapped in an enormous loneliness … The walls that security companies have built round houses and factories have become transformed into walls between people.

The South African social structure was changing. Whites, no matter what their skills or lack of them, used to be guaranteed a job – that was one of the reasons for setting up apartheid in the first place. But in 1984 Cardoso encountered the phenomenon of white unemployment. Former colleagues from university had taken unrewarding clerical jobs because the alternative was unemployment. 'Non-whites' were now moving into jobs where, 10 years before, a black face would have been unthinkable. It was the same in education. When Cardoso was thrown out of South Africa, only 150 of the 11 000 full-time students at Wits were black, coloured or Indian. Nine years later he found that fully 16 per cent of the student body was 'non-white'. 'The regime has tried, at great speed, to create a black middle class which it envisages as a buffer between itself and the demands of the great mass of black workers,' Cardoso argued.

> But the creation of this class has not arisen merely because the regime is convinced of its economic usefulness. It is also the result of countless popular struggles against South Africa's labour laws, and against racial discrimination at work. Working class demands and student struggles throughout the 1970s were perhaps the principal force leading the regime to adopt a strategy for coopting a part of the black population.

Those struggles had impacted on the distribution of wealth. 'Undoubtedly the greater part of the cake is still gobbled by the whites, but the black middle class is now sitting at the table.'

❖

On 25 May, Cardoso was invited to give the Fairbairn Memorial Lecture to the South African Society of Journalists in Johannesburg. Here he could tell other professionals how he envisaged journalism – and it was emphatically not a vision of neutrality. Journalists had to choose: 'We either contribute to bringing peoples together by accentuating decolonisation and each people's contribution to the common road of humanity, or we contribute towards the reproduction of the humiliating and mediocre relations of domination.' For Cardoso, African (and especially South African) journalism had to be decolonised, and he hit hard at the stereotypes regarding Mozambique so prevalent in South Africa, and largely borrowed from the west.

> As Mozambican journalists, we have often been asked: Does Mozambique follow the Soviet, Chinese or Yugoslav model? Most people who ask this do not know that the question itself is an insult, because they are not conscious of the preconceptions on which it rests.

> Theories, like empires, take time to die. And some theories die many years after the death of the empires that gave them birth. Such is the case with the theory that views local conflicts as mere extensions of the conflict between east and west.

There were blocs headed by the US and the USSR, and 'the rest of the world is just scenery, a mere passive instrument of the only two blocs capable of making history'. This was the prism, Cardoso argued, through which far too many editors had viewed Samora Machel's trip to various western countries in 1983. It was said that Mozambique was 'turning' to the west, and the crudest variants of this position were either that 'Mozambique has recognised the failure of socialism' or that 'Mozambique was abandoned by the socialist countries'. Cardoso was honest enough to admit that stereotypical analysis was not a monopoly of western or South African analysts. Some of the country's eastern European allies believed that Mozambique 'was moving straight and naively into the mouth of the evil capitalist wolf'.

In Mozambique itself, however, 'we merely reaffirmed some old principles' – such as that the country 'non-aligned in its foreign policy, and socialist in its choice of development, was seeking more friends and fewer enemies'. Mozambican journalists asked such questions as: To what extent has the west concluded that war in southern Africa is against its own political and economic interests? and: To what extent could western interests in a southern Africa free from war coincide with Mozambique's interests in building a strong and independent nation? Thus Samora Machel's European tour had wildly differing interpretations. 'For some, it was a political matter to be analysed as to its objectives and nuances, its pros and cons. For others, it was simply a matter of making reality conform to the pre-established theory that the existence of two world bosses is immutable and all-embracing.'

Nor was the reliance on cold-war clichés just a case of mental laziness. In the South African case it was permeated with racism.

> Under its skin, deep inside its veins, there is the racist premise that the peoples of the so-called third world are not makers of history. Either they are dominated by the west or they are automatically dominated by the east. The religious dichotomy good–bad, heaven–hell, is thus reproduced in politics with the insidious coincidence that those who are in the middle – the specta-

tors, the non-makers of history – are the non-whites of the world.

According to the east–west conflict theory, the African must choose. And to have to choose between east and west is to accept a secondary role in the act of fashioning the destiny of the world. It means one is condemned forever to have a political, economic, ideological and cultural boss.

He went on to attack those African journalists who have their feet in Africa, but their heads somewhere in the metropoles of the old colonial empires.

Our people make history but this history appears in our media completely distorted. It is digested via interpretations made in distant capitals, and brought here through the telex machine and the satellite, and above all, via the colonised brains of many of us.

Cardoso's vision of an independent journalism had nothing to do with who owned the media. He wanted independence from western stereotypes, from models made for other realities and other times, models that some African journalists 'apply so uncritically that they end up insulting the history of their peoples . . . It will suffice to draw your attention to the fact that many African media treat genuine guerrilla movements as "terrorists" and classify as "guerrillas" groups of bandits.' Cardoso proudly staked out his position, a position he would defend to the end of his life:

As an African journalist, I refuse to be dominated by definitions and models in the formulation of which neither I nor my people have participated. To be independent, therefore, means first of all to reject the claim of universality for norms and rules resulting from specific processes of a reality foreign to mine. Either I am independent in this way or I will not be able to participate on a par with journalists of other countries, regions and continents in fashioning any decisions pertaining to the media. Without this independence, someone else will be the microphone and I the loudspeaker.

A side-effect of Nkomati was that AIM could open an office in South Africa. The man chosen to be correspondent was Leite Vasconcelos, taking advantage of the fact that Vasconcelos was going to Johannesburg anyway for medical treatment. The South Africans created bureaucratic obstacles to Vasconcelos's accreditation, but in the end they had little option but to accept. Vasconcelos was able to start work in October 1984. From then right through to the late 1990s, AIM had a reliable correspondent in Johannesburg (first Vasconcelos, and later Maria de Lourdes Torcato). The South African regime now expected the Mozambican government to control the press. A clause in the Nkomati Accord banned propaganda that incited 'war of aggression', and Pretoria wanted to interpret this as 'No more articles critical of apartheid!' At the meetings of the joint security commission post-Nkomati, Oscar Monteiro recalled, the South African side 'brought in articles, quotations, transcripts of Radio Mozambique programmes'. To these complaints, the Mozambican negotiators shrugged their shoulders and told the South Africans, 'We don't control the press.'

❖

Meanwhile there was still no sign of the war winding down. Quite the contrary: the MNR was now regularly hitting the power lines from Komatipoort to Maputo, plunging the city into darkness. Trains and buses in Maputo province came under attack. Mozambican patience had its limits, and in late September Jacinto Veloso warned that continuing violence was endangering the Nkomati Accord itself. On 1 October, Veloso was in Pretoria and the South African government tried to lure his delegation into face-to-face talks with the MNR general secretary, Evo Fernandes. Veloso refused, and so the South Africa foreign minister, Pik Botha, and Magnus Malan had to shuttle between the room where Veloso's delegation was sitting and the one where Evo Fernandes was waiting. Veloso steadfastly refused any 'political discussion' with Renamo.

The final result was a document known as the Pretoria Declaration, which Botha read out in the presence of Veloso and Fernandes. This said: '1. Samora Moises Machel is recognised as the President

of the People's Republic of Mozambique. 2. Armed activity and conflict within Mozambique, from whatever quarter or source, must
stop.' Two other short points said that South Africa 'is requested to
consider playing a role in the implementation of this declaration',
and a commission for implementation would be established. As far
as the Mozambican government was concerned, the document
meant that, in recognising Machel as president, Renamo also recognised the Mozambican state and all its institutions. Renamo denied
there was any such commitment. The Mozambicans, Cardoso
included, believed that the South Africans had pledged to persuade
Renamo to accept an offer of amnesty, and disband. But the regime
sold the Declaration to international public opinion as the start of
'political negotiations' between Maputo and Renamo.

Reality burst in on 24 December 1984. That was when a captured Renamo fighter named Arnaldo Martins spoke at a rally held
by Machel in the town of Manhiça. He said he had been arrested in
South Africa, handed over to Renamo, and given military training.
But this was not before Nkomati, or even shortly after Nkomati – it
was in October 1984, when the South African government was supposedly trying to implement the Pretoria Declaration. Machel
remarked that, although Renamo had its 'publicity headquarters' in
Lisbon, South Africa was responsible for the violence. 'Let's make no
mistake,' Machel said, 'South Africa is the key to the problem, and
that's why we signed the Nkomati Accord.'

On the first anniversary of Nkomati, there were no celebrations.
Cardoso's editorial pointed out that 'a year after the agreement,
Mozambican workers and peasants are still being killed and maimed,
foreign citizens working on development projects are gunned down
or kidnapped, vehicles are still ambushed and burnt, economic
installations destroyed. The aggression, in short, continues.' And
much of it indisputably came from South African soil. The sabotage
of the transmission lines carrying electricity to Maputo was the work
of gangs operating from the South African side of the border, and
where else but South Africa could the planes violating southern
Mozambican airspace come from? This article admitted what much
of the AIM newsroom had argued right from the start – that South

Africa may well have disregarded the Accord 'because it saw the agreement as a mere tactic, a first step in a vaster plan, the goal of which was to force Mozambique to accept sharing power with the bandits'.

There were some scraps of comfort to be salvaged from the wreckage of Nkomati. Prior to the Accord, western governments 'were sympathetic to Pretoria's argument that Mozambique posed a military threat. Yet Mozambique's full implementation of the agreement, and the South African government's non-implementation of Nkomati, must now lead those governments to see Pretoria as the main threat to peace in the region.' But Cardoso had to conclude: 'Whatever gains may have been won because of Nkomati, for Mozambique they are dwarfed by the continuing terrorist violence. One year after the signing of the agreement there is very little to celebrate.'

As relations with Pretoria deteriorated, those with the ANC improved. Moses Mabhida, general secretary of the South African Communist Party, had been one of the ANC exiles harassed by Mozambican security when the Nkomati Accord was signed; but when he died on 8 March 1986 the Mozambican government gave Mabhida a state funeral with full military honours, at which the speakers were Machel, Oliver Tambo and Joe Slovo, once again a welcome guest in Maputo. Machel described the communist leader as 'an elder brother' who had chosen 'to bid farewell to life here, on the borders of his own country' rather than seeking more advanced medical care elsewhere. 'The racists hate South African communists with a special venom,' said Slovo, and the life of Mabhida, son of a peasant family expelled from their land by white settlers, showed up the falsehood of 'the myth that communists are strange people from far-away places who import foreign ideas that are dangerous for Africa'. Symbolically, Machel, Tambo and Slovo laid their wreaths on Mabhida's grave simultaneously.

'The Freedom of the Wind and the Scent of the Morning'

South African duplicity was fully exposed when, in August 1985, the Renamo headquarters fell. This base, named Casa Banana after a long-defunct shop, nestled in the foothills of the Serra de Gorongosa, half-way between Beira and the Malawian border. The offensive against Casa Banana was officially described as a joint operation between Mozambican and Zimbabwean forces, but in reality the decisive role was played by Zimbabwean paratroopers. This was a significant shift in strategy. Previously the Zimbabwean troops had simply defended installations vital to Zimbabwe's own interests, such as the Beira–Zimbabwe railway and pipeline. At a meeting in Harare between Machel, Mugabe and Nyerere on 12 June, it was agreed that the Zimbabwean troops would go on the offensive. Visiting Casa Banana on 5 September, Machel declared optimistically, 'We have broken the back of the snake.' But he admitted, 'The tail will still thrash around for a while.'

In its haste to leave Casa Banana, the Renamo leadership had abandoned piles of documents, including diaries kept by Joaquim Vaz (later to become Renamo general secretary). These proved conclusively that the South African military had never taken the Nkomati Accord seriously, with contacts between South Africa and Renamo continuing to within days of the Zimbabwean paratroopers storming Casa Banana. The government gave a press conference at which Sérgio Vieira, now security minister, unveiled the Gorongosa documents. Copies were made available (with a translation into English) for both local and foreign media.[1] Cardoso acquired copies in advance, which gave AIM a head start on the rest of the world's media in breaking the story. And the story was one of breathtaking duplicity. Although Nkomati was not signed until 16 March 1984, a 'gentlemen's agreement' had been reached at a meeting three months earlier that, while the formal treaty was being drawn up, neither side would infiltrate men or equipment into the territory of the other. It was perhaps naive to regard anyone in the apartheid establishment as a 'gentleman': the South African military took advantage of those three months to pour weaponry into Mozambique so that Renamo could continue the war regardless of the non-aggression pact.

The captured diaries gave the dates and places of the weapons drops, and lists of the equipment promised by the South Africans. The liaison between South African military intelligence and Renamo was Colonel Charles van Niekerk. He had struck up a close relationship with Afonso Dhlakama, and the Renamo leader referred to him frequently in the diaries as 'my friend Commander Charles'. Despite the resupplies prior to Nkomati, by June 1984 Renamo was running low on ammunition. The Gorongosa notebooks recorded the messages between Dhlakama and Van Niekerk as Renamo begged for more. 'Friend Commander Charles, we no longer have war material, mainly in the southern and central areas of country,' radioed Dhlakama on 16 June. 'We want to remind our friends of the pledge they gave to keep up support for us clandestinely … We need ammunition to sustain the war in the central areas of the country.' Not only were resupplies arranged, but in September Dhlakama was in Pretoria, where he held discussions with Van Niekerk's superiors right up to the head of the SADF, General Constand Viljoen. The diarist diligently scribbled down Viljoen's words as he told Dhlakama, 'I agree with a joint strategy for putting Machel out. Because we want to remove the Russians from our region of southern Africa, we have to employ a joint strategy to be able to defeat communism.' Viljoen promised to be on Renamo's side 'until final victory'.

The documents also threw a fascinating light on what was going on behind the scenes when the Pretoria Declaration was drawn up. Pik Botha was trying to negotiate a Renamo recognition of Machel as president at the very moment that the South African military were pledging support for Renamo's effort to overthrow the government. Such was the antagonism between the military and Pik Botha that Viljoen told Renamo not to trust the 'treacherous' Botha, and even bugged the room where Botha was to meet with the Mozambican delegation so that Renamo could eavesdrop. The Renamo diarist wrote: 'They will install microphones in the negotiating room to listen in on the talks between Pick [sic] Botha and the Mozambican delegation: it will be very advantageous for us. In this way we will know Pick Botha's plan and Frelimo's.' One of the most startling revelations in the documents was that a government member, the deputy foreign minister, Louis Nel, shuttled between Pretoria and Gorongosa in mid-1985. Van Niekerk saw Nel as an ally of the military, and told Dhlakama to convince him 'that Renamo will win this war'. Nel's last clandestine visit to Gorongosa was just nine days before Casa Banana fell.

Machel now felt strong enough to summon a South African minister to Maputo. He confronted Pik Botha with the Gorongosa documents, and Botha had to admit their authenticity. On his return Botha held his own press conference (to which only South African journalists were invited), at which he tried to depict the violations of the Nkomati Accord as 'technical'. Yes, it was true that South African planes had dropped supplies to Renamo, and that Renamo members had been ferried in and out of Mozambique by plane and submarine. It was true that South African troops had built an airstrip for Renamo, and that Nel had flown into Casa Banana to confer with Dhlakama on at least three occasions. But it was all done with the best of intentions, Botha claimed. The violations were merely 'technical'. Any aid given to Renamo was 'humanitarian', and the only guns provided were to protect the South African personnel working on the clandestine airstrip. All this was justifiable, claimed Botha, to push the government and Renamo to the negotiating table. Even by apartheid standards, this was an extraordinary level of mendacity. Nobody who was not already committed to the regime could possibly have believed Botha. The English-language South African press rebelled, with both the Johannesburg *Star* and *Business Day* remarking that government promises no longer had any value.[2]

South African spokesmen contradicted each other. PW Botha tried to override his foreign minister and dismissed the documents as 'communist lies'. The new deputy foreign minister, Ron Miller, promised an inquiry, but Pik Botha said there would be no inquiry. Cardoso wondered how the South African cabinet could continue meeting amid such distrust among its members. 'What the South African government should have done was implement the Nkomati Accord and drop the bandits, instead of trying to put them in power after signing an agreement which historically, necessarily, implied the acceptance of the legitimately installed power in Mozambique,' he wrote.

> From manoeuvre to manoeuvre, from dishonesty to dishonesty, the South African authorities had built the tension that now reigns amongst them. Sometimes, far from the South African stage, there is a tendency to imagine that South Africa has very elaborate and sophisticated strategies, but reality seems to show that the highest South African officials are almost naive in their simple approach, the fruit of their own racism.

The Gorongosa documents and Botha's semi-confession were valuable instruments in the Mozambican armoury when Machel visited the United States on 17–21 September 1985. He could go to the Reagan administration and say, 'You wanted us to sign an agreement with Pretoria – we have kept our side of the bargain, they have not.' The battle for western imposition of sanctions against South Africa was now sharpening, and Reagan had already bowed to pressure by announcing selective sanctions. The Front Line States discussed the strategy Machel should use in his discussion with the US administration at a meeting in Maputo, two days prior to his departure. It says something for the trust in which Machel now held Cardoso that he was among those asked to transcribe the tapes of the Front Line leaders' private discussions. Machel was to carry the message that Africa wanted complete isolation of the apartheid regime – this, and not Chester Crocker's doctrine of 'constructive engagement', was the way to ensure democratic change.

Relations with the United States were on the mend as the 1981 expulsion of the CIA ring faded from memory. After years in which the position was vacant, a skilled career diplomat, Peter de Vos, was appointed US ambassador to Maputo. The US administration also had hopes that it could 'wean Mozambique away from the Soviet Union', a phrase repeatedly used in the mid-1980s. At the same time, dealing with Reagan looked to be tricky. Although he had not yet been diagnosed with Alzheimer's disease, the US president's poor attention span was already notorious. Quiet advice to Machel before he left was: 'If you have anything important to say to Reagan, get it in within the first five minutes.'

Machel's charm seems to have worked on Reagan – at least, the talks were described as cordial, and Reagan did publicly condemn the South African support for Renamo. Machel diplomatically praised Reagan for the US sanctions (even though the measure had been taken against Reagan's will). 'This is a first step, and first steps are always important,' he said. 'We said the American administration should increase the pressure to eliminate apartheid.' When Machel was interviewed by a US television channel, the question of Mozambique 'turning to the west' came up, and the following exchange took place:

> *Reporter:* Do you think there will be some change in relation to the Soviet Union after your visit to the United States?
>
> *Machel:* Do you think the Soviet Union is boss in Mozambique? You want me to change things so that Washington is the boss? You think that the Soviet Union is my boss, and that I'm here to see if I can change my boss? Look here, I've only ever had one boss in my life, and that was Portuguese colonialism … I am visiting the United States as head of state of the People's Republic of Mozambique, and not of one of the republics of the Soviet Union. I haven't come here to exchange anything. I don't have any boss. Or rather my boss is my people, and I don't want any other boss.

When Samora told his US interviewer that he had never had any boss since he rebelled against Portuguese colonial rule, this inspired Cardoso to some rapid notes on Mozambican Marxism:

> The president has no boss on the field of ideas, he has no theoretical or ideological mentor. Neither Marx nor Lenin are the 'bosses' of Samora Machel. They are companions in struggle on the long road of revolutions, they are comrades from whom the contributions specific to their epoch are taken, and to whom the contribution of the revolutions of today's epoch is delivered, like flowers for their graves, and new chapters for their science.

Those who read Marx, Engels and Lenin as if their works were secular bibles were acting in an anti-Marxist fashion, Cardoso argued,

> because Marx and Lenin were not bosses, they rejected property in its deepest and most perfidious sense: the ownership of one epoch by another.

> Based on the idea of having no boss, and testing it at each step, all political practice can only have as its companions the freedom of the wind and the scent of the morning. So here is an appeal to future generations: do not commit against Samora Machel the crime he has not committed against Marx, Engels and Lenin.

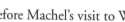

Shortly before Machel's visit to Washington, an off-the-record meeting to which Cardoso was invited threw a harsh spotlight on what was really happening in the army. Machel, other politburo members, and about a hundred people who had organised celebrations of the tenth anniversary of independence met on 13 September 1985, and Machel chose to brief them on his concerns about the army. Machel bitterly regretted the relaxation of 1980. 'We were drunk on the victory over Smith. We gave no importance to training the army,' he admitted. They had fallen into 'populist' errors. 'There are officers without quality, but we promote them. Now we don't demote anybody. During the armed struggle, a commander who lost more than five men was demoted.' Cardoso wrote it all down in his notebook. Machel wanted new blood in the army: 'Generals aged 58 or 63 should retire.' Such remarks in front of an audience of over a hundred were bound to find their way to the generals concerned, who might not be enthusiastic about the idea of forced retirement. 'We need a military career structure,' Machel said. 'You can't build an army out of conscription. Compulsory Military Service is a national reconstruction service. Two years and they leave.'

Machel revealed that on 3 June he had visited the barracks at Boane, west of Maputo. At the end of the afternoon the helicopters flew off again – but the president was not on board. 'All the soldiers believed I had gone back to Maputo. At about 19.00, music began to play in the camp, and later all kinds of guns, including anti-aircraft cannon, were firing into the air.' He turned to a reporter attending the meeting who had once been a commando in the Portuguese army. 'It was like that in the Portuguese army in '69, '70. Shoot before sleeping. Fear.' He told his generals, 'The problem is fear. Our soldiers are afraid.' That same night he called for 150 soldiers from a special unit in Maputo. 'They went to Boane, and we arrested 250 soldiers.' Work started on rehabilitating Boane, with Machel visiting the place every day. 'There was no more nocturnal shooting.' Although Boane was still not in a fit state to receive new recruits, '200 youths appeared, sent there with their heads shaved and without undergoing medical inspections. I was furious. I said it was necessary to find who was responsible.' He called two prominent officers, Guideon Ndobe and Dinis Moiane, 'saboteurs', and ordered them to apologise to the 200 recruits. Rebelo declared, 'Sometimes we think that Comrade President is not informed, but we see that he is informed.' Machel retorted, 'I wasn't informed. I found out.'

Cardoso would later recall this meeting as a sign of the deep malaise within the armed forces, and of Machel's increasing isolation.

❖

Despite all the optimism arising from the capture of Casa Banana, the war was now seriously affecting life in the capital. Renamo was mounting ambushes against all roads and railways leading out of Maputo, and in late 1985 even made hit-and-run raids into outlying suburbs of the city. As if to mock the Nkomati Accord, Renamo saboteurs crossed the border from South Africa on 5 December and blew up a railway bridge just eight kilometres from where the agreement had been signed. Maputo was not exactly under siege, but foreign embassies issued instructions to their staff that they could only leave the city by air. Most Mozambicans did not have that option – they could risk the roads, or abandon plans to see family members elsewhere in the country.

With Renamo hitting the power supply regularly, Maputo was frequently plunged into darkness. With the transmission lines down, the electricity company, EDM, switched over to an expensive and obsolete power station fired by coal and gas. This could not produce enough power for the entire city, and so a scheme of rotating power cuts took effect. One bit of the city would be blacked out for a few hours, then the next. This played havoc with industries and services, and led those who could afford it to buy generators. Initially, AIM had no generator – so, thanks to an inspired idea of Lima's, we dangled a wire into Radio Mozambique and borrowed some of the power from its generator – enough to run the telexes and a few lights at any rate, but not the air-conditioners or the lift. We got very used to walking up and down five flights of stairs and to working with no air-conditioning in the stifling heat and humidity of the Maputo summer.

These were days of great austerity. Cardoso lived that way too, and never viewed his position as a means of enriching himself. Indeed his personal file at AIM includes letters detailing expenses on trips abroad, where he tried to account for every penny. AIM made official declarations even for tiny sums – such as this one of 12 June 1986: 'The director of AIM, Carlos Cardoso, is carrying 35 US dollars for official business abroad, starting on 12/6/86.' The idea that every cent should be accounted for would come to seem rather quaint in the post-Machel Mozambique of structural adjustment and capital accumulation by any means possible.

❖

It was in 1985 that *Tempo*'s book division, Cadernos Tempo, published a slim volume of Cardoso's poetry under the title *Directo ao Assunto* (To the Point). Mia Couto remarked that it would be harder to find a less poetic title. The book is a compilation of jottings, most in the form of poems but including some prose fragments, from Cardoso's notebooks. The poems are highly compressed, often playing with words in a way which makes them almost impossible to translate. Most of the pieces are Portuguese aphorisms. They included perhaps the shortest and most succinct justification of liberation wars ever penned:

> Sometimes the underdeveloped kill
> So that they may no longer
> Be obliged to kill.

There is also a brief tribute to Ruth First, written within days of her murder in August 1982:

> This thing about the dead not talking,
> Well, I don't know.
> Because from some of the dead
> Baobabs of rage spring up
> Among the grasslands of our hesitation.

But easily the most memorable is the aphorism which summed up Cardoso's attitude to journalism: 'In the business of truth, it is forbidden to put words in handcuffs.'

❖

1985 also saw one of the visionary schemes that led the more sceptical of his colleagues to dismiss Cardoso as 'crazy'. He decided to make his own contribution to the struggle for food security by persuading children to plant pawpaw trees. He set out to collect as many marbles as possible: they would be offered to children in exchange for planting pawpaw seeds. Despite the opposition of much of the newsroom, Cardoso signed a formal cooperation agreement, in the name of AIM, with the Casa Velha Cultural Association, represented by Machado da Graça, the purpose of which was 'the transformation of marbles into pawpaws'. AIM would acquire 'the greatest possible quantity of marbles' and deliver them to Casa Velha. For its part, Casa Velha would collect pawpaw seeds. Children were to take the seeds and plant them. When the plants were 30 centimetres high, they would bring them back to Casa Velha and receive their reward – five marbles for each plant. There would be extra prizes for those who planted most trees. AIM and Casa Velha would decide jointly where to replant them.

In a marginal note, Cardoso admitted that AIM 'is aware of the danger that requests of this nature may bring to its image as a producer of news'. But he argued that this was a way of fighting the racketeers. Pawpaws were on sale in the markets for outrageous prices. His idea was to produce large quantities of this nutritious fruit, which could be offered to barracks and military hospitals, thus assisting the army, and sold to everyone else for half the price charged by racketeers.

Cardoso obtained 26 000 pawpaw seeds and little plastic bags from a contact in the ministry of agriculture. Foreign visitors to AIM were asked to bring marbles with them. Astonishingly, Cardoso was so convincing that many obliged. He had no hesitation in asking the director of the Zimbabwean News Agency, Farayi Munyuki, for marbles – a Casa Velha member was visiting Zimbabwe and could pick them up. The Chinese, the North Koreans, the East Germans – they were all asked for marbles. The campaign was formally launched on 14 March: 142 children turned up at Casa Velha, and all took away little bags each containing four seeds. Others came to pick up seeds later.

But in the middle of a war you can't run a news agency and an agricultural campaign at the same time. The campaign ran out of steam: there was nobody who could devote sufficient time to it while the first pawpaw trees grew. And there was the problem of storage space for all those marbles. Cardoso put them in a friend's house. Disillusion set in. On 17 December 1985, Cardoso wrote in his notebook: 'Inevitable, I said. I've just been (13.30) to Jorge's house to fetch the 15 000 that were stored there, and found nothing. Just a few hundred. The rest were stolen when his house was recently burgled.'

Some pawpaw trees did grow. The first one was handed back by a child in late December, and Cardoso duly provided the five marbles. A few dozen others survived in the backyards of several friends.

CHAPTER 11

The Press in the Service of
the Counter-Revolution?

In late March 1986 Cardoso spent two weeks in Nicaragua at a time when the US Congress was discussing President Reagan's plan to give a further 100 million dollars' aid to the 'Contras' fighting against the Sandinista government. In the Nicaraguan case, ruthless destabilisation directed by Washington eventually worked, and the Sandinistas lost power. But in 1986 there was still a great deal of confidence, and it rubbed off on Cardoso. He was pleased to find that Samora Machel had made quite an impact when he visited Managua in 1982. He met Nicaraguans who had a basic knowledge of southern Africa and who compared their own situation to that of Mozambique. They would ask the question: 'Comrade, how are you getting on over there? Is it as tough there as it is here?' 'The similar circumstances in which Nicaragua and Mozambique find themselves have overcome geographical distance,' Cardoso wrote.

Cardoso found that Sandinista soldiers were well cared for, with decent support for those disabled in the war, and for war widows. Ordinary Nicaraguans told Cardoso that supplies meant for the soldiers did indeed reach them and were not diverted by officers or by civilian middlemen. When Cardoso visited the front he could see for himself that the soldiers were properly supplied. 'All the soldiers had uniforms, all had boots, and all were sent other items of clothing in addition to their regular uniforms. They all had a regular and varied diet, and all were allowed regular journeys home to see their families.' The contrast to the growing disorganisation and corruption inside the Mozambican Armed Forces (FAM)[1] was unstated but obvious.

Nicaraguan officials believed there was a real threat of intervention by US forces themselves, and drew up scenarios to cope with this – ones that involved abandoning the main cities to the invaders, and carrying on the war from the mountains. Could the Nicaraguans beat the US army? For both the Sandinistas and Cardoso the reference point was Vietnam, where the greatest military power on earth was humiliated. But the US had learnt from Vietnam: although it could still choose to use overwhelming force (as in the invasion of Grenada), it preferred to resort to proxies (Unita, the Contras, the women-hating mujaheddin of Afghanistan) and wage what became known as 'low-intensity conflicts', the academic term for what we in southern Africa had always called destabilisation.

Cardoso asked a lieutenant in the Sandinista army if the key US aim was to stir up popular dissatisfaction with the government. 'Yes,' he replied. 'They are applying military pressure to create the conditions for popular discontent. Our people are facing serious problems, and our government is unable to satisfy all the people's needs. We make mistakes in the management of the economy, because we are still learning.' It sounded remarkably like Mozambique. And in both cases, enthusiastic supporters of the government, such as the Sandinista lieutenant or Cardoso, believed that the enemy tactics would backfire, and the people would eventually become more united around the revolutionary leadership.

They were wrong. They underestimated the enemy. In 1986 nobody fully understood that destabilisation works. It is an effective, low-cost way of getting rid of inconvenient governments or radically altering their policies. It would eventually remove the Sandinistas from power and fundamentally change the nature of Frelimo's power.

❖

A major government reshuffle took place on 24 April 1986, and Cabaço was replaced as minister of information by Teodato Hunguana. This came as an unwelcome surprise for Hunguana, since he had applied to leave the government and was under the impression that Machel had agreed. Three years earlier, in 1983, his career had seemed finished when Machel sacked him as justice minister. But a few months later he was back in the government, albeit in the junior post of second deputy minister of the interior. Now, without any prior consultation, he found himself promoted to a full minister again. The party discipline of the time meant there was no way of refusing. 'Being a minister was receiving a task from the party, full stop,' Hunguana explains. Within the media, Hunguana's appointment was welcomed. Here was a relatively young intellectual, trained in law and known as someone with an open and modern approach. But Hunguana had little political clout within Frelimo. He was not a member of the Central Committee, and the senior figure in charge of the media remained Rebelo in his position as Central Committee secretary for ideological work.

Hunguana soon found that other members of the government were leaning on him to rein in the press. 'They wanted me to order the media to shut up – and I wouldn't do that,' he recalled. One minister who felt he was running into repeated problems with the media was Manuel Jorge Aranda da Silva, minister of domestic trade. 'Aranda had lots of difficulties with the media, which made him lose his temper, which worsened his relations with journalists,' Hunguana said. 'He came to me, and I told him to meet with the journalists.' Aranda da Silva took this advice, and a tempestuous meeting between the minister and several dozen journalists took place on 30 July 1986 at the ONJ. He brought with him piles of press cuttings which, in his opinion, showed that 'objectively the media serves the counter-revolution'. He said that 'infiltrators' had been found in many walks of life, so logically there must be some infiltrators in the media too. Mia Couto thought that Aranda da Silva was targeting him in particular, left the meeting early, and protested to Hunguana. Calane da Silva was so furious that he never spoke to Aranda da Silva again. 'He accused us of doing the enemy's work, but the people were dying of hunger and that was his ministry's responsibility,' said Calane. Many of the journalists thought the meeting had gone disastrously. Cardoso was not so sure: he believed a dialogue between ministers and the media, no matter how stormy, was better than distrustful silence.

The meeting with Aranda da Silva was immediately followed by the second conference of the ONJ. The organisation was moribund: it had virtually collapsed. When its first general secretary, Rafael Maguni, became Mozambican ambassador to Zimbabwe in 1980, Frelimo seemed to have lost interest in the ONJ, but Rebelo sent Manuel Tomé to renew the organisation as from 1984. 'For a year and a half I prepared the second conference and I received no guidelines,' recalled Tomé. He felt the ONJ had been abandoned. But at the conference that all changed. The relationship between the Frelimo ideology department and the ministry of information suddenly became very clear. It was Rebelo, not Hunguana, who chaired the meeting and made the keynote speech. The minister was marginal to events.

To the delight of the AIM delegation, Rebelo made the very same criticism of the media that Cardoso had been making since 1982. It did not cover the war, which

> appears only sporadically in our media. The media give the picture of a country that does not exist, that does not correspond to current reality. Our media are thus losing credibility among the people. Even more serious is the fact that, in most cases, the war only appears in our media through the actions of the bandits; the activity of our own forces only appears sporadically and occasionally.

But after the opening speech, the conference went steadily downhill; for a serious approach to the war would mean letting reporters accompany the military – and journalists who went with military units might see things that could embarrass the official line.

Cardoso was the voice of dissent at the conference. Not that Cardoso opposed Frelimo; instead, on the second day of the conference, he said something that at the time was far more heretical. He suggested that Frelimo might change, that Frelimo was not immutable but might degenerate. It might become something that journalists could no longer support. Cardoso was telling the head of the party's ideology department that journalists' loyalty could not be taken for granted, and that journalists might make their own minds up as to whether Frelimo was still worth supporting.

For Rebelo this was intolerable: here was a journalist behaving as if he was just as much a valid judge of what was good for the country and for the revolution as the party leadership was. Rebelo lost his temper. He interrupted Cardoso's speech and told him to sit down. This was almost unprecedented in Mozambican meetings. An unwritten code was that people, even if talking nonsense, were allowed to finish their speeches. 'It was natural to lose my temper,' Rebelo recalled. 'We still had the idea that we were pure. We were convinced that Frelimo had the correct line, and there was nothing wrong with its leaders. Cardoso's speech sounded like a provocation.' Joaquim Salvador, sitting next to Cardoso, recalled that Rebelo was 'beside himself with rage', quite unlike the dispassionate figure senior journalists knew. 'He flew into a rage probably because he and Cardoso were rather similar,' said Salvador. 'They were both men of integrity and fixed in their ideas.'

On the final day, Cardoso sat in silence as the national secretariat was 'elected', by imposition of a list selected by the party. All the enthusiasm had gone. Cardoso noted, 'the only spontaneous round of applause was for Manuel Tomé when it was announced that he was the new general secretary.' 'Absolutely diabolical' was how Cardoso summed up the conference in his diary. 'Machiavelli would feel outdone in terms of demonic imagination. It is hard for me to watch a man who is so incorruptible and patriotic behaving so incompetently from the point of view of handling the party's policy in the delicate sphere of ideology.'

Hunguana's first meeting with journalists occurred on 9 August 1986, just days later. As reported in Cardoso's notes, the minister was taking a rather humble, open line. Hunguana dissociated himself from Aranda da Silva. The claim that the media was counter-revolutionary 'worried me', he said. 'I must state clearly that this is not the general attitude inside our government.' He was clarity itself when it came to members of the government telling the media what to write. It was illegal, Hunguana declared, for ministers to give orders to the press. This was the first time a minister of information took the law seriously, and stated clearly that the party should act within the law.

Cardoso pointed out that, unlike any other sector, in the 11 years since independence, despite all the shortages, all the frailties and shortcomings, the media had never halted production. Apart from power cuts, Radio Mozambique had never gone off the air. *Notícias* had never missed an edition. He received a warm round of applause from the 150 or so journalists present. 'I said that the government should at least learn to appreciate this,' he wrote in his diary.

Cardoso was in Lusaka in September 1986 attending a round-table discussion on 'Apartheid and the African Media'. Here he extended a critique that he had made in 1984 of the liberal South African press to the media of independent Africa. Cardoso declared:

> The present state of the African media is tragic. Many of us editors and sub-editors of Africa are spiritual neo-colonies of the news agency transnationals. We give the multinationals our newspapers, we give them our TV networks, we give them the loveliest and most influential voices of our radio announcers to air their opinions, their news items, their arguments, and after all this, we pay them handsome sums of money every month.

In short, the 'New International Information Order' was not working because too many African editors preferred to serve obediently the multinational media companies. 'This mental slavery clouds our vision, inhibits our creativity, diminishes our sense of sovereignty at the level of information, robs us of the passion and beauty of our struggle for well-being and happiness,' Cardoso declared. He attacked those who reproduced the South African and western description of Renamo as 'guerrillas' or 'anti-communists'. There were western media who 'carry more stories about the bandits in a month than they had about the liberation movement in a decade. This should not shock or surprise us. It is the task of those media to do exactly this. But it should shock us to see so many African media using the same terms.' The term 'civil war', so frequently used to describe what Mozambicans called 'destabilisation', is not a value-free term, Cardoso argued. 'It is not a "professional," "journalistic" term. It is a political term.'

The problem was not restricted to journalists.

Many of our ministers and other civil servants are no different from us editors ... They analyse Africa through the eyes and the minds of the multinationals or the prominent western papers. They spend more time reviewing with great passion what such and such a western newspaper said than thinking how to improve their own media. And they would rather pay the multinationals than pay for the consolidation of Pana.

❖

In 1986 Cardoso was called several times to the presidential palace for off-the-record briefings with Machel. During these talks he received the distinct impression that the president was an increasingly lonely figure. Years later Cardoso recalled one occasion when Machel had called him and Alves Gomes to the palace. The details had faded with time, but Cardoso recalled two startling phrases used by the president. He told the journalists, 'I have no strategy' and 'I am lost.' Later Cardoso would reflect that this conversation was 'a further indication that behind the staged unity of the Frelimo leadership, Samora Machel was almost completely isolated at the top'.

CHAPTER 12

Disaster at Mbuzini

If there was a decisive date in the crisis leading to Samora Machel's death it was 11 September 1986, when Machel flew to Malawi to warn the aged dictator Hastings Banda of the possible consequences of continued support for Renamo. Machel had planned to take a contingent of both Mozambican and foreign reporters with him. He had invited all the foreign correspondents in Maputo. But at Maputo airport the delegation was told that Banda had vetoed the presence of any foreign journalists. Machel was furious, and as soon as he arrived in Malawi he had an official ring AIM and ask Cardoso to organise an airport press conference to be held as soon as he returned.

That press conference was Machel's last. In it he proudly restated Frelimo's commitment to a non-racial Mozambique, and expressed visceral contempt for Banda. 'We don't have any elite yet. We are the pioneers and champions of the region, the People's Republic of Mozambique,' Machel declared.

> I stress – People's. The people in power. It's not the majority, it's the people in power. We don't care if they're black, white, mulatto or Indian.
>
> When the Mozambican ports belonged to the Portuguese, Malawi did everything so that the world would send its goods via those ports. Everything to fight against Frelimo. For Malawi, everything from the whites is good. When we proclaimed independence, the ports of Nacala, Beira and Maputo were entirely at the service of Malawi. But they didn't like it, because

the ports were now black. Malawi has complexes ...
We went to Malawi to tell them this.

The South African soldiers, the South African military security, they're in charge, they dictate the politics of Malawi. The South Africans have installed themselves in Malawi to destabilise Mozambique.

'Is it the Malawian government?' a reporter asked. 'How many Malawis are there?' Machel responded. 'I said the South African military use Malawian territory to destabilise, to destroy the People's Republic of Mozambique. They do it with the police, the army and the security of Malawi. It's the Malawian government.' What will Mozambique do? 'First, put missiles all along the Malawian border. We've got plenty of missiles, they just don't have a target. Secondly, close Malawi's route through Mozambique to Zimbabwe and South Africa. Let them arrange some other route.'

Following these open threats to the only African government allied to South Africa, the noises from Pretoria took on an increasingly harsh and belligerent tone. A landmine explosion in the bantustan of Kangwane on 6 October, in which six South African soldiers were injured, was the excuse for the apartheid military to menace Machel. On 7 October a South African source rang Cardoso and translated the latest threats made by Magnus Malan from Afrikaans into English. Malan blamed the Mozambican government for the landmine blast. The Nkomati Accord and landmines 'cannot exist side by side,' said Malan. 'If President Machel chooses landmines, South Africa will react accordingly.' If Machel 'allows a Moscow-inspired revolutionary war against South Africa, he must also be prepared to take responsibility. If he chooses terrorism and revolution, he will clash head on with South Africa.' The deputy foreign minister, Ron Miller, followed up this sabre-rattling with threats of renewed military action against Mozambique: 'Mozambique has to decide its priorities – the peaceful benefits of the Nkomati Accord or confrontation with South Africa. If Mozambique is allowing its territory to be used by the ANC, it will have to run the risk of strong reaction from South Africa in an attempt to defend itself from the ANC.'[1]

Western diplomats frowned and made the habitual calls for solving problems through negotiation. Mozambican spokesmen said Malan was simply trying to shift responsibility for the breakdown of Nkomati. Aquino de Bragança, in his last conversation with Cardoso, remarked,

> Malan is incapable of solving the problems caused by the crisis in South Africa and naturally wants to export the problems to us. Those in power in South Africa push the theory that subversion is external to South Africa, and they forget that practically the whole world, including many South African establishment figures and businessmen, understand perfectly that the causes of subversion are internal.

The South Africans increased the stakes with a sudden announcement that no more Mozambicans would be recruited to work in the gold mines. A government note of 8 October declared: 'No further recruitment of workers from Mozambique will be allowed as from today, as a result of the activities of the African National Congress and the South African Communist Party who are responsible for the continuing deteriorating security situation on the common border.' Mozambicans currently working on the mines would complete their contracts, but would then have to leave and their contracts would not be renewed. This was potentially a body blow to the Mozambican economy, given the weight of the remittances from the 55 000 miners in the balance of payments. The cost to Mozambique would be about 50 million dollars a year, a third of the country's total foreign exchange earnings.

Unnamed military spokesmen, cited by the South African Broadcasting Corporation (SABC), claimed that ANC guerrillas had 'regrouped' in Mozambique and had 'many times this year' crossed the border into the Transvaal. They made much of the fact that Joe Slovo had been seen in Mozambique on several occasions with high-ranking government officials. (This was no bold coup of South African intelligence – Machel and Slovo had stood shoulder to shoulder, very publicly, in March at the Maputo funeral of Moses Mabhida.) On 11 October the Mozambican government accused

Pretoria of preparing a direct attack against Maputo with the intention of installing a puppet regime: South African commando units had already been infiltrated, warned Sérgio Vieira. At the same time, there was 'massive infiltration of bandits' into Tete and Zambezia from Malawi.

The Front Line States held an emergency summit in Maputo on 12 October. The militant declaration issued at the end of the meeting claimed: 'South Africa has already embarked on the road of fascism and of war against the peoples of southern Africa.' The summit backed the Mozambican denunciation of Banda, and denounced 'the complicity of the Malawian government with the Pretoria authorities in the terrorist campaign against Mozambique'. Malan went on the offensive again on 15 October, warning that the Front Line leaders must 'share the responsibility' for the ANC's 'acts of terror' and 'would have to suffer the consequences of ANC attacks launched from their countries'.

As regional tensions were rising, Samora Machel, on 11 October, held his last-ever informal meeting with a select group of reporters. Albino Magaia recalls that he had never seen the president in such a mood before: for the first time Samora seemed afraid. This opinion is not shared by all those who met him in his final days. Mota Lopes and Aquino de Bragança talked with Machel one evening deep into the night, and Mota Lopes had the impression not of fear but of 'great concern, not only with the external and regional situation, but also (perhaps above all) with the internal situation, particularly at the highest levels of the Frelimo leadership. A deep, very serious and agonising concern, at the weakening of Frelimo and of the officials who were surrounding him.'

Machel's meeting with the journalists also went on for many hours. When the presidential protocol politely suggested it was time for his guests to leave, Machel insisted that they stay longer. In such meetings the president let journalists know the things that a head of state can never say in public, things which Cardoso scribbled diligently into his notebook. Machel did not hide his loathing for Banda and Mobutu of Zaire. Banda was 'a fascist, a black Nazi, with all the characteristics of the European fascists ... He kills his collaborators with such ease.' Mobutu is 'a megalomaniac. He's vain, so profoundly vain.' Such regimes 'are terrorists towards their own peoples. They're subservient, and they lick the boots of the colonialists.' He also gave a thumbnail sketch of what the IMF wanted from Mozambique: 'Privatisation of the railways and ports, of the schools, of the hospitals. That's what the IMF is saying in the negotiations. They've attacked our revolutionary gains and our life.'

But Machel also asked the journalists what they thought of the current situation. Cardoso later recalled, 'I had uppermost in my mind the whole adventurist behaviour of the South African military hierarchy over the years and the recent threats by General Malan. I spoke of these things and told the president that the conclusion I drew was "They are going to try to kill you."' Machel smiled. Scarcely had Cardoso finished speaking when he replied, 'They've already tried. In November 1985 they infiltrated bazookas into Mozambique that were to have been used to assassinate me.' Machel paused for a moment before adding, 'I am in their way. I have not sold out to anyone. My hands are clean.'

Cardoso did not restrict his fears to private briefings. On 15 October he wrote the article 'Samora: A possible target?' in which he argued that, if the South African military did carry out their threatened raids, then the president himself would be among their targets. Some of Malan's remarks, he noted, were specifically directed at the person of Samora Machel. He had declared that Machel 'appears to have lost control of the situation' and warned that if Machel 'chooses terrorism and revolution' then South Africa would 'act accordingly'.

The apartheid media marched to Malan's tune, in what Cardoso read as a softening-up operation to prepare the South African public for a direct strike at the Mozambican president. The SABC carried items trying to link Machel with the Portuguese ultra-left group FP-25, some of whose members were facing terrorism charges in Lisbon. The *Citizen* called on the South African military to 'take out' targets in Maputo, and claimed that ANC leaders plus Machel had left Maputo to take refuge on the nearby island of Inhaca. The *Sunday Times* claimed that Joe Slovo was 'once more' the brains behind ANC 'terrorist activity', and was operating from a flat on Julius

Nyerere Avenue in Maputo. Cardoso noted, 'One person who really does live and work in Julius Nyerere Avenue, and who is of significance for Pretoria, is President Samora Machel himself.'

He argued that the military now dominated South African politics and required a permanent state of war to keep that position.

> The political power of the South African generals lies precisely in the fact that they are in charge of war and destabilisation, with enormous weight at the highest levels of decision making in Pretoria. The generals need destabilisation. It is the guarantee of their internal power. Without it, they would be unemployed.

> Malan and his colleagues seem involved in an operation designed to get rid not only of an obstacle called Samora Machel, but also of the embarrassingly sovereign and independent Mozambican state – a state that refuses to do what it's told, but whose decisions, right or wrong, are taken in Maputo and nowhere else.

There was one worrying precedent for the situation facing Mozambique in October 1986, Cardoso concluded.

> When the Portuguese colonial rulers of Mozambique felt control slipping out of their grasp, they tried to regain the initiative by organising the assassination of the first president of Frelimo, Eduardo Mondlane, in February 1969. Those who murdered him believed that by eliminating the top leader, they could also eliminate the roots of anti-colonial resistance. Forces of the same nature, equally lacking in imagination, equally soaked in crime, seem today prepared to follow their example and murder the Mozambican president.

This article was submitted to *Tempo* for publication in its next issue. *Tempo* blanched: was this not speculative, scaremongering, alarmist? So they did not publish. In fairness, it must be said that some of Cardoso's colleagues at AIM, including myself, shared the *Tempo* position. I was reluctant to translate the article into English. Was it not unduly pessimistic? I asked. I have never made a worse error of judgement. Three days later, President Samora Machel lay dead among the wreckage of the presidential aircraft on a bleak hillside at Mbuzini, just inside South Africa. Too late, the next issue of *Tempo* did carry Cardoso's article.

On Sunday 19 October, Machel flew to Mbala in Zambia, where he, Kaunda and José Eduardo dos Santos were to confront Zairean dictator Mobutu Sésé Seko over Zairean support for Unita. It was an open secret that much of the American aid to Unita was channelled via Zaire. The Front Line strategy was clearly to knock out or intimidate those regimes that were cooperating with Pretoria: first Malawi, and now Zaire. When Machel left Mbala, it was already dusk. His Zambian hosts suggested he stay for the night. But Machel was a man in a hurry: he had a meeting with the military hierarchy scheduled for the following morning, at which he intended to make sweeping changes in the FPLM general staff. So the plane returned at night – and never arrived at Maputo airport.

After communications between the Maputo control tower and the cockpit were interrupted, a search was begun. The air force and the navy looked for any sign of the plane, on land or at sea. But they were looking in the wrong place. Only at 06.50 the following morning did the South African foreign minister, Pik Botha, telephone Sérgio Vieira to inform the Mozambican government that a plane travelling from Zambia had crashed on South African soil. To confuse matters, the initial South African message said the plane had crashed in Natal, whereas in fact the disaster had taken place in the Transvaal, just five kilometres north of the point where the Mozambican, South African and Swazi borders meet.

On the morning of 20 October, the AIM newsroom was subdued. The message announcing the crash, read by Marcelino dos Santos, was broadcast repeatedly. It did not actually announce Machel's death, but all hope was extinguished by the funeral music that the radio played. At home, Cardoso made some phone calls and discovered that a delegation was about to leave for South Africa, headed by Vieira. He learnt that Vieira was taking Kok Nam to photograph the crash site, but apparently nobody from the written media had been contacted. Cardoso phoned Hunguana and insisted that at least one reporter from the written media should go.

Hunguana agreed and five minutes later rang Cardoso back, telling him to go at once to the airport. Vieira had been given a free hand by the Frelimo politburo to select the delegation, and immediately accepted Cardoso's name.

Cardoso called in at AIM first. Just before 09.00 he rushed into the newsroom, ordered that no one was to write anything more about the crash until he returned, then rushed out again. Cardoso's rehabilitation was complete – he was one of a handful of journalists accompanying a government delegation on the most tragic mission in the country's history. But these were the days before e-mail and satellite phones. From Mbuzini there was no way for Cardoso to contact AIM. So the rest of the world had the story of Machel's death – from the version given out by Pretoria – but the Mozambican media did not.

After stopping first at Komatipoort, where Pik Botha met them, Vieira's delegation arrived at Mbuzini at about 13.00. The scene was desolate, with the bodies of victims, covered with sheets and blankets, scattered over a radius of some 30 metres around the fuselage and tail of the ruined plane. The South Africans had already placed Machel's body in a hermetically sealed plastic bag inside a coffin. A South African doctor opened the coffin and bag so that Vieira could formally identify the president's body. Cardoso wrote:

> The bag was opened from the head downwards, but my first strong feeling that I really was looking at the body of Samora Machel came when I saw his right hand, resting on his abdomen. Those hands in life never stopped moving. They are engraved on the memories of many Mozambicans through personal contact with the President, through photographs and films, through the many meetings and rallies he addressed. Only later did I notice a small portion of the beard that had become famous across the world.

No autopsy could be carried out at the crash site, and in any case 'the Mozambicans could not bear to look at the still and silent body of the man whose image in their minds was one of enormous vitality. One of the Mozambicans collected some stones to mark the exact spot where Samora's body was found.' Vieira's delegation then had to identify the other bodies, a process which lasted for two hours, recalled Cardoso, 'and was extremely painful, particularly for those who had close friends among the victims'. When this task was complete, Vieira asked the South Africans to withdraw, and the Mozambican delegation gathered around Samora Machel's coffin. Vieira called for a minute of silence, at which point he too began to weep but was checked by some gentle words from the deputy foreign minister, Hipolito Patricio. Kok Nam caught the delegation's last tribute to Samora on film; his remarkable photograph depicts perfectly the awesome silence and dignity of the desolate scene (see page 178).

Nine people, all of whom were sitting at the back of the plane, survived the crash. Almost miraculously, one of Machel's bodyguards, Fernando Manuel João, had no serious injuries and was able to walk away from the crash to seek help. But the 33 others on board were dead. They included Aquino de Bragança, Fernando Honwana (who Cardoso believed was being groomed as a possible successor), Muradali (who had became Samora's private secretary), Daniel Maquinasse, and the transport minister, Alcantara Santos.

That night, when Cardoso returned, the world could finally receive a Mozambican version of the tragedy. A second government communiqué was now released, which did not quite accuse the apartheid regime of murdering Samora Machel but clearly suggested that the crash had been criminal in origin. There was not much rest for AIM reporters in the ensuing week. The agency had to cover a national outpouring of grief, relay reactions from around the globe, and start probing the reasons for the crash: were the South African military involved, and if so, how?

The plane crash led to violence on the streets, not of Maputo but of Harare. Angry demonstrators attacked cars driven by white motorists: in Zimbabwe, 'the whites' were being blamed for Samora's death. These incidents horrified the AIM newsroom, and led to an editorial on Samora's anti-racism aimed specifically at the neighbouring countries, and penned by Cardoso and myself. Samora never saw the enemy in racial terms, but as a social system. In the struggle against the Smith regime, AIM said pointedly, 'Samora stressed that it was not white Zimbabweans who were the enemy, but the anti-democratic minority regime.' Furthermore, the regime could change its colour and remain the enemy, 'which was precisely what happened in 1979, with the creation of the short-lived "Zimbabwe-Rhodesia" with a black man, Bishop Abel Muzorewa, as Prime Minister.' As for South Africa, Samora 'held firmly to the belief that white South Africans, particularly Afrikaans speakers, were indeed Africans, even if their racism refused to allow them to admit it. He often told Afrikaners that their racism was keeping them away from their true place in Africa.' He had always hoped that one day he would visit a liberated, nonracial South Africa. We wrote that one of the best tributes to Samora's memory 'is to continue the fight to build non-racial societies, in South Africa and elsewhere, and eliminate the pernicious idea that a person's worth has something to do with the colour of his or her skin'.

Meanwhile disinformation was freely flowing in the South African media. There was speculation about the weather and about the competence of the crew. But it was easy to check with the meteorological office and discover that the weather was fine on the night of 19 October. Cardoso also looked up the flight records to find that the same Soviet crew had landed at Maputo airport 65 times, and 70 per cent of these landings were at night. One of the nastiest bits of disinformation was the use made of the Soviet survivor, Vladimir Novoselov. The regime organised a press conference around Novoselov's hospital bed, in which he allegedly said that his experience as a pilot was the only thing that had allowed several of the passengers to survive. The Johannesburg *Star* claimed that Novoselov had tried to belly-land the plane. 'My flying instincts must have taken over,' he was quoted as saying. None of the journalists at this press conference bothered to ring up Maputo for some confirmation. It was up to Cardoso to put the record straight shortly after AIM received this story over the wire: Novoselov was not a pilot, he was the flight engineer, and had been sitting at the back when the plane crashed (which was why he had survived). The real pilot, Yuri Novodran, was among the dead.

Grotesquely, the South Africans had organised a press conference to be addressed by a severely wounded airman in an intensive care unit. The translation from Russian to English was given by a South African military interpreter. None of the journalists present bothered to check the translation. There was a carefully arranged photo opportunity when PW Botha's wife delivered a bouquet of flowers to Novoselov. All in all, it was an effective way to distract attention from the question of how the crash had occurred.

The funeral took place on 28 October. Late October is usually pleasantly warm in Maputo, but that day was one of the coldest I could remember in the Mozambican capital. Other mourners agreed – the chill winds and occasional burst of rain out of a squally sky were entirely unseasonal, as if the elements themselves were mourning the passing of Samora. His coffin lay fittingly next to that of Eduardo Mondlane: the man who created Frelimo and the man who led it to victory were now reunited. Not until after Samora's funeral could Cardoso get anything like a full night's sleep. 'I slept for some seven hours,' he wrote in his diary. 'I collapsed. Naturally. It was the longest week in the suffering of this people. It was a week without sleep.' He reckoned he had worked 16 to 20 hours a day.

> In work there was an escape. The only escape. Not to think about the old man.

> I'm tired, psychologically shattered. He is dead. So is Aquino, and Fernando, and Maquinasse. They were among the best of this elite of ours ... It's as if part of the Mozambicans' heroic epic has disappeared ... I shall sleep now. To wake up to what Augusto[2] calls 'Mozambique: page two'.

CHAPTER 13

Accident or Murder?

The Mbuzini story was much more than the outpouring of grief for the untimely loss of an inspiring and much-loved leader: it was also an investigation into what many Mozambicans believed was the assassination of their head of state. How could a plane, piloted by a highly experienced crew in good weather and clear skies, be so wildly off course as to crash into a hillside in South Africa? Given the open threats against Mozambique in the preceding weeks, it is hardly surprising that fingers of suspicion were pointed at Pretoria. But how had they done it?

The first indication that there might have been some kind of electronic sabotage came from an unlikely source. Sérgio Vieira recalls that, when he arrived at Komatipoort on his way to Mbuzini on 20 October, South African police commissioner Johan Coetzee, after offering condolences, blurted out, 'Minister, you know what my crew is saying – you have to look for a beacon over there.' And he waved in the direction of the mountains. So South African police helicopter pilots, less than 24 hours after the crash, believed that the Tupolev had been lured off course by a pirate navigational beacon. The standard omnidirectional radio beacon used to guide planes in to airports is known as a VOR. The Soviet crew should have been following the Maputo airport VOR; but what if somebody had erected, in the vicinity of the Lebombo mountains, another VOR, broadcasting on the Maputo frequency?

On 21 October I took a call from the Johannesburg office of UPI (United Press International). The UPI correspondent thought AIM should know that he had received an anonymous call from a man claiming to be a South African air force officer, alleging that he knew the South African military had planted a 'decoy beacon' somewhere in the border region, and it was this that caused the plane to crash. Lima rang up from the US. He said that a US air force officer had told him it was quite possible, by using electronic equipment on the ground, to cause an aircraft to deviate from its flight path while the pilot still believed he was on the correct route. The officer said he was familiar with the Tupolev 134 and knew that the South African military possessed the technology to interfere in the Tupolev's navigational system. In this way they could create a different flight path that could deceive the pilot. Thus our sources, thousands of kilometres apart, had the same suspicion – that this was not simply pilot error, but that the plane had been deliberately lured from its correct course.

The South African government certainly behaved like men with something to hide. At one point Pik Botha announced that alcohol had been detected in the bodies of the dead Soviet crew. This statement was technically correct, since alcohol is produced naturally in the human body during decomposition – but Botha was clearly suggesting that the plane crashed because the pilot was drunk. Indeed, this was a line pushed by South African officers who interrogated survivors. Despite his serious injuries, Vasco Langa, a protocol officer in the foreign ministry, was interrogated in hospital in the days following the crash by a South African air force major, who told him that the Soviets were drunk. Since contact with the crew was part of Langa's job, he knew this was untrue. But the major insisted that 'the airplane crashed because the Russians were drunk'.

A more effective diversion was the sudden release on 6 November of a document allegedly taken from the crash site. Pik Botha gave a press conference that evening, claiming the document proved a Mozambican–Zimbabwean plot to topple the Malawian government. When news of that press conference reached AIM, Cardoso immediately phoned Hunguana. This was the first Hunguana had heard of Botha's claims. 'I almost vomited,' he later recalled. 'This is a vulgar attempt to turn the victim into an accused,' he exclaimed to Cardoso, 'to turn the person who has been attacked into an attacker, to turn the country that has been invaded into an invader, to present the country that has been destabilised as the destabiliser.' He had no idea whether the document Botha presented came from the presidential plane or not, but declared: 'We alert the international community that something extremely serious is taking place – South Africa is doing all it can to hinder the normal process of the investigation into the death of President Samora Machel.'

Shortly afterwards, Hunguana's words were winging across the world in an AIM dispatch. Hunguana recalled this incident as an example of Cardoso's professionalism: Cardoso's prompt response to Botha's press conference 'helped neutralise the South Africans' plans'. Indeed, at every stage AIM was on top of the story, and Pretoria found it could not issue statements without a response from Maputo. This time, government members responded when AIM rang them, and did not delay for days before releasing crucial information.

One of the key areas probed by AIM was the South African radar system. The obvious question was: Why was the South African air traffic control system not used to warn the pilot that the Tupolev was off course and in danger of entering South African airspace? The South Africans dismissed this – they claimed the plane had been flying so low that it dropped off their radar screens, and that their controllers therefore assumed it had landed in Maputo. Pik Botha claimed on 1 November that the Tupolev 'just disappeared from the screens. No-one monitoring that radar could or would have imagined that there was anything strange about it.'

Botha painted a picture of a rather primitive and inefficient radar system, monitored by inattentive staff. This story was blindly accepted by the docile South African media. But a little investigation by AIM, using published South African sources, showed Pik Botha up as a liar. Over 10 years earlier, South Africa had addressed the problem of planes 'disappearing' from radar screens. At Mariepskop, on the edge of the Drakensberg mountains, an early-warning system was set up, designed to alert against 'hostile aircraft approaching South Africa'. The apartheid regime boasted about this. The Johannesburg *Star*, back in February 1975, wrote of how this radar system 'can pick up most aircraft movements from a large chunk of Botswana in the west, to Rhodesia in the north, to southern Mozambique and Natal in the east. Height finders are positioned nearby. They can calculate the height of any aircraft picked up by the scanner.' This material was fed by computer into the headquarters of the South African radar defence system at Devon, which worked out whether any approaching aircraft was 'friend or foe'.

In 1982 the system became even more sophisticated with the acquisition of the Plessey AR-3D computerised radar system. Plessey itself boasted that the system provides 'a complete picture of the air situation for the central command staff'. A complete picture; not a partial picture from which something as large as a Tupolev-134 could mysteriously disappear. Furthermore, in March 1985 a new low-altitude radar network had become operational along the border with Mozambique. Pik Botha had boasted of the new system and his words could be found in the South African press of the time, just 19 months before the Mbuzini crash. This system was supposed to monitor illegal flights, and one of the planes Botha said it followed landed at Inhaca island, in the bay of Maputo. In other words, this system's 'radar horizon' was pretty well at sea level. Also in March 1985, the whole eastern Transvaal border area was declared a 'special restricted airspace', and Malan announced that 'all possible technological aids are being used to ensure its effectiveness'. To obtain authorisation to enter this restricted area, pilots were supposed to approach air force headquarters. Yet the Tupolev went straight into the restricted area, and no attempt was made to dissuade it.

By November 1986 Botha had conveniently forgotten his earlier boasts of South African radar capabilities, and the South African media committed worse acts of self-censorship than anything in Mozambique. They had the material on the radar systems in their own archives, but they refused to use it. Underfunded and understaffed though it was, AIM under Cardoso could write about the South African radar system, while even the 'liberal' South African media shut their eyes and ears.[1] Some absurd theories were floated in the South African press. Perhaps the most grotesque was the claim that three villages in the Kangwane bantustan had a configuration that the Soviet crew might have mistaken for a runway. But none of these villages had electricity – so we were asked to believe that an experienced pilot could mistake a series of cooking fires and oil lamps for runway lighting.

Although the Tupolev's 'black box' flight recorders should have been taken at once to Moscow for decoding in the presence of Mozambican, South African and Soviet experts, Pretoria stalled, delaying the technical investigation for over a month by finding one pretext after another to hang onto the black boxes. It was not until 24 November that they were finally taken to the USSR. On 16 January, the international commission of inquiry formed by the three countries directly involved issued its 'factual report', which included the transcript of the cockpit voice recorder (CVR). The transcript showed that, when the plane made its fatal turn to the south-west, the captain was surprised and asked, 'Couldn't it be straight?' The navigator replied, 'VOR indicates that way' – meaning that he believed the plane was following the Maputo airport VOR. 'VOR indicates that way' – this was the key piece of evidence which indicated that Brigadier Coetzee, the man who phoned UPI, and the US officer who spoke to Lima, were right. There had been another beacon, one powerful enough to drown out the Maputo beacon and lure the plane to disaster.

Cardoso contacted Guebuza, now transport minister, who told him it was crucial to find out what VOR the plane had been following. 'The plane was following signals from a VOR which was not the one in Maputo,' he said. 'It was this VOR that caused the plane's fatal turn away from its normal route.' The factual report also stated that

> during the on-site investigation an abandoned camp-site was found on the South African side of the border approximately 150 metres south-east of the place where the aircraft initially contacted the ground. Witnesses on Mozambique's side of the border informed that a tent on the site had been removed on the day after the accident.

So the commission of inquiry asked the South African police at Komatipoort to investigate 'who erected a large tent on the site and when'. The police found an employee of the veterinary services who had patrolled this section of the border in September and October 1986. The report stated, 'He frequently saw members of the S.A. Defence Force camping at the place. Their tents were, however, small.' The report added, 'The company commander of the army unit in the Komatipoort area has no knowledge of any camps with large tents in this particular area.' So the plane crashed within shouting distance of a military tent. Cardoso declined to speculate on what it contained, but suspicions were aroused in Maputo that the tent had housed the mystery beacon.

Later, in 1988, a Renamo representative in Lisbon, Paulo de Oliveira, defected to Mozambique. He told reporters that on 19 October 1986 he was contacted from South Africa and told to prepare for a major Renamo claim. But some hours later that order was countermanded. At the time we did not float any theories; but it seems quite possible that the intention behind luring the plane off course was so that it could be shot down, and Renamo would then triumphantly announce that it had killed the president. The mystery tent might have hidden somebody armed with a heat-seeking missile, but the plane was flying so low that he got no chance to use it before the Tupolev crashed.

With the CVR transcript before him, Cardoso now wrote one of the most difficult articles in his career: an account of the last 10 minutes on board the doomed Tupolev. It was difficult, first because he had to acquaint himself with some basic notions of avionics, and secondly because the Soviet crew did indeed make serious mistakes. Some in the media were content merely to attack Pretoria over the phoney beacon, but Cardoso opted for the complete story.

The crime the Soviet crew committed was not one of incompetence, much less drunkenness. Theirs was the crime of the experts, the crime of over-confidence, believing in their own capacities rather than in their instruments. Yuri Novodran had flown in and out of Maputo dozens of times. The Tupolev had followed the Maputo VOR dozens of times. What could possibly go wrong? So, despite Novodran's initial surprise at the turn to the south-west, a few seconds later the crew turned to trivial matters such as orders for drinks to take home. Novodran 'was psychologically prepared to go home: which is incorrect from the point of view of work discipline', Cardoso noted. A few minutes later Novodran swore when he could not see the city. He immediately assumed that Maputo was suffering from another of its regular power cuts. He did not even consider the possibility that the reason he could not see the lights was that the plane was nowhere near Maputo.

Conversation with the Maputo control tower followed. It was a tragic dialogue of the deaf, with the controller misunderstanding the crew's questions, and the crew misunderstanding his answers. Thus the controller authorised an ILS (Instrument Landing System) approach: but the crew could not register the Maputo ILS because they were so far away. 'ILS out of service?' asked the crew. 'Affirmative,' replied the controller. But while he imagined he was telling the crew that the ILS was functioning, they took him as confirming that it was not functioning. The exchange was fatally ambiguous, since at no point did the controller clearly indicate that the runway lights were on – which would have alerted Novodran to his true situation.

As the crew puzzled over their inability to spot the city, the Ground Proximity Warning System (GPWS) sounded. This is a loud noise alerting the crew that they are about to hit the ground. The only thing Novodran should have done was climb, and very rapidly. But this highly experienced Soviet pilot ignored a life-saving instrument. Cardoso could only surmise that Novodran preferred to trust hs own instincts to the equipment. He still imagined 'that he was flying towards Maputo at the safe altitude of 3000 feet above flat terrain, and this may have led him to believe that something was wrong with the GPWS.' The plane's radio altimeter was not working, and so Novodran, confident of his own abilities and believing he knew where he was, assumed that the GPWS was also unreliable.

Cardoso remarked on the oddity that nobody in the cockpit so much as mentioned the GPWS. On the tape nobody says, 'What's that noise?' There is no indication from the CVR that they noticed or even heard the warning. So did something else happen on board to stop the crew from reacting and taking the plane up – something that had left no record? Of course the South African government pounced on any indication of Soviet blunders to exonerate themselves from responsibility. Cardoso replied that it would be a mistake to examine only the last few tragic seconds, for the origin of the disaster was 10 minutes earlier – it lay in the turn to the south-west provoked by the mystery VOR. 'Had that VOR not interfered, the plane would have continued its trajectory north to south-east, to the right of Maputo, and would have been able to see the city perfectly,' Cardoso wrote, and concluded:

> From South Africa's point of view, it is important to persuade public opinion that, even if there were a phoney VOR, the crew could technically have avoided the crash. It is not in their interest to make a detailed examination of the reason for any human error. From Mozambique's point of view, it is important to clarify whether the technical failings have technical explanations, or if they arise from a criminal action exterior to the plane. If there was a crime intended, even if we suppose that it was technically possible for the crew to have avoided disaster, then this has drastic implications for the immediate future of the country.

Once the factual report was out, South African cooperation in investigating the crash ended. Pretoria had done the minimum required of it by the international regulatory body. Now it rejected Mozambican demands for investigation of the VOR the plane had been following. Instead the South Africans organised a hearing of their own into the disaster, under Judge Cecil Margo, which was largely successful in deflecting criticism of the government. The Margo Commission was not remotely impartial. But, even though neither Mozambique nor the USSR was represented at the Margo Commission, there was the occasional awkward question from South African lawyers. Thus, Pik Botha was asked why he had falsely suggested that the Tupolev crew were drunk. Margo intervened to halt further cross-examination on those lines.

Predictably the Margo Commission blamed the Soviet crew, and both the Mozambican and Soviet authorities rejected these findings. Margo's report was released on 9 July 1987, but Guebuza insisted that the work of the international commission of inquiry was far from over. 'Conclusions can only be drawn after all the facts have been investigated,' he said, 'and particularly this new and vital element – where was this VOR, was it a decoy or not? But the South Africans, in their usual intransigent and arrogant fashion, continued with their own inquiry and sent us the report.'

The series of articles written by Cardoso on the circumstances surrounding Samora Machel's death won him the ONJ's first prize for investigative journalism, which he received from President Chissano's hands at a ceremony in April 1988. But well before then, others had read Cardoso's articles and reacted in a very different way. In late June 1987, Magnus Malan declared that he would not tolerate 'the export of revolution', not only in the sense of violent upheaval but even in the form of anti-apartheid propaganda. In an article of 30 June, Cardoso wrote: 'This is the first time that a leader of the apartheid regime has made it so clear that Pretoria will try to impose on journalists and politicians in the Front Line states the same level of censorship that operates against journalists inside South Africa itself.'

On 9 July, the SABC celebrated the conclusion of the Margo inquiry with an attack on AIM and on Cardoso in particular. We were all described as 'Soviet agents'.

> Soon after the crash Soviet masterminds had begun to design and effect an intricate disinformation strategy. Moscow coopted the assistance of Soviet agents of influence within the Mozambican government agencies. The Mozambican media participated fully in this campaign and served to give momentum to the entire operation.
>
> Only days before Machel's death, Carlos Cardoso, the director of Frelimo's propaganda instrument, AIM, and a hardline Marxist, speculated that South Africa was likely to retaliate for a landmine blast in which six South African soldiers were killed. In an article, Cardoso explicitly stated that President Machel was a likely target for an assassination attempt.

At this stage in the SABC report a photograph of Cardoso appeared on the screen. 'Cardoso later emerged as a key figure in the Soviet-designed disinformation strategy,' the SABC continued. 'In his capacity as director of AIM, he originated a vast percentage of the total disinformation output.' The SABC also attacked Lima – his report from Boston 'is the first sign of a Soviet attempt to float the false beacon theory in the west'.

This was followed, a couple of days later, by a formal letter to the government from Colin Patterson, head of the South African trade mission in Maputo, protesting against Cardoso's articles. Hunguana showed Cardoso the letter. Patterson wrote:

> I find it disappointing that Mozambique has so slav-ishly followed the Moscow line on Mbuzini. What makes the matter even sadder is that Moscow knows the truth and is trying to defend its reputation and position in Africa, whereas Mozambique has appar-ently allowed itself to be pushed into taking a point of view wholly unsupported by the evidence, and the findings of world experts in order to further its own inexplicable smear campaign against South Africa.

Then came an implied threat: 'In this way, I am afraid, Mozambique has gone dangerously far out along the limb of distrust and suspi-cion, as far as the South African government and people are con-cerned.'

At a distance of a decade and a half, the Soviet conspiracy rant-ings of the SABC and Patterson are merely laughable. But at the time they seemed loaded with menace. Cardoso regarded the use of his picture by SABC TV as a thinly disguised death threat. For a period he took to sleeping in different houses every night. This was not paranoia. The murder of Ruth First had shown that South African death squads could reach into Maputo when they chose. And on 29 May 1987, South African commandos had struck again into the heart of the city, attacking a house used as a clothing store by the ANC, and murdering three Mozambicans (whom they might have mistaken for ANC members).

❖

As the years passed, questions arose about Mbuzini, questions that were never answered. Were the South African military the only guilty ones – or did they have collaborators in Mozambique? The South African generals certainly wanted Machel eliminated, and they had the means to eliminate him. Using the principle of Occam's razor, there was no need to invoke anyone else. But Machel had been making enemies elsewhere, including within the armed forces. Calane da Silva recalls that he had wanted to change the FPLM's military strategy but had been blocked. Machel wanted to use former commandos in the colonial army as shock units in the war against Renamo. These highly trained soldiers had caused problems for Frelimo in the 1970s, and Machel respected their military skills. Those who had become Mozambican citizens were fully rehabilitated after the 1983 meeting between the party leadership and 'those compromised by colonialism'.

Machel wanted new units, headed by these men, to wage counter-guerrilla warfare – and they would be under his command, independent of the general staff. But the rest of the military hierarchy objected, and the idea never got off the ground. Similarly, attempts to promote rapidly young officers trained in the Soviet Union met with obstacles. The result was that, although the FPLM had modern Soviet helicopter gunships (just as good as any helicopter in the South African air force), it was rarely able to use them effectively. By 1986 Machel had decided on a thorough reorganisation of the military, and he was honest enough to announce it in advance. 'Samora talked a lot,' remarked Calane da Silva. 'He said he would reorganise the army and the South Africans overheard him.'

Cardoso revisited Mbuzini in an article written for the tenth anniversary, published in *Mediafax* on 18 October 1996. He recalled the meeting he had attended at the Central Committee offices in 1985 with Samora 'clearly attempting to swim against the tide of carelessness and corruption into which high-ranking officers were letting the army fall'. He recalled earlier remarks by Samora in mid-1981, when he had complained to Cardoso and Vasconcelos that the rest of the politburo were restraining him. He was not carrying out the type of political offensive that he wanted because 'these people won't let me'.

One prophetic and chilling remark of the president stuck in Cardoso's memory. Samora warned, 'So that 100 000 people don't die today, a million will die tomorrow.' In other words, Samora was prepared for 100 000 deaths immediately in a war with apartheid, since he feared that the death toll would be much higher if apartheid were allowed to continue to exist and to ravage the region. He was right. When the UN, in 1989, published the report *South African Destabilisation: The Economic Cost of Frontline Resistance to Apartheid*, it estimated the Mozambican death toll at 900 000, mostly children who would have lived if health posts had not been destroyed, transport sabotaged, and agriculture disrupted by South Africa's surrogates. By the end of the war, in October 1992, the death toll had probably reached a million or more. But there were no backers for a quick thrust to overthrow apartheid. The Soviet Union was more worried about Afghanistan than southern Africa, and would not support anything that smacked of 'adventurism'.

Cardoso now thought that the cautious Soviet approach was one of the factors that pushed Samora to seek an understanding with Botha at Nkomati. In 1986, Cardoso recalled, the president seemed a lonely figure. 'The president was increasingly alone, at the top, in the ominous clouds of the party leadership, trying to keep Frelimo healthy and the state efficient. He was the Socratic gadfly, stinging within the state, which he was so desperately trying to tame.' Several of those interviewed for this book agree that Machel seemed increasingly isolated. 'It was obvious that Samora was in crisis in 1986,' said Cabaço. 'This led to an increase in authoritarian behaviour, and an increase in decisions taken alone.' 'Decisions ceased to be collegial,' Luís Bernardo Honwana recalled. 'Towards the end of his life, Samora was taking decisions on his own. Relations were becoming formal, reduced to protocol. People were hiding their opinions from Samora, and no longer identified with the decisions.'

Samora's honesty was perhaps his downfall, Cardoso wrote.

> He told his adversaries within the armed forces general staff and he told the party leadership, perhaps out of loyalty to their past record as liberators of the country, what he intended to do: dismiss almost the entire gen-

On the bleak hillside at Mbuzini, the Mozambican delegation salutes the coffin of Samora Machel. Cardoso is second from the left.

eral staff, replacing them with the young officers trained in the USSR. And he even told them the date of the changes: 20 October 1986. A meeting to change the leading figures in the armed forces was set for 07.00 that morning. But on the night of the 19th, that meeting with the general staff was postponed *sine die* because the presidential aircraft crashed at Mbuzini.

So was there a Mozambican hand in the conspiracy against Samora Machel? 'Yes, there is a mountain of circumstantial evidence – such as the personal threats made by Malan – and the factual evidence on the South African side of the border,' Cardoso responded. 'But on this side there is a series of questions about radars and misunderstandings between the airport tower and the pilot, questions about the lights, and much else to be clarified.' After 'the moral and political collapse' of the ensuing decade,

> I am tempted, in moments of bitterness, to think that Samora's death was a game of silences. From their side, without a word being said, the question would have come 'Can we?' And from our side, without anybody saying anything, the answer went 'You can.'
>
> In other words, perhaps the deed was done on the other side of the border, but today I think that on this side there were people who secretly cracked open the champagne.[2]

'The Reality is War, the Media Talks of Peace'

A IM held a party to celebrate its tenth birthday in December 1986 – it should have been held in November, but the Mbuzini tragedy and its aftermath forced a delay. 'Ours has been an apprenticeship full of inadequacies, and often tumultuous,' Cardoso told the AIM workforce. 'Organisationally, we are still terribly weak, and our administrative skills provoke laughter or pity, and almost always frustration.' But the quality of the journalism produced had been fine, he stressed. 'Today we can say, with justified pride, that as to the truth of the events reported by us, we only got it wrong two or three times in more than five years.'

The 'greater truth' was the right of the Mozambican people to sovereignty, social justice, wellbeing and peace.

> Without this truth we would be reduced to spectators of the history of our country and of the region. Because of it, we are actors in this history … Our enthusiasm has pushed us forward. It is a force that cannot be measured, but without which our profession would be empty, and our hearts deserted.

AIM's staff, he was sure, would continue to give of their best so that to future generations of reporters and photographers we can say that there was some glory in having been journalists at the start of our nation. The force of some of our journalistic work is due to this, to the fact that we don't have to wait for a tranquil tomorrow to know how to taste the adventure of the tumultuous dawn.

Meanwhile, Cardoso was finally to obtain the status of director that we had all informally given him before. He became director in early 1987, thanks to Hunguana overhauling the way the ministry of information functioned. Hunguana was starting with a clean slate – Machel had died before he could give him any instructions on how to handle the press. So Hunguana took his own decisions. The first was to bypass the Frelimo ideology department. He noted that AIM had no director: Cardoso's formal rank was still that of chief news editor. It was widely assumed that any attempt to promote him to director in name as well as fact would run into opposition from the DTI, the department of ideological work. Hunguana reasoned: 'Either Cardoso was trustworthy, in which case he should be appointed director, or he was not and somebody else should be appointed.' He considered Cardoso a good professional 'despite certain reservations, given his nonconformist temperament. He was a rebel, in the positive sense of the term.' And so the minister decided to appoint him – but did not consult the DTI.

Hunguana had effectively gone over the head of Rebelo, and never again would the DTI play a determinant role in the media. 'The DTI was in charge of the media area, but after 1986 there was a clear understanding that this kind of management had to change. I decided to marginalise certain mechanisms,' said Hunguana. He also formalised the 'editorial council' in the ministry. The previous ministers had tended to deal with the media directors individually, discussing matters with them one by one. The editorial council brought the minister together with all the directors and editors at least once a week. Sixteen years later it is easy to dismiss this as just a measure to control the press. But Hunguana regarded it as 'a measure of democratisation. Everyone could speak. That was the intention.'

Initially Cardoso was enthusiastic about Hunguana and the fresh air that seemed to be blowing through the ministry corridors. But his relations with Hunguana began to sour because of the AIM office in Nampula. Salomão Moyana opened the office in March 1986. But two months later a new governor was appointed. He was the former secretary of state for cashew, Gaspar Dzimba; and the promotion of

Dzimba to run the most populous province in the country turned out to be one of Machel's most serious errors of judgement. For Dzimba thought the governor's office should control everything that happened in the province – particularly the press. A month after Dzimba's appointment, Moyana found there was something odd about recent arrests of petty criminals in Nampula. They turned out to be men who had served prison sentences in northern re-education camps and been released – but with no transport home. These ex-prisoners had been able to make it as far as Nampula, where they hoped they might be able to hitch a lift south on military aircraft at the Nacala air base. They had no money and no food, and so resorted to crime in order to eat. Some police officers regarded them as a convenient pool of labour, and employed them as domestic servants in their homes – but then did not pay them. Moyana found one case of a former prisoner who was severely tortured because he was suspected of stealing from his new employer's house.

When Moyana tried to hear the police version, the Nampula commander took out his pistol and put it on the table. And, just to make sure Moyana had got the message, he told him he was 'at risk of your life', should he publish the story. Moyana sought an audience with Dzimba and told the governor of the death threats. Dzimba set up a commission, headed by a senior civil servant, to investigate. The commission discovered that everything Moyana had told the governor about the ex-prisoners was correct. Moyana then met with Dzimba, who told him his story was quite accurate – but he couldn't publish it. Moyana tried to persuade the governor: after all, this was a story that would make him look good. Here was a case where abuses were discovered, the governor investigated, and the guilty policemen were punished. What was wrong with that? Moyana recalls Dzimba telling him: 'You can't publish because Samora won't like it. It's a violation of human rights, and the president does not like that.' In vain did Moyana say this was precisely why it should be published, so that the president could see that a governor he appointed was active on the human rights front.

The next stage was a meeting involving all the other journalists in Nampula. Dzimba told Moyana to read out his story, and to his sorrow he received no support from the other journalists. 'My colleagues said I should not publish,' he recalled. That same day Dzimba set up a 'press analysis office' headed by Ricardo Malate, then the Radio Mozambique delegate in the province, which was to vet any articles being transmitted outside the province. Moyana regarded this as nothing short of a censorship office, and refused to have anything to do with it. He told Dzimba he was responsible to the director and chief news editor of AIM, and the decision as to whether his stories were published would be taken in Maputo, not Nampula. So Moyana sent the story on the police employing ex-prisoners as cheap labour to Cardoso, with an explanation, and it appeared in June 1986.

Dzimba had made other, more powerful enemies – notably the provincial military commander, Eduardo da Silva Nihia, who took strong objection to the governor's apparent contempt for the main ethnic group in the province, the Makuas. So Machel made his last visit to Nampula, where he carpeted Dzimba, demanding respect for veterans of the independence war such as Nihia. There is little doubt that Machel was planning to sack Dzimba – but the tragedy at Mbuzini intervened, and Dzimba's stewardship of the province continued for several more months.

The governor had not forgiven Moyana for the story on the police, and awaited a chance for revenge. Shortly after the introduction of structural adjustment measures in January 1987, a government team went to Nampula to explain them. Led by the agriculture minister, João Ferreira, it held a meeting with all the senior cadres in the province, including journalists. The meeting was supposed to discuss the government's economic recovery programme; but Ferreira was annoyed by an article that had appeared on the state poultry company, Avicola. He asked who had written it, and Moyana said it was his work. Ferreira called him 'mediocre', and Moyana retorted that the ministry of information, not the ministry of agriculture, was the body that decided whether journalists were mediocre or not. This was a courageous thing to say to a minister in a semi-public gathering. The response was glacial. 'He insulted and threatened me, and forced me to remain standing throughout the meeting,' Moyana recalled. Dzimba chipped in, saying this was a journalist who was always creating problems. On the spot, Ferreira announced that he would have Moyana arrested. This was little more than bluster: the meeting ended, and nobody hauled Moyana off to jail.

But, for Moyana, it was an unpleasant and humiliating experience. He informed Cardoso, who was furious. Cardoso phoned Hunguana and demanded that he do something about it – otherwise he had better find a new director for AIM. This was the first time that Cardoso threatened to resign. The next day Hunguana met with Cardoso. 'My reporter is being threatened – you must take action,' Cardoso told him. And the minister did – he sent a commission headed by Albino Magaia to Nampula to see if Cardoso's accusations were correct. The delegation was there for a week, meeting separately with Moyana and with the other Nampula journalists. Radio journalist Saide Omar backed up Moyana's version of events, and prepared a document on Dzimba's interference in the work of the media, and his manipulation of the Nampula radio station.

A week later, Hunguana sent a message directly to Moyana. It said, as far as Moyana could recall 15 years later: '1. The AIM delegation in Nampula is abolished. 2. Journalist Salomão Moyana should present himself in 48 hours at the ministry of information for new orders.' In addition, Ricardo Malate and Saide Omar were transferred to Maputo, and a new radio delegate was appointed. Moyana phoned Cardoso, only to find that the AIM Maputo office knew nothing about the minister's orders. Cardoso was beside himself with rage, and Moyana could hear him banging on the table. Once again he threatened to resign. Hunguana had not consulted him before sending the message to Moyana, and Cardoso had not even received a copy of Magaia's report.

Within the requisite 48 hours Moyana was back in Maputo, and reported to Cardoso and to Hunguana. The minister appeared to be having second thoughts, since he gave Moyana the option of returning to Nampula. That looked like a non-starter – Moyana had done as instructed, closed the AIM office and handed over the keys. So Hunguana transferred him to *Notícias* – much to the annoyance of the paper's director, José Catorze, who said there were no vacancies.

Confusion reigned. Moyana was sent back to Nampula, but not to re-open the AIM office. A short while later a place was found for him in *Notícias*, where he stayed for six months before moving on to the Sunday paper *Domingo*.

Moyana and Omar were entirely vindicated in May 1987. On the strength of further complaints about Dzimba's tribalism, the Frelimo politburo set up a commission of inquiry, and Dzimba was told to take a holiday. The commission did not publicly humiliate Dzimba, but he did not return. With Dzimba out of the way, perhaps AIM could return to Nampula. Cardoso fought for the restoration of the AIM office, arguing that, if the minister objected to Moyana, then somebody else could be appointed. But Hunguana refused, and so AIM was again reduced to the anomalous status of a national news agency which had offices abroad (in Lisbon and Johannesburg), but none in any of the country's provinces.

When he was justice minister in the early 1980s, Hunguana had faced similar problems with provincial governors protesting against judges; and in these cases the prudent option was to withdraw the judge. 'The governor was appointed by the head of state, and the judge by the minister' – it was an unequal battle, and to protect the judges Hunguana thought it better to pull them out. He argues that a similar rationale lay behind the 1987 decision to close the AIM Nampula office. If that was so, he was being excessively cautious; for Dzimba was a lightweight compared with the Niassa and Cabo Delgado governors (senior Frelimo figures Aurelio Manave and Armando Panguene) who had given him headaches as justice minister.

❖

On 1 August 1987 the representative of the Norwegian development agency Norad, Arthur Sydnes, invited Cardoso to a dinner at his house. Also present was a young Norwegian lawyer named Nina Berg. She was in Mozambique as part of a team from the law faculty of Oslo University, doing field work on Mozambique's unique system of local people's tribunals and the way they could be used to empower women. Her research was aimed at seeing whether in practice the people's tribunals were implementing the gender equality stipulated in the constitution. Sydnes's wife was also a lawyer, and was pleased to meet a delegation of fellow Norwegians from her field – hence the dinner party.

Nina knew little about Cardoso beyond his name: indeed, although she was an activist on the Norwegian left, she knew little about Mozambique because her solidarity work in Norway had concentrated on South Africa. At the dinner party the two met and started talking. Samora Machel was among the topics of discussion. 'It was obvious that Carlos was still very affected by the death of Samora,' Nina recalls. 'He was not very joyful when I met him.' But the following day Cardoso contacted her, and a love affair blossomed. Nina left Mozambique after six weeks, and when Cardoso took his holidays in February 1988 he went to Norway and stayed with Nina.

But by then a great deal had happened.

Renamo now appeared to regard southern Mozambique as a free-fire zone, and a series of grisly massacres occurred. The worst took place on 18 July 1987 in the small town of Homoíne, in Inhambane province. In the bloodiest single incident in the war, a heavily armed Renamo unit stormed into the town killing everyone they could find. Some were heard to shout, 'We've come to finish off the people of Samora Machel.' The total death toll came to 424. Renamo did not dispute that a massacre had occurred – it tried to thrust the blame onto the Zimbabwean troops. But the Zimbabwean army had never operated in Inhambane, and surviving Homoíne residents had no doubt that the attackers were 'Matsangas'.

AIM found and interviewed an American Mennonite missionary and agronomist, Mark van Koevering, who was in Homoíne working for the Mozambican Christian Council on a seed multiplication project. He too had no doubt who was responsible. 'Having lived through this, I think it's important, especially for Americans, to realise that this is not a civil war. These people are not fighting for any ideal. They're fighting to create terror,' he said. Van Koevering attacked the far-right American supporters of Renamo. 'The argument that people like Mr Helms [North Carolina senator Jesse Helms] offer that this is a democratic movement to liberate the people of Mozambique is complete foolishness,' he added.

On 10 August it was the turn of Manjacaze, a town in Gaza, where Renamo butchered 92 – a death toll that would have been much higher but for the courage of a tiny FPLM garrison that kept the attackers at bay for five hours, allowing most of the residents to escape. Two months later, Renamo switched its attention to the main north–south road, Estrada Nacional No. 1. Trucks moved in convoy, usually under military escort, along the road, a fragile lifeline linking the capital to Gaza and Inhambane. On 16 October came the first Renamo attack on a convoy: 53 people were killed as vehicles were fired upon in the area of Taninga, 80 kilometres north of Maputo. This should have led to increased security at Taninga, but it did not. On 29 October Renamo struck at much the same place, destroying 80 vehicles, including buses full of passengers. The death toll was 278. The carnage shocked western diplomats taken to the scene. Surveying the desolation, US ambassador Melissa Wells had no hesitation in describing the ambush as 'banditry and terrorism', while the UNDP resident representative, Arturo Hein, said: 'For me, the authors of this attack are bandits and terrorists who kill without justification.'

Initial media response to the Homoíne massacre had been painfully slow: three days passed before the news got to the outside world. The local military command had seen no urgency in taking journalists to the massacre site. Rebelo was certainly aware of the problem of credibility, and once again an attempt was made to ensure some form of liaison between the military and the media. Rebelo chaired a meeting on 7 October, essentially between top military figures and DTI staff. The minutes of this meeting stated the problem clearly: 'There is no information strategy on the war. The information produced contains no analysis, it is sometimes inaccurate, and it always arrives late.' There were more stories in the media about Renamo atrocities than about 'the combat actions of the FAM'. This 'has negative effects, giving the idea that the armed forces do not defend the public and our economic and social projects.'

This meeting clearly agreed with many of Cardoso's concerns, as the minutes show:

Speed in releasing information plays an important role, inside and outside the country. Internally, if we are quick, it will be us and not the enemy to inform our people on how the war is going, which will avoid distortions; and, for those abroad, if we put out the information first, that information will be more credible.

The meeting decided to set up a press office in the offices of the general staff, to be manned by an FAM officer and an experienced journalist. It was to coordinate its activities with the party, the ministry of information, and the national political commissariat of the FAM.

The general staff was to tell the provincial military councils to grant access to journalists 'to cover combat actions'. Information on the war was to be released immediately, and the press office was to compile all information on FAM and Renamo activity. 'Other in-depth reports, of an analytical nature, should be drawn up by the reporters chosen by the media. These journalists will meet regularly with military officers for briefings allowing them to gather background information,' the meeting decreed. It even suggested giving some journalists military training so that they could become war correspondents, while soldiers of a certain academic level could be trained in journalism skills.

A working group was set up to implement these decisions, including representatives from the main media (Fernando Gonçalves was to represent AIM). But once again the initiative was still-born. The working group scarcely met, and all the decisions were quietly forgotten: for the military, it was business as usual.

But AIM did have one positive experience with the military. As from late 1986, Gil Lauriciano became the nearest thing the media had to a war correspondent. Lauriciano was initially a technician, but in 1985 he asked to switch to the newsroom. Cardoso had doubts about his ability to write, but Lauriciano's persistence paid off, and as from the 1986 general elections, shortly before Machel's death, he started to travel with the army. Cardoso sent him to Zambezia, which was then being overrun by Renamo infiltration from Malawi. The man in charge of military operations there was General Lagos Lidimo, who demanded to see Lauriciano's dispatches. Lauriciano refused, ignoring empty threats that he would be shot. He insisted that the only person who would alter what he had written was Carlos Cardoso.

And so articles on the war in Zambezia began to appear. They were not mere propaganda, but they did show the army in a fairly good light. 'Lagos eventually understood that journalists were not so dangerous after all,' commented Lauriciano. The following year, the army actually invited Lauriciano to cover the 1987 counter-offensive in Zambezia. 'They wanted the same journalist, and they left me alone to write my articles,' he recalled. 'Lagos became almost a friend.' But this experience was isolated. The army high command did not take the risk of trying to generalise this to other reporters.

❖

The wave of massacres coincided with further threats against the Front Line States from Magnus Malan. On 16 September he told the SABC that 'counter-measures' against the ANC did not mean 'action against terrorists alone. Counter-measures also mean that leaders of countries from which terrorists operate will be accountable for their part in murder and destruction caused by terrorists.' He then picked out Chissano by name, along with Robert Mugabe, Kenneth Kaunda and José Eduardo dos Santos. Their support for the ANC, he threatened, meant that 'the future of their countries would be in the balance', since South Africa 'would be forced to act, if it considered this to be in its interests.' Cardoso noted that the last time Malan had threatened a Front Line leader by name, his target had been Samora Machel in October 1986, just two weeks before the Mbuzini crash. Further threats came on 14 October, in a speech made by Malan when opening a new air base in the northern Transvaal. He accused the Mozambican government of being 'directly or indirectly involved in the physical export of violence to South Africa'. 'The spreading of revolution has to be prevented,' he menaced. 'We expect President Chissano to pull his weight in this regard, or we will have to take steps to neutralise terrorists in his country.'

On 16 October, Malan included AIM in his threats against Mozambique – this was the third time in the space of a few months that the apartheid regime, or its broadcasting services, had specifically menaced AIM. In an editorial entitled 'Malan and us', Cardoso replied:

> We've got the message, we understand what it means. The minister's threat is an order transmitted to the South African bodies that deal with destabilisation. It's an order to the bandits inside Mozambique to put bombs in our offices, to send us booby-trapped letters, and to see to it that some of us 'mysteriously' turn up dead on street corners at night. We fully understand. The message is clear. Either we shut up, or something unpleasant may happen to us.

After the Taninga massacre and Malan's threats, the AIM staff met, and Cardoso wrote on their behalf to the ONJ general secretary, Manuel Tomé. The AIM reporters thought 'the current situation merits the urgent and organised attention of all journalists through the ONJ.' Cardoso asked for a meeting with Tomé to present a detailed report on the South African government's attempts 'to impose censorship in Mozambique'. Journalists were prepared to play a role in civil defence, and 'a passive attitude towards the extremely serious problems we are facing is the most effective way for the enemy to demobilise us'. The AIM journalists still believed that 'the people's war against armed banditry is the only way to defend sovereignty, to eliminate the armed bandits and to weaken apartheid'.

What Cardoso did not tell the rest of the newsroom was that he also wrote to Hunguana, suggesting that he be relieved of his duties as director of AIM in order to concentrate exclusively on handling information on the war. After the massacre at Taninga, he wrote,

> It's obvious that the media should prepare for a profound change in the way it works ... The media can make an enormous contribution to dissipating the present climate of despair and immobility, particularly in Maputo city, which is a terrible weapon in the hands of Pretoria.
>
> The reality of the country is marked by war. Everything depends on what happens in this area. But the media speaks of a country of relative peace.

The gross disparity between what was happening on the ground and what was reported in the media 'helps create a climate of alienation'.

The result is a gigantic lie which serves Pretoria perfectly. People speak of war, but don't find this reflected in the media. There are those who argue that normal, rather than war, programming is necessary so that the sources of foreign support believe there is enough stability. A massacre undoes this in one blow.

Cardoso noted the frequent criticism from military leaders that the media 'has more news about the actions of the bandits, and is thus playing the enemy's game'. He rejected the accusation. 'News and reports on the activities of the bandits, as well as visits by diplomats to massacre sites, help show the true face of apartheid and of banditry internationally. The mistake does not lie in speaking about the bandits. They are a part of our reality.' For the press to say nothing about massacres and the other crimes committed against civilians every day 'would be to remove all credibility from the media – and from the Party and the government'.

Cardoso thought it perfectly possible to report on combat from the army's side, on bravery shown by Mozambican troops, to interview soldiers, to add news from the rest of southern Africa, and thus 'we will have a climate of taking the offensive'. 'The only way to fight the racism of apartheid is for the media to show by facts, and not by slogans, that the historic initiative, the strategic initiative, the initiative in creating systems, lies in the hands of men and women whom apartheid considers "inferior."' If the media went onto the offensive, this would help demoralise the enemy and 'help immensely the anti-destabilisation forces inside South Africa to use better arguments against the militarists whose basic strength is in the weakness of our response, and when that response exists, the fact that the anti-intervention sectors don't know about it'.

Cardoso's proposal was that he leave the post of director. A director-general could be appointed to deal with all the administration while he concentrated exclusively on editorial matters. Coverage of the war, he thought, would be a matter for close coordination between AIM and Radio Mozambique. He wanted this idea discussed in a meeting of media directors, chaired by Rebelo, and with Hunguana present. 'This proposal is the fruit of months of thought, made urgent by this phase of massacres,' Cardoso concluded.

Yet Hunguana knew full well that the real problem lay in the army, not the media. He replied: 'The real problem your letter raises does not refer to the media, I have no doubt of that.' Politely, he rejected Cardoso's proposals: 'In my view the better functioning of the media does not necessarily arise from any of the proposals in your letter, taken individually or together.'

But by the time this letter arrived on his desk, Cardoso was no longer in Maputo. He had flown to Luanda to cover a Front Line summit, and found himself, almost by accident, covering the key military conflict of the entire southern African war, as South African troops closed in on the embattled Angolan town of Cuito Cuanavale.

CHAPTER 15

Under Fire from Friend and Foe

The largest conventional battle ever fought in southern Africa raged round the small Angolan town of Cuito Cuanavale from September 1987 to March 1988. It resulted from miscalculations on both sides – but eventually unlocked the door leading to Namibian independence. The Angolan army, Fapla, miscalculated in imagining that a mid-1987 offensive against Unita in Cuando Cubango province, the sparsely populated territory which the Portuguese had called 'the lands at the end of the world', would be a limited affair. They did not envisage a massive South African response to rescue Unita. But much the worse miscalculation was by the South Africans: they did not realise that Fapla was now a battle-hardened force capable of withstanding the South African Defence Force (SADF), nor that a major South African thrust into Angola would trigger renewed Cuban commitment to the war.

The Angolan offensive began in July 1987, without Cuban support. Later, Cuban sources were to tell Cardoso that the Cuban high command disagreed with the timing. They argued that, if Fapla were to strike against Unita supply lines south of Cuito Cuanavale, then it should have started several weeks earlier – for in September and October rain comes to Cuando Cubango, threatening to turn this normally semi-arid area into a swamp. However, Soviet military advisers agreed with the offensive. A Cuban source told Cardoso: 'There was agreement between the three – Angola, Cuba and the USSR – on the major strategic questions, but there were various frictions between Cubans and Soviets, and sometimes between Soviets and Angolans over tactical issues.'

The South Africans announced that the Fapla goal was to seize Unita headquarters at Jamba, and the SADF intervened massively in September, catching Fapla units by surprise at the Lomba River. Fapla suffered heavy material losses, but most of its men were able to retreat in good order across the river, and fell back to Cuito Cuanavale. Ferocious fighting developed around Cuito Cuanavale, which Fapla decided must not fall. At this stage Fapla was on its own: the Cubans formed a rearguard hundreds of kilometres to the north. Indeed, the Cubans had not been involved in front-line fighting since 1976, when the initial South African drive on Luanda had been defeated. But now Fapla needed reinforcements. Recalling this period, a top Fapla officer told Cardoso: 'It's not easy for the troops, in the heat of combat, under massive fire from the South Africans, to accept the policy of Cuban non-involvement.'

In November, Magnus Malan made an extraordinary announcement: the South African president, PW Botha, and four of his ministers (Malan, Pik Botha, finance minister Barend du Plessis, and education minister FW de Klerk) had visited the southern Angolan battlefront to encourage the SADF forces there. Malan said Botha's visit was to demonstrate his 'personal responsibility' for an operation which had cost the lives of 23 South African soldiers so far. (The Angolans said the real figure was 10 times as high.) Malan's announcement came on the eve of a Front Line summit in Luanda, dominated by the military situation in Cuando Cubango. Cardoso went to cover the summit and ended up staying in Angola for six critical weeks. Cardoso found the Front Line leaders convinced that it was the death of white South African soldiers that was the immediate cause of Botha's visit, and that his action 'means more, not less, war'.

But Kenneth Kaunda's opening remarks were a veiled warning to the Angolan government not to bring the Cubans in. After briefly claiming that Botha's visit was 'a clear indication' of Fapla efficiency, he praised the Angolan government for not moving Cuban troops south. Kaunda said the US was putting pressure on Dos Santos to use the Cubans 'because they wanted an excuse to bring other western forces to join the South African forces in order to transform the struggle into an east–west conflict'. He congratulated Dos Santos for 'not falling into this trap'. The US had suffered 'a political defeat', he claimed. 'You outmanoeuvred them.' Was this ignorance or naivety on Kaunda's part? Perhaps he did not know that Dos Santos had already requested more troops from Havana; or perhaps he suspected it and was trying to prevent their deployment.

Although AIM had a longstanding agreement with the Angolan news agency Angop, Cardoso chose to operate, not out of the Angop offices, but from the delegation of the Yugoslav agency Tanjug: for the Tanjug correspondent, Nikola Vadjon, had excellent contacts in both the Angolan and Cuban military, whereas the tightly controlled Angolan media, with a few exceptions such as the TV programme *Opção*, simply reported official statements on the war.

Cardoso rapidly concluded that the battles in southern Angola could be decisive for the entire region. But the Angolan version of events received virtually no coverage in the western or South African media; so Cardoso instructed AIM to ensure that his dispatches from Luanda were all translated into English and distributed as widely as possible, particularly to the South African press. Thus AIM reports from Angola began to appear in the Johannesburg *Star*, much to the annoyance of Magnus Malan. Cardoso thought his stories were published in the South African media because the editors of those papers knew 'that the SADF give little or no information, they don't want to see their country's name always linked to aggression … and they know that AIM is in the middle ages of news agency journalism, but it doesn't tell lies'. On several occasions Cardoso gained access to General António dos Santos Franca 'Ndalu', the Fapla chief of staff – the man who was running the war. In mid-November, Ndalu told Cardoso he expected more heavy fighting between Fapla and the SADF in the coming weeks; the fighting was then only in Cuando Cubango, but he expected a front to open in the neighbouring province of Cunene as soon as the SADF moved its 8th motorised division across the Namibian border.

Ndalu gave a candid assessment of Fapla losses – 242 dead, 16 missing, 728 wounded. The Angolans had also lost 126 vehicles, 27 tanks, four helicopters and two MiGs. Ndalu claimed the South

Africans had lost 230 men (many of these were SADF black soldiers and had not been acknowledged), 12 tanks, 24 other vehicles and 39 planes. The last figure is a gross exaggeration – but Fapla anti-aircraft fire had certainly brought several planes down, mainly unmanned drones but also some Impalas and Mirages. As for the purpose of the initial Fapla offensive: 'We never told our soldiers that the aim of the operation was to take Jamba. That was made up by the South Africans.' Ndalu said the real purpose was to cut the Unita supply routes which ran through 'an area between Cuito Cuanavale and the Lomba River'.

On 27 November Arnaldo Ochoa Sanchez, the general who headed the Cuban forces in Angola in 1975–76, sent a clear signal of a more active Cuban role. In a message to the Cuban military mission in Angola, he declared: 'The present moment demands that we maintain the highest level of combat readiness to repel any aggression, playing our role as defenders of the territorial integrity and sovereignty of the People's Republic of Angola, and of the right of the heroic Namibian people to independence.' Magnus Malan sneered at the Cubans: he claimed they had 'abandoned' Fapla and preferred drinking and womanising in the cities to doing any fighting. This was a spectacularly foolish gaffe; for, at the very moment Malan was speaking, fresh Cuban forces were crossing the Atlantic.

It was Cardoso who announced their arrival. A dispatch of 5 December proved to be one of the major scoops of his career. He had confirmation from a source in the MPLA leadership that 'a considerable number of fresh Cuban forces' had recently arrived in Luanda. A Cuban source then told Cardoso that the 50th division of the FAR (Revolutionary Armed Forces of Cuba) was on its way to southern Angola. And Ochoa Sanchez was with them.

Cardoso's report drew two denials. One was from Malan, who, in an 'informal briefing' for South African journalists in Cape Town, said that for AIM to report on Angola was 'like going to Moscow to find out what was happening in Los Angeles' (it was not clear whether he was trying to tar Cardoso as an agent of Moscow, or was simply unaware that Cardoso was in Angola). AIM's credibility was 'very low', he claimed, and he described the purpose of Cardoso's reports as 'to bolster the image of the Cuban and Angolan forces'. In any case, the SADF wasn't worried about Cubans, he added, since they were not 'real fighters'.[1] But the second denial came from the Angolan government itself. In an interview with the BBC, Deputy Foreign Minister Venancio de Moura denied that there were any Cuban reinforcements, or that Cuban forces were heading southwards.

Cardoso's story was entirely accurate, and he stuck to it. In a telex conversation with me he said, 'Please do not worry too much about possible contradictions between AIM and Venancio de Moura. This profession was never without contradiction.' He was clearly irritated by the messages that were reaching him from Mozambican officials. 'I'd love not to have more pressure on journalistic coverage than the gargantuan ones that apply here in Luanda. Anyway, the military here are so much freer and more self-confident in dealing with information than "civilians," who seem to be under all sorts of pressure from the Americans.'

A worried Arlindo Lopes sent a message to Cardoso on 8 December. Was he aware of Venancio de Moura's interview? And, in a suggestion that AIM should exercise self-censorship, he asked: 'Is publicising these facts in the interests of the Angolan authorities?' The following day Teodato Hunguana sent a message advising Cardoso of the denial, and adding: 'Even if the arrival of new Cubans is true, we should stress the fact that the South Africans are taking a beating from the Angolans and play the Cuban factor "low-key."' Neither Lopes nor the minister suggested that Cardoso was lying or had got the story wrong.

Later Cardoso recalled thinking to himself, 'There are new Cuban troops in Angola. It's a fact, it's true, and journalists have the duty to tell the truth, particularly when it's as simple as this.' He sent a lengthy reply to Hunguana, insisting not only that his story was accurate but that it was in the interests of the Angolans to raise the hypothesis that the Cubans were about to enter the battle for Cuito Cuanavale. He told Hunguana that his MPLA source was none other than the ideology secretary, Roberto de Almeida, and wrote:

> Possible re-entry of Cubans in no way removes Fapla
> merit in having severely pounded SADF. Entry of

Cubans might wound some national sentiment, but many Angolan officers want the Cubans in, because in combat zones, when they don't enter, all the logistics they control remain inactive. This has already happened, because the Cubans had orders not to open fire. And it cost Fapla lives.

So yes, the role of Fapla in the battle should always be stressed, Cardoso agreed, but 'without omitting the vital importance of the Cubans'.

Despite Venancio de Moura, any attentive observer could deduce that the Cubans were not twiddling their thumbs. Both Fidel Castro and José Eduardo dos Santos were in Moscow in early November for the celebrations of the seventieth anniversary of the Bolshevik revolution, and both held discussions with Mikhail Gorbachev. A few days later Jorge Brisquet, of the Cuban Communist Party politburo, was in Luanda – bearing a message from Castro. Clearly Dos Santos had asked Castro for further military help, but the Cuban leader could reply only after discussions in Havana.

The UN Security Council had set the date of 10 December for the withdrawal of all South African troops from Angola. Cardoso concluded that Angola and Cuba 'are giving Pretoria a clear warning that they intend to carry out the Angolan demand that all South African troops should be out of Angolan territory by 10 December'. On 8 December, even the stodgy official daily *Jornal de Angola* warned that a Fapla offensive with Cuban support could arise 'after our country has tried by all means to find a diplomatic solution to the conflict fomented by racist South Africa'.

Heavy fighting continued in Cuando Cubango, and Ndalu told Cardoso that the SADF was intent on capturing Cuito Cuanavale but was no longer prepared to risk its air force. The town was pounded by the SADF's long-range G5 and G6 artillery. TV reporters from *Opção* were helicoptered in to Cuito Cuanavale. Their footage showed a downed South African plane, and an SADF mobile artillery piece captured intact. The buildings in the town were ruined, but the Fapla units were still there. On 8 December the SADF attacked a Fapla column travelling from the provincial capital, Menongue, to Cuito Cunavale. This was just hours before the head of the South African army, General Jannie Geldenhuys, announced that the SADF was withdrawing after 'successfully completing' its mission. 'If this is indeed a South African withdrawal from the Cuito Cuanavale area, it would show that the South Africans have no stomach for a major battle with the Cubans,' mused Cardoso. But in fact it was nothing more than a half-hearted attempt to make the west believe that the South Africans would indeed be gone by the UN deadline.

On 10 December itself, José Eduardo dos Santos praised the 'renewed commitment' of Cuban forces 'in the trenches' side by side with Fapla, and the Angolan radio reported the arrival of another Cuban general, Raul Tomassevic. The deadline passed, and on 11 December Dos Santos warned the South Africans of a repeat of the 'victorious campaign' of 1975–76. Angola could 'resort again to assistance from our friends and allies from Cuba'. Since the South Africans had not withdrawn, Fapla would 'expel the racist aggressor'.

On 13 December Cardoso had another exclusive, based on 'a high-ranking Fapla official' (probably Ndalu): the Angolans were now prepared to move Cuban forces south of the Moçâmedes railway, not only to relieve the pressure on Cuito Cunavale but also to recover all the territory the SADF had been holding since 1981 in south-eastern Cunene. The Moçâmedes railway is the southernmost line in Angola, running from the port of Namibe to Menongue. Angola and South Africa had reached an understanding in 1984 that all Cuban forces would move north of the Moçâmedes railway to facilitate a South African withdrawal from Cunene. 'We carried out an inspection,' said Cardoso's military source. 'The South Africans had effectively withdrawn to Namibia. Two days after we completed our inspection, they re-entered Angola and they have been inside Angola ever since. It's clear they don't respect any agreement they sign. We're tired of this.'

When Cardoso returned to Maputo, Cuito Cuanavale was still being shelled, and it was still unclear whether the Cubans would indeed enter the battle. Back at the AIM office, Cardoso was regularly on the phone and telex to Luanda, contacting his Cuban and

Angolan sources, and the ever-willing Nikola. On 5 January came the first report that the Cubans were on the front line: Cardoso's sources reported that Cuban reconnaissance units had clashed with the SADF on a small scale in late December. Some Cubans were now stationed at Cuito Cuanavale. In the second week of January, Cuito Cuanavale came under the worst shelling yet – an average of 170 to 200 of the massive G5 and G6 shells fell on the town every day. The Angolans responded with air strikes against SADF positions. But the air force in question was the Cuban one; this was acknowledged by none other than Kenneth Kaunda, who told Prensa Latina journalists that 'Cuba's determination to save Angola is more than welcome'. This was the first mention of the Cuban air force. It appeared on Pana and was given prominent play by Cardoso at AIM (but was ignored by the Angolan media).

The Unita office in Lisbon then claimed that Fapla had withdrawn from Cuito Cuanavale. Cardoso rang up Carlos Henriques of *Opção*, who said he had visited the town on 28 January: although the airfield was damaged, the local Fapla command was still inside Cuito Cuanavale. Henriques gave the chronology. The SADF had massively attacked the Fapla 21st brigade on 13 January. It withdrew from front-line positions, and over the following two days it became evident that the SADF intended to advance on the town. On 15 January the air force went into action, and its MiG-21s, MiG-23s and Sukois did 'serious damage' to the SADF positions – the incident referred to by Kaunda. At the moment of the worst South African bombardment, the Fapla command did pull back from Cuito Cuanavale, but it soon returned. That the town was still firmly in Fapla hands was clear in the third week of January, when the Cuando Cubango provincial commissar, Francisco Tutu, held a rally there, and Ndalu paid a visit at the head of a large politico-military delegation. All this was faithfully relayed by AIM to the best of its ability, in Portuguese and English, to the rest of the world.

And once again the Angolan authorities, far from expressing any thanks, tried to gag Cardoso. In February 1988 Arlindo Lopes sent a worried message to Hunguana conveying a protest from the Angolan department of information and propaganda (DIP). It declared: 'The People's Republic of Angola is seriously concerned at the dispatches AIM has been distributing in recent months on the military situation in Angola, particularly since the most serious aggression was launched.' The Angolans claimed that Cardoso had committed 'abuses of trust, in that in particular cases he published information given to him by Angolan officials "off the record" on the basis that they were talking to "a comrade."' Worse still, DIP claimed that 'some of the information published by AIM objectively damaged certain strategic and tactical measures taken by the Angolan authorities'. It even blamed Cardoso's dispatches for 'unnecessary losses of men and equipment', adding that 'the gravity of some of the information published causes Angolan diplomacy embarrassment'.[2]

Foreign ministers of the Front Line States met in the Tanzanian town of Arusha on 26–27 January 1988, and the Angolans complained to the Mozambican minister, Pascoal Mocumbi, about Cardoso's work. Mocumbi, however, cannot have been greatly concerned, since it was not until three weeks later that he sent a letter to Hunguana (dated 18 February) outlining the Angolan complaints. Mocumbi said he had been under the impression that Cardoso's stories 'were written in agreement with the Angolan authorities and in their interest'. The puzzled foreign minister asked Hunguana 'to take appropriate measures to clarify this matter and to avoid similar situations in the future'. At much the same time the SADF, oblivious of any friction between Luanda and Maputo, were denouncing both AIM and Angop as 'leaders in the propaganda campaign'.

May 1988 was a crucial month. As the South Africans pulled back from Cuito Cuanavale, serious discussions began on Namibian independence, in the form of quadripartite talks in London between Angolan, South African, Cuban and United States delegations. On the margin of these talks, for the first time Ndalu and other Angolan military figures met with South African generals. Cardoso, citing 'a reliable source', was the first to reveal this meeting. But the Angolans had hoped to keep it quiet, so Ndalu issued a routine denial.

At much the same time Tanjug carried a story, from Cuban sources, that Fapla, FAR and Swapo forces were driving towards the border and were now 200 kilometres south of the Moçâmedes railway. Cardoso attempted to confirm this story from 'official' Angolan sources, with a predictable lack of success. He put it out anyway, citing Tanjug. A telex conversation between Cardoso and Vadjon a few days later has survived. 'You stirred up a thousand demons with that story' (on the military meeting), remarked Vadjon. He was suspected, correctly, of passing information to Cardoso, and said the Luanda authorities fired 'artillery salvoes against me'. Cardoso was worried this time: had their sources got it right? Vadjon was sure they had. He was also convinced that the reason the South Africans went to London was the Fapla–FAR drive towards the border. If the South Africans did not now talk peace seriously, 'they'll have Cubans in Namibia before they can blink'. Initially the South Africans said there was no such drive south. But on 16 May Malan warned that if Swapo, 'protected by Cubans', moved any closer to the border, that would be 'the spark that lights the fire'.

Once again Angolan protests landed on Mozambican desks. Roberto de Almeida sent a telex message to Hunguana on 6 May 1988:

1. Journalist Carlos Cardoso (AIM) phones up Angolan colleagues, including the director of *Jornal de Angola*, seeking to confirm stories he says were given to him by Cuban sources here.

2. This does not seem correct to us, since the contact most clearly indicated for AIM is Angop.

3. He must be held responsible for any less than truthful items published in the Mozambican media.

This time the MPLA ideology chief was saying that even the official daily was no good as a source: AIM should only be allowed to use Angop!

The most extraordinary Angolan protest came from Angop itself – a telex signed by 'General Management' even threatened to cut off relations with AIM because of Cardoso's reporting. The Angop management said it had been asked by Almeida

to express our disappointment and concern at the casual way that AIM reports on the military situation in Angola. Although, in the best spirit of collaboration and comradeship, we have duly warned about the reliability of the Angolan and Cuban sources or pseudo-sources which AIM says it contacts in Luanda by phone, we note that AIM continues with the same practice of sensationalism and disinformation.

Angop was particularly annoyed by Cardoso's scoop on the meeting (described by Angop as a 'pseudo-meeting') between Ndalu and the South African military in London 'on the margin of the talks'. For Angop, if the Angolan general denied the meeting, it couldn't have taken place. 'If this practice and the sensationalist stress given by AIM to the struggle we are waging in Angola persists, we shall be forced to review the ties of collaboration between Angop and AIM.' Angop director Julio Guerra did not put his own name to this – so the telex message looked very much like direct MPLA interference in Angop–AIM relations.

Despite the anger of one of Mozambique's traditional allies, the ministry of information did not gag Cardoso. Indeed, Hunguana cannot remember whether he even bothered to reply to Roberto de Almeida.

If I did, I would have told him that the articles are the responsibility of the journalist, not of the minister, that they were signed by Carlos Cardoso, not by the minister of information.

Our attitude towards the media was always different from that of the Angolans. We didn't have the concept that journalists are government functionaries. We never regarded journalists simply as civil servants. Even before the transition to pluralism, there was debate. It was not a simple case of a minister giving orders to a civil servant.

Events speedily vindicated Cardoso, for on 9 June there was a named Cuban source to confirm what had previously come out of anonymous sources in the military mission in Luanda. And that source was none other than Fidel Castro. A Prensa Latina dispatch gave Castro's account of the siege of Cuito Cuanavale. He confirmed that in mid-November the Angolan authorities asked Havana to strengthen its military presence in Angola; Castro promptly agreed, regarding the situation as identical in essence to the South African invasion of 1975.

Among the Cuban decisions was to send their best MiG-23 pilots to Angola, thus allowing the Fapla–FAR forces to achieve air supremacy. Cuban forces were flown in by helicopter to Cuito Cuanavale to strengthen the Fapla garrison on 5 December. Fidel's account of the ensuing battles was much the same as Cardoso's, with the major South African offensives coming on 13 January, 14 February, 25 February, 12 March and 23 March. The SADF was repelled with heavy losses, and African history now had a new landmark 'before and after Cuito Cuanavale', said Castro. He confirmed the Fapla–FAR–Swapo drive south: the allied forces had built a new airstrip, and the best Cuban anti-aircraft weaponry was now in southern Angola. The allied forces were just 50 kilometres from the border: Pretoria wanted to negotiate 'because it has come up against a force that it had never before encountered,' said Castro.

The final battle took place near the Calueque dam, and began on 20 June, immediately before the talks between Angola, South Africa, Cuba and the United States were due to resume in Cairo. The SADF opened hostilities with a long-range artillery attack on an Angolan–Cuban position at Tchipa in Cunene. The Cubans responded with air strikes against a South African motorised unit moving towards Tchipa. Malan and Pik Botha claimed the fighting endangered the talks; the Angolans, however, believed that the SADF now took very seriously the prospect of a Fapla–FAR offensive across the border into northern Namibia, and were prepared to negotiate in earnest. The South African resolve crumbled, and less than six months later, in December, the final agreement on Namibian independence was signed in New York, plus a timetable for Cuban withdrawal from Angola.

Later, as he compiled his Angolan material for a tentative book (which was never published), Cardoso dismissed the facile arguments appearing in the west to explain why Namibia was suddenly on the road to independence after decades of UN failure. The breakthrough was attributed to the clever diplomacy of Chester Crocker, or to a supposed change in Soviet policy towards southern Africa, or to a change of heart in Pretoria. Cardoso argued that the real change was military: South Africa had lost control of the skies over southern Angola, and had battle-hardened Angolan and Cuban troops approaching the Namibian border. 'South Africa agreed to negotiate and signed the agreement on Namibian independence because it had no choice.' It was changes in the relation of forces on the battlefield that led Pretoria 'to accept partial defeat, rather than risk total defeat, which would mean the complete collapse of apartheid in South Africa, provoked militarily in Angola and Namibia'.

Cardoso stood by the integrity of Nikola and of his various Angolan and Cuban sources: they had been proved right throughout. 'On no occasion did what they told me about the facts prove to be untrue.'

❖

Despite the tensions over Cardoso's Angolan reporting, an Angop representative was present when AIM hosted a conference of the Pana Southern Pool in Maputo from 28 May to 2 June 1988. Cardoso defended his Angolan coverage, pointing out that it had thrown Malan onto the defensive and, through AIM's contacts with the more liberal of the South African media, had given South African whites, usually so ignorant about what was happening in the region, some insight into what their government was doing.

He revisited Malan's attack on AIM of December 1987 and his remark that the Cubans were 'not real fighters'. Yet for more than a decade Pretoria had used the supposed 'Cuban threat' as the justification for intervening in Angola.

> This case shows that a single news item forced General Malan to deny what he had been saying for many years – namely that the SADF had been fighting the Cubans. A single news item generated the indirect recognition that the SADF had been fighting, not Cubans or Soviets, but Angola's Fapla army. We believe that many South Africans became a little wiser.

Cardoso commended those editors in South Africa who had taken the risk of using AIM reports, thus giving an alternative view to that of Pretoria. 'They have played an important role in fighting public ignorance, which is a very dangerous weapon indeed in the hands of militarists,' he said. AIM had shown that the region's news agencies could have an impact within South Africa, 'diminishing the scope of the lies and ignorance upon which the regime bases its policy of regional aggression.'

At the closing session of the conference, Hunguana made it publicly clear that he retained his confidence in Cardoso, whatever the Angolan government might think. He warmly praised AIM, which had functioned with 'dynamism and efficiency', and he committed the government (a commitment never fully met, since Hunguana did not hold the purse strings) to 'make greater investments in training and ensure that AIM receives more politically and professionally tried workers'. He praised the vigilance shown by AIM and the rest of the Mozambican media in not echoing the propaganda of Pretoria. 'It is this active vigilance that saves us from being victims of the disinformation orchestrated from Pretoria,' said Hunguana. 'We believe that if every member agency of Pana adopts this vigilant position with firmness and conviction, a great deal of disinformation can be neutralised.'

Probably Cardoso had an input into this speech (which was distributed in English), since Hunguana went on to attack those African media that read the situation in Mozambique through concepts eagerly spread by Pretoria – a point AIM had been making for years.

> When we echo or let pass information material that originates in South Africa, our passivity ends up by becoming a complicity with the apartheid regime … Africa above all cannot ignore or have distorted knowledge of what is happening in Angola, Mozambique, Namibia, South Africa itself. Pana and the agencies represented at this meeting have a particular responsibility for impeding the disinformation coming from Pretoria and circulating the information coming from our agencies.

In this speech Hunguana also attempted to formulate how the media slotted into Frelimo's overall vision, 'not as a power, but as an instrument of power'. The media were thus 'inevitably anti-colonialist, anti-racist and definitely anti-apartheid'. But how active or passive should they be? Hunguana opted for 'an information that serves by inquiring, examining, questioning and investigating'. He added a caveat: there was a risk that the media 'could fall into the practice of acting as a power that judges, arbitrates or decides'. The risk included 'provocation and sensationalism without responsibility for the consequences'. But Hunguana declared that he was ready to take those risks, as the option for a questioning, investigative journalism was the only one that could lead 'to the growth of the media in terms of professional rigour, ethics and political responsibility. Any other option would inevitably lead to discrediting information and its professionals.'

In practice, this position – yes, please examine and investigate, but don't try to influence policy – was quite untenable. For who was to draw the line? Who was to determine when an investigative reporter was examining and when he was arbitrating? On such conceptual rocks the notion of the media as 'an instrument of power' would eventually founder.

By mid-1998 Cardoso was tired of being a director. He reached the conclusion that the burden of running the agency was getting in the way of his journalism. Even though AIM had employed an administrative director since 1986, Cardoso believed that too much of his time was being spent on administration. Lima held quite the opposite view: that in reality Cardoso was not spending enough time on the routine, bureaucratic tasks needed to ensure the smooth running of a news agency. 'I was always critical of Cardoso's management style – he was chaotic in terms of organisation,' Lima recalls. 'He was opposed to methodology, to order. He was anti-system.'

As the agency expanded, taking on more staff, so the need for proper routines increased. But disorganisation at AIM was not due simply to its voluntarist director. There were harsh objective factors. It was never going to be easy to run a news agency with an erratic power supply, as Renamo sabotage regularly plunged the city into darkness. Nor could the best work be extracted from staff in the technical section who were frequently hungry – particularly after the sharp fall in real wages that accompanied the 1987 currency devaluation and shift towards a market economy. When Lima was in the United States in 1987, he bombarded Cardoso with critical letters on the AIM administration and finances. He worried that precipitate decisions by Cardoso would harm AIM's always fragile financial situation. 'Management decisions are putting at risk the viability of projects that are genuinely generated from initiatives by AIM and its journalists [such as the now flourishing photographic department],' he warned.

Journalists were better paid than most of the AIM staff – but not by very much. Suddenly the lack of a properly defined career and wage structure for the state-owned media became an issue. Writing in March 1988, Fernando Gonçalves warned Cardoso that unless reporters' wages were improved, the AIM newsroom threatened to become 'ungovernable. That is the logical consequence of the delay in approving the professional career structures. With journalists earning 12 000 meticais (just US$27 a month at the official exchange rate of the time) it becomes impossible to demand good articles.'

AIM was sometimes subject to criticism that now seems incomprehensible. Thus there were even claims that, while the government and Frelimo were doing all in their power to make the visit of Pope John Paul II in September 1988 successful, AIM was trying to sabotage it. At one editorial council meeting, Hunguana attacked AIM for its anti-clerical stance. Lima retorted that this claim, retailed by some of the *Notícias* management, was simply untrue. Lima and Cardoso had both stressed to the AIM reporters that we should be as thorough and accurate as possible during the Pope's visit. But this did not mean leaving our critical faculties at home. AIM did not forget that Roman Catholicism had been the official religion of colonial rule, and that Catholic priests had blessed Portuguese troops going into battle. Nor did we believe that there was one rule for interviewing ordinary mortals and another for interviewing cardinals. So, at a Maputo airport press conference shortly before the Pope's visit, I asked the cardinal of Maputo, Alexandre dos Santos, a few tough questions. In some quarters, this was regarded as an unseemly thing to do, and was probably the origin of claims that AIM was opposed to the papal visit.

In the event, the papal visit passed off smoothly and AIM covered it intensively. Our reservations about the Pope seemed shared by Chissano, who was visibly irritated that throughout the three-day visit the Pope could not bring himself to mention the word apartheid. This led Chissano, at the moment of John Paul's departure, to discard his prepared speech and give the Pope a polite lecture. 'Apartheid and colonialism still exist,' he declared. 'They are abominable evils that should be eradicated once and for all from our planet.'[3]

At a meeting on 5 October, Hunguana said the coverage of the visit had been 'positive'. He admitted that AIM's blanket coverage had been excellent. The same meeting, however, showed some of the pressures Hunguana was facing. On the one hand he was worried that opinion pieces had almost disappeared from the press. On the other hand, according to Cardoso's notes from the meeting, he wanted to set up 'very simple mechanisms, which should express unequivocally the political leadership of Minfo. We must know beforehand the contents of tomorrow's paper, otherwise we are not leading.' This sounded as if the minister was calling for a return to censorship: in reality, he wanted some form of defence against other ministers who criticised him when they read something they didn't like in the press. 'I don't like giving justifications, particularly in a situation where I have to say "I didn't know."'

As reported by Cardoso, the minister declared: 'An analysis office within the national directorate of information will immediately start work, with the purpose of establishing a dynamic relationship with the newsroom councils in the media. The media managements must submit future contents to this office.' This was a wildly impractical scheme, and was never implemented. Hunguana was quite frank about his problem: he was being shouted at down the phone by more senior figures. 'These phone calls happen every day,' he said. He even thought he might be facing the sack. 'I am prepared for these two possibilities: to be removed as minister, or for Minfo to be abolished.' (In fact, neither was to happen – at least not in the immediate future.)

In December Cardoso was one of the Mozambicans invited to

address a European Conference on South African Aggression against Mozambique and Angola in Bonn. His speech highlighted Renamo's role as 'an external instrument' of the South African military 'in a complex power struggle within South Africa'. He argued that the 'promoters of generalised terrorism in Mozambique' had developed 'a substantial economic interest in war', and warned that those same forces might well use the Renamo 'model of brutality' inside South Africa itself in an attempt to break popular anti-apartheid organisations.

This was Cardoso's last major public appearance as AIM director. He wanted to leave the job, and repeatedly attempted to submit his resignation to Hunguana. At first the minister refused to accept it: Cardoso told me that he had to submit three resignations (though it was never clear whether they were all in writing) before Hunguana bowed to the inevitable.

CHAPTER 16

The Battle for Press Freedom

Hunguana finally accepted Cardoso's resignation in January 1989. He appointed Ricardo Malate, who had been chief news editor at Radio Mozambique, as the new director. Hunguana was evidently reluctant to let Cardoso go, but he said that by then 'it was no longer possible to resist Cardoso's pressure to resign'. Hunguana admits that the logical successor to Cardoso was Lima; but the minister did not trust him. 'Fernando Lima simply did not give me the same sense of security I felt with Cardoso,' he said.

When he introduced Malate to the AIM staff on 7 January 1989, Hunguana made a point of praising Cardoso's work: under Cardoso's 'dynamic leadership', AIM had won 'prestige and credibility' in the outside world. 'No valuable work is undertaken without difficulty,' Hunguana told the meeting. 'And we had immense difficulties with AIM and with Cardoso. That's very good, because it means we didn't have a simple functionary heading AIM, but a journalist who never stopped being a journalist.' He referred delicately to the row over Cardoso's reporting from Angola. Perhaps AIM had ignored 'state rationale', said the minister, but he acknowledged that from a professional point of view the articles had been fine.

Although no longer director, Cardoso had no intention of leaving AIM. He assumed that, with his hands free of administrative work, he could devote himself fully to journalism. But Lima believed Cardoso had made a serious mistake in surrendering the power and prestige that went with the title of director. He thought Cardoso was naive to imagine that, just by giving up administrative tasks, he would be free to publish more. The immediate challenge was the

Frelimo Fifth Congress. Those of us who had covered the Fourth Congress looked forward to it. The Fourth had been an exhilarating experience, and we mistakenly assumed that the same relative openness and friendly attitude to the media would characterise the Fifth.

In the run-up to the congress, the ONJ swung into action, hoping to influence events. Cardoso was minute-taker on 9 June 1989 at a meeting where it was announced that a document on the media had been drawn up inside the party leadership and had been sent by Rebelo to other members of the politburo for their comments: apparently, the party leadership wanted to ensure a consensual position before embarking on any discussion with journalists. The reaction was cool. 'Who makes the consensus, them or us?' asked Calane da Silva, while Machado da Graça wondered if Rebelo intended coming to the ONJ once more to transmit guidelines. José Catorze thought the days of guidelines were over. After Machel's meeting with the press in 1975, 'journalists became sort of propagandists for the party – but today the situation is different, which leads us to rethink our role. All of society and the party itself are being rethought, as well as the party's political line.' Salomão Moyana protested, 'The media doesn't have to reflect the party's position in every paragraph. We don't know what the party thinks, nor does the party tell us what it thinks.'

Prominent journalists were now thinking in terms of press freedom – Calane da Silva stressed, 'Press freedom can exist in a one-party state' – and of a press law to lay out clearly the rights and duties of journalists. But who would draft such a law? 'If we wait for the Ministry of Information to draft the law, then we'll go on waiting,' remarked Lina Magaia. The ONJ sent a document to the party later that month, insisting on proper access to sources:

> When we speak of access to sources of information, we don't just mean giving journalists the facts that, at any particular moment, are in the interests of a structure or an official to publish, but access to knowledge about policies, as well as the situations and facts which allow journalists to understand so that they can inform.

They argued the impact on society 'which is not properly informed by its media, and seeks out the foreign media easily accessible by radio'. This resulted in a lack of credibility, not only of the Mozambican media, but also of 'our government, which is in charge of a media without credibility'.

Once again journalists decried the media's failure to inform the public of the military situation. Repeatedly attempts had been made to ensure that journalists had access to Mozambican military sources, and could cover FPLM actions. 'Working mechanisms were proposed ... but either they were not put into motion, or they were started, but there was no continuity.' The ONJ also warned of the spread of corruption. 'Today one notes a savage process of private accumulation. Since the low level of economic activity does not allow accumulation based mainly on the direct exploitation of labour, it rests heavily on the illicit appropriation of goods, on trafficking in influence, on fraud, on theft.' But when reporters tried to cover this, 'they face various barriers, from lack of access to sources of information, to a refusal to cooperate, and the fact that some areas are considered taboo.'

Did Frelimo take any notice of such documents? Possibly they had a cumulative impact on the opening up that took place a year later, in 1990, in the debate over a new constitution. But in 1989, Frelimo seemed to go into reverse. Those who expected the Fifth Congress to show the same *élan* and enthusiasm as the Fourth were sadly deceived. Whereas everything bar the elections had been in open session at the Fourth Congress, most of the Fifth was behind closed doors. To make matters worse, the party did not make clear beforehand what was open and what was closed: selected journalists could cover otherwise closed sessions, but it was far from clear what, if anything, they could write about them.

Frelimo was in a jittery mood, and not merely because of the war. This was the congress of the U-turn, at which Frelimo dropped Marxism-Leninism and ceased describing itself as a party of the worker–peasant alliance. Now it was to be 'a party of all the people', a phrase that was never adequately defined. But the congress documents gave no explanation for the switch: in fact, they did not even acknowledge it. The term 'Marxism-Leninism' simply disappeared.

Of course, in off-the-record meetings aimed mainly at party members, the change was explained. I attended one such meeting in Maputo, at which Manuel Tomé asked why the party no longer described itself as Marxist-Leninist, and Rebelo gave a detailed reply. But for the public there was no such explanation. The official ideology of the past 12 years was just to be forgotten. And much of the media obediently forgot: *Notícias*, *Tempo* and Radio Mozambique all simply reported the content of the new Frelimo statutes and programme without bothering to mention the old ones. At AIM we had more respect for history, and wrote articles pointing out that Frelimo had dropped 'Marxism-Leninism' and comparing, in detail, the old statutes with the new ones. Since the AIM news stories were being stuck on walls in the congress premises, this soon stirred up anger in some quarters – so much so that a worried Malate told AIM reporters, 'Don't make comparisons.' But by then it was too late, and the stories had been distributed.

The party line on the media was far from clear. At the congress, Hunguana called for both a continued state monopoly on media ownership, and democratisation of the media. His speech declared: 'This democratisation occurs under the firm and clear leadership of the party and the state, and not at the convenience of individuals or small groups of individuals.' But, from our point of view, easily the worst aspect of the congress was the harassment that AIM journalists suffered. Cardoso, Gil Lauriciano, Cassimo Ginabay and I were all, at one stage or another, banned from the proceedings. The excuse for banning Cardoso was contained in a letter signed by the Snasp director, Amade Miquidade: 'For having given his credential to a foreign journalist during the Fourth Congress, we suggest that Carlos Alberto Lopes Cardoso be dispensed from covering this event, since he does not merit the trust of this body.'

The 'foreign journalist' was myself, and the story was entirely untrue. Cardoso and I both had credentials for the Fourth Congress, and both received 'Diplomas of Honour' for our work then. There had been a minor incident in 1981, when Cardoso lent me his credential for the closing session of a sitting of parliament. Had Snasp confused the two events? – and if so, why had they waited so long before pouncing? In the joint letter of protest we wrote later, Cardoso noted that eight years had passed, during which he had covered events of enormous importance for the country without any expression 'of distrust on the part of any security body ... I still do not know the real reason for this action against me. I await clarification.' My part described the allegation made by Miquidade as 'false and absurd'. I still had my own Fourth Congress credential and could quote its number. I also had a credential for the Fifth, to enter the congress hall as a translator. I had been asked to translate the Central Committee report into English, a task which took much of the preceding week. But in the congress hall a Snasp agent identified me and seized my credential, thus expelling me. I had never felt so humiliated in Mozambique before. I noted that my reward for translating a key congress document 'seems to have been my expulsion from the congress'.

Although an AIM journalist had translated the Central Committee report, the document was being treated as if it were secret. Cassimo's crime was to have acquired a copy from a congress official, to whom he had identified himself as a journalist. It was whispered that he had obtained it 'illicitly', and he too found his credential confiscated. The same thing happened to Gil Lauriciano, who was one of the select few entitled to attend closed sessions. He obtained a copy of the speech given by the finance minister, Abdul Magid Osman, quite openly, and signed for it. This did not stop a Snasp agent seizing it from him and confiscating his credential.

As interim news editor (Lima was absent), Fernando Gonçalves defended us – what Gil and Cassimo had done, he said, 'was no more than comply with their professional duty ... The number and nature of the incidents involving AIM journalists suggests deliberate action directed against the way this agency works.' Cardoso and I received individual apologies from Rebelo and Matsinha, but there was never any explanation as to why the agency had been singled out for this malignant treatment by Snasp.

Cardoso's thoughts were never far from the unfolding crisis in South Africa. Apartheid was now visibly shaking, and the new president,

FW de Klerk, was beginning to marginalise the military. Yet violence was threatening to run out of control. Cardoso feared that the surrogate armies and death squads created under apartheid would now destabilise South Africa itself.

In this frame of mind, he drafted an open letter to De Klerk, to which he obtained the signatures of 74 prominent Mozambican intellectuals (these included the internationally renowned poet José Craveirinha; the country's best-known painter, Malangatana Valente; and the scientist Orlando Mendes). The letter appeared simultaneously in Portuguese and in English on 14 January 1990, in *Domingo* in Maputo and in the *Sunday Star* in Johannesburg. It declared that Mozambique had suffered

> one of the most terrible genocides in the history of Africa. The aggression that our country has suffered cannot in any way be described as a war. A war is directed against the armed forces of a state. A war, though it involves destructive acts, prepares the conditions for insurgents to take over the government. This is not what is happening in Mozambique. In our country, the violence is directed fundamentally against civilians, wiping out human lives and destroying economic infrastructures.

The letter argued that the aggression was not aimed at replacing one government by another, but merely at its own reproduction, 'making Mozambique non-viable as a nation, and threatening to extend chaos to the whole region'.

Cardoso accepted that significant changes were happening in South Africa under De Klerk – but at the same time Renamo was still receiving support from South African soil.

> The first condition for the establishment of peace in our country is the eradication of all mechanisms conceived in the light of the 'total strategy' of Pieter [*sic*] Botha to destabilise the region militarily. In order to cancel this tragic heritage, it is imperative that all the forces in South Africa that still use armed violence to achieve political change in Mozambique be neutralised.

The letter warned of the impact on South Africa too. 'The survival of these mechanisms not only keeps the threat against southern Africa alive, but establishes a disastrous legacy of destabilisation in South Africa itself.' The signatories urged De Klerk to act, not out of generosity but to defend the peaceful future necessary for the entire region, including his own country.

At the same time, Cardoso prepared an appeal to the South African anti-apartheid forces, signed by the same group, calling on them to make 'an end to all acts of destabilisation launched from South African territory' a condition for negotiations with De Klerk's government:

> The apartheid system that still oppresses you is the same that initiated the oppression against the Mozambican people. There are not two apartheids, one that operates in South Africa, and another in the region. The Mozambicans who died as victims of terrorism perished under the same flag of struggle that covers your dead.

The policy of terror rehearsed against Front Line States was now being turned against the South African people. The letter warned that it was just a matter of time before South Africa itself fell victim to 'the holocaust launched against Mozambique'.

So the signatories appealed to anti-apartheid forces: 'Make your voices heard for peace in Mozambique.' For to delay any longer, 'to hold off until the end of apartheid, threatens the stability and well-being of future generations'. Cardoso was convinced that regional integration needed the industrial powerhouse of South Africa, and needed it intact, not in ruins. He feared that, far from an orderly dismantling of apartheid, the whole system might collapse in a welter of violence. Looking back now, with South Africa stable and relatively prosperous under a democratic government, it is easy to scoff at such fears. But in early 1990 the ANC was still outlawed, Nelson Mandela was still in jail, and collapse seemed all too likely as apartheid's proxies ran amok in the townships and in KwaZulu-Natal.

Change was inevitably on the way in Mozambique too. The half-way house of the Fifth Congress – a one-party state without its

Leninist justification, and with the confusing 'party of all the people' – soon proved hopelessly inadequate. The Soviet bloc was visibly crumbling, and Mikhail Gorbachev had made clear his intention to allow political pluralism in the Soviet Union. Furthermore, many in the Frelimo leadership, Chissano included, had reached the conclusion that, sooner or later, the government would have to negotiate, not with Pretoria but with Renamo. The political discourse had changed: it was no longer about smashing armed banditry but about winning peace. In 1989, feelers went out to Renamo via clergy and the Kenyan and Zimbabwean presidents, Daniel arap Moi and Robert Mugabe. Initially the government said it was sticking to a set of 12 principles sent to Renamo, which demanded acceptance of the established order, and a recognition that the constitution could be changed only by the will of the people.

In December the Frelimo Central Committee endorsed the one-party state – just when several of the top leaders were considering jettisoning it. 'The creation of a multi-party system is not a demand raised by the Mozambican people,' the Central Committee stated. But a month later, in January 1990, Chissano unveiled the draft of a new constitution which eliminated all reference to Frelimo's 'leading role' and took no position at all on the one-party state. The question of political pluralism versus the one-party state was to be decided in a nationwide debate on the constitution.

The draft constitution was a remarkably liberal document. The Leninist 'unity of power' disappeared, to be replaced by the standard 'separation of powers' familiar to western constitutional lawyers. It stressed the rule of law and the independence of the judiciary, and abolished the death penalty. It granted workers the right to strike – a right which they were already seizing as Chissano spoke. A strike wave (mainly over wage demands) spread across the country from late December 1989 – even though strikes were not merely illegal but were security offences which could, in theory, be dealt with by military courts. Most of the standard personal freedoms were granted under the draft: freedom of worship, freedom of expression, and freedom of assembly and association. But it said nothing, not a word, about freedom of the press.

Indeed, three days before Chissano unveiled the draft constitution, Hunguana intervened in *Notícias*, sacking its director, José Catorze. The sacking was eminently political: for, two days later, Hunguana warned against anti-communism in the media, in what was read as a reference to the *Notícias* coverage of events in eastern Europe. 'Primitive anti-communism belongs to the most reactionary and fascist-leaning tendencies in any part of the world,' said Hunguana. 'It is not a tradition in our country.' True – but how could anyone seriously regard the cautious Catorze, a man of proven loyalty to Frelimo, as a 'primitive anti-communist'? Lima suspected that the problem was the *Notícias* coverage of various corruption scandals in the disintegrating Soviet bloc: in some quarters, these might be seen not as genuine coverage of a story of international interest but as a disguised attack on Frelimo.

At the same time Calane da Silva resigned as television news editor, in protest at administrative interference in TV news coverage by the ministry of information. Calane recalls that he and Catorze were the critical voices on the ministry's editorial council throughout 1989. 'Teodato got angry with us. We were in favour of total openness. We had to report the strike wave. We couldn't lie about it.' Such events, together with the absence of any reference to the media in the draft constitution, provoked several leading journalists to meet informally to discuss how they could bring press freedom into the constitution. The driving spirit behind the group was Leite Vasconcelos, and its other core members were Cardoso, Albino Magaia, Fernando Lima and Ricardo Rangel.

They decided to draw up a petition entitled 'The Right of the People to Information', and gather as many signatures as possible from the newsrooms. This was quite unprecedented, and took the ministry, the party and the ONJ leadership by surprise. The petition called for the inclusion of an article in the constitution 'to enshrine the right of citizens to complete and truthful information, and the right to express themselves freely through the media'. And 'since we believe that there are currently serious problems that limit the effectiveness and credibility of our media, we propose that some methods and rules ensuring press freedom be implemented straight away.'

There had been significant gains in the 15 years since independence: the signatories believed that 'in our country a national media has been built that seeks to identify with the great aspirations of the Mozambican people'. Nonetheless, the media 'lacks credibility among our people', and one of the fundamental reasons for this was 'the tendency of government bodies to use the media as instruments'.

The group that drafted the petition had nothing against state ownership of the main media – in fact, they thought it necessary 'to guarantee its national character ... State ownership should ensure that the media is at the service of the people, but this principle has been confused with the tendency to put the media at the service of government bodies.' True, there was no institutional censorship in Mozambique,

> but the limitations on access to official sources, the interference in editorial decisions, and various forms of institutional pressure on the media generate a climate of intimidation that leads to frequent self-censorship ... This promotes distortion of reality, encourages rumours, ensures that our media does not deserve credibility – which reflects indirectly on the party and the government – and ensures that many citizens seek in the foreign media the news that our media omits.

Not all the interference was government policy: there were those who took advantage of the absence of press freedom to promote their own image and 'cover up individual responsibility for mistakes, disorganisation, negligence, incompetence, misuse or theft of state property'.

The indictment did not stop there. The petition listed the ways in which the media had been intimidated.

> There have been unjustified detentions of journalists; journalists have been threatened with detention, expulsion and punishment, often by those who have no legal power to interfere in the media; journalists' work has been banned, or there have been attempted bans, sometimes by those who have no legal power to intervene in the media; there have been cases where leaders have publicly humiliated journalists.

Recently there has been a worsening trend to blame the media for events caused by objective and well-known social phenomena. Worse than this, media officials and journalists have been summoned to hear gratuitous accusations of subversion, agitation, promotion of instability and even banditry.

The demands raised were very simple. All editorial decisions should be the responsibility of the director of the medium concerned, 'advised by an editorial council composed of democratically elected journalists'. Journalists should be guaranteed access to official sources of information, with due safeguards for 'state secrets, matters that are sub judice, and protection for privacy'. As for those who felt offended by anything that appeared in the press, instead of making threatening phone calls they should resort 'exclusively to the right of reply and to the courts'.

The petition gathered 162 signatures but caused alarm in some of the more conservative quarters of the media. Those who were worried about what the party or the ministry might think declined to sign. In some cases pressure was brought on journalists not to sign, and there were even a few cases of people who signed and were then persuaded to withdraw their names. As events showed, it was the timid or the downright hostile who were out of touch with current Frelimo thinking – for the party was moving inexorably away from the one-party state, and political pluralism ought to imply relaxing Frelimo control of the media. 'If you're going to adopt a multi-party system, how can you prevent press freedom?' mused Hunguana. 'Once pluralism was introduced, there could be no return to the old system of running the media.' The promoters of the petition thought they were swimming against the tide, but Hunguana believed that press freedom would have come about with or without the petition. 'Perhaps the virtue of the document was to clarify things.'

There is a flaw in Hunguana's argument that political pluralism more or less inevitably entails press freedom. For there are plenty of nominally pluralist societies where press freedom is at best tenuous. Zimbabwe is a flagrant example: this is, in principle, a multi-party society, but Zanu-PF controls public broadcasting much more ruthlessly than Frelimo ever controlled Radio Mozambique. Laws inherited from the colonial power are used against journalists; and, if these are not sufficient, new ones are passed in an attempt to muzzle all criticism of the regime. Cardoso and the other promoters of the petition were aware that it is perfectly possible to multiply the number of parties while shackling the press – hence the need to ensure press freedom on journalists' terms before the political system opened up.

A meeting with Chissano himself took place on 29 May at the ONJ, which ran on into the small hours of the morning. There were moments of tension, and at one point, uncharacteristically, Chissano lost his temper. This was the meeting at which Cardoso bade a fond farewell to the journalism of the 1970s (in the speech cited at the start of chapter 3). In those days, 'There was no "me" the journalist and "them" the leaders.' Instead there was the exhilarating idea 'that I was a comrade in my post, that my leaders were comrades in their posts, and that we were all responsible to each other in the struggle to eradicate misery.' These were years that would never be repeated. It had been a privilege to live through a period 'in which politics and morality went together, in which nobility of intentions was palpable in the very act of governance'. In the immediate post-independence period 'Frelimo, as the main critical conscience of society' led journalists like Cardoso to grant 'the term "official" all the dignity and burden of truth normally related to the verdicts of just, moral and efficient legal systems'. But there was no going back to this age of innocence. 'Nothing is eternal. These phases of governance are also not eternal.' The rules were changing, and 'bit by bit the "us–them" dichotomy is being established in society'. He attacked the information ministry for ordering *Notícias* not to publish articles he had written on bank frauds, including one based on an interview with deputy attorney-general Sinai Nhatitima. 'I ask what legal, moral or political right a minister has to prevent a deputy attorney-general from communicating with the public,' said Cardoso.

But while Chissano may have been irritated by the pressures for press freedom, he understood that the old way of running the press was no longer viable. Frelimo now voluntarily abdicated: it would no longer seek administrative control over the media. When the Frelimo

Central Committee met on 5–9 September, it reworked the draft constitution and included press freedom and the right to information. The press freedom clause was drafted by Hunguana, met most of the demands raised by the petition, and was unanimously accepted when parliament approved the constitution in November 1990.

Cardoso was not there to savour this victory. He had left AIM – and, astonishingly, he had dropped out of journalism altogether. 'He was completely frustrated and burnt out,' commented Orlanda Mendes. Besides, Cardoso was now a father. His son, Ibo, was born on 22 April 1989, and he needed to spend more time with his family. He took three months' unpaid leave in 1989, from late August through to late November. He was also finding it difficult to publish some of his opinion pieces. He submitted an article entitled 'Maputo and the question of power', and in a handwritten note at the top of the article, dated 7 February 1989, he scribbled 'José Catorze refused to publish this. "We know perfectly well I cannot publish this in *Notícias*," he told me.' Why not? Doubtless because in the article Cardoso had written in acidic terms about the government's inability to defend the population, and of the growing gulf between the capital and the rest of the country. He warned that Maputo had become a dangerous ivory tower 'reproducing the illusion that some magic hand will put an end to the holocaust overtaking the Mozambican people'.

After he left the director's chair, Cardoso found an increasing trend not to publish his more outspoken views. When Cardoso wrote a speculative piece after Herman Cohen, the US deputy assistant secretary of state for African affairs, visited Maputo, on 15 July Malate wrote in the margin: 'It does not seem prudent to me, in an AIM dispatch, to enter into speculation on the official policy of the government.' Malate highlighted parts of the article that 'raise delicate questions whose approach has been considered premature and inopportune. It's because of this that we have been promised a press conference given by the head of state. I think we should wait.' In other words: Don't write, wait for the president to speak.

Cardoso's article asked: 'Did Cohen tell Chissano that the South African militarist sectors involved with armed banditry are finally being forced to respect the Nkomati Accord?' He noted that Magnus Malan was no longer centre-stage. The apartheid regime was changing, and within a few days Chissano would be meeting the new leader of the National Party, FW de Klerk. 'Will De Klerk guarantee that South African support for the armed gangs will definitely end?' wondered Cardoso. The part which Malate particularly disliked read:

> The worst scenario would be that of De Klerk offering guarantees, entering the second phase of the peace process – direct dialogue between local bandit chiefs and the Mozambican authorities – only to find the South African military recreating the MNR, with this or another name, so that the war continues, so that there is another dialogue, and bit by bit Mozambique hands power over to the local representatives of apartheid. Dialogue itself would cease to be the means to a solution, and would become an integral part of destabilisation.

Cardoso had always written speculative pieces, sometimes badly misreading the situation but more often catching the logical thrust of events and the various scenarios they might produce. And sometimes he would make uncannily accurate prophecies. Now Malate was telling him not to speculate any more.

Then there were the articles on fraud and corruption that Cardoso mentioned in the meeting with Chissano. He had interviewed a prominent prosecutor, Afonso Antunes, who told him of a major bank fraud in Nampula involving officials of the ministry of the interior linked to local businessmen. When he spoke to the deputy attorney-general, Sinai Nhatitima, he asked him outright whether any members of the government were involved in bank frauds. The reply was cautious: with regard to the cases in his office's hands, 'I can tell you that we don't yet have any, let us say, direct involvement of any member of the government.' Again *Notícias*, apparently under pressure from the ministry, was reluctant to publish this material.

At that time the government was preparing the ground for negotiations with Renamo. It circulated its 12-point document to embassies, containing principles – notably a renunciation of violence, and acceptance of the legitimacy of Mozambican institutions – on the basis of which a dialogue with Renamo might take place. Naturally, diplomats leaked this document to Mozambican and foreign journalists. AIM acquired a copy, Cardoso confirmed its authenticity, and he, Gonçalves and Lauriciano put their names to an article about it entitled 'After Angola, Mozambique?' It was not published. In his notes for a meeting at the ONJ, Cardoso scribbled, 'Once again Mozambicans have to switch to foreign radio stations to find out what is happening in their country. It's a disgrace for all of us, the party, the government, the media.' He later wrote, in what seems to be a draft letter addressed to Chissano (it is not clear whether it was sent):

> We were told that the document sought, solely and exclusively, to provoke international reactions to the principles it contained as a basis for dialogue ... If the objective was not to provoke an internal discussion, then that was foiled because a large number of citizens already know about the document. You just have to listen to the BBC, the Voice of America and South African radio, which many thousands of Mozambicans do regularly.

Chissano went public with the 12 principles on 17 July 1989. Only then did *Notícias* acknowledge their existence.

In December 1989, Cardoso started a weekly column, simply called 'The Opinion of Carlos Cardoso', in the Sunday paper *Domingo*. But the article that was to have appeared on 17 December was rejected. Entitled 'Recipe for chaos', it dealt with what Cardoso called 'the trend towards a re-feudalisation of power in Mozambique'. The *Domingo* management told him it was 'too pessimistic, apocalyptic'. From Cardoso's own papers we know what it said:

> From a primitive but organised phase of capital accumulation, we are moving into a savage accumulation. With their national points of reference destroyed, with the aggression making it impossible to defend and nourish any cultural alternative, and even though they

cling like shipwrecked mariners to the remote echo of the word Mozambique, millions of Mozambicans are returning to their ancestral loyalties of family, clan, tribe and region. It's their defence in a desperate survival action ... Thus there rapidly emerges a *chapa-cem* bourgeoisie,[1] unable to affirm itself as an autonomous capitalist class, doomed to be the local agent of the international pillage of our resources.

From the vantage point of the early twenty-first century, that sounds an entirely accurate prediction of what Mozambique was becoming. Within a few years there would be those who could stand up in parliament (the Renamo intellectual, David Alone, for instance) and defend, as the most natural and sacred thing in the world, 'the ancestral loyalties of family, clan, tribe and region'. Today, Cardoso continued, the country was experiencing 'the chaotic phase of accumulation against which any morality is as useless as preaching to stones. If this situation lasts a few more years, without an end to the war, tribalism and localism will win political legitimacy, waged by local aristocracies competing among themselves.' The nightmare was a future of coup and counter-coup, of cities full of armies of child soldiers, from which organisations such as Renamo could be born over and over again. It was a grim prophecy. It did not entirely come true, because its premise, the war, was brought to an end. But it was not a wild fantasy, as any glance at events in parts of west Africa in the 1990s bears out.

When *Domingo* declined to publish this, Cardoso protested that the article was intended as one of a series. Next week, he would have provided a balancing piece: the article 'would have a framework through the following articles, which would deal with the opposite trend – that of regional integration – and so on with future pieces'.

Cardoso did not give up. He suggested expanding his vision of the two possible futures – regional integration within SADCC, or a chaotic descent into warring quasi-feudal states – into a booklet, drawing heavily on his experience in Angola. It would be published as one of the occasional booklets issued by *Notícias*. Cardoso started a draft of this booklet, which opened characteristically with a statement of the right and need for Mozambicans to take part in regional debates: 'I thought it urgent that Mozambicans take part with all possible vigour in the public regional debate on the present and future of southern Africa, otherwise the content of this debate will be imposed on us by the huge South African intelligentsia and by their powerful media.' But the book was never completed, and it is not clear why.

Cardoso was now tired and frustrated. Once again he decided to go on leave with his family. This time he applied for unpaid leave of 11 months. Technically he had no right to this, since he had taken unpaid leave in 1989 as well. But it is always possible to bend the rules – and they should certainly have been bent in the case of the agency's best writer, and the man who had put it on the international map. But Malate stuck to the letter of the civil service regulations:[2] Cardoso could not have any more unpaid leave. So Cardoso wrote a one-sentence letter of resignation announcing that he was leaving AIM as from 31 August 1990. Thus Cardoso took no part in what should have been a crowning triumph: the passage in 1991 of one of the most liberal press laws anywhere in the world. Instead, he was in Scandinavia, living with Nina in Oslo but frequently fleeing to Copenhagen when he felt oppressed by the formal Norwegian lifestyle.

❖

When he returned, in 1991, Cardoso astounded his friends by telling them that he had given up journalism. He was sunk in pessimism, and had already told Nina that he would never return to the media; he thought he might take up poetry or music. Instead, he took up painting. To some, this merely confirmed that Cardoso was indeed 'crazy'. But Nina held that, although the work itself was 'absolutely nuts', it preserved Cardoso's sanity 'by making him concentrate on something. He did not become an addict, or an alcoholic, and he did not sit in the corner moaning.' Mia Couto recalls that Cardoso had been deeply depressed – but when he visited him one day, he found him painting and 'enthusiastic for the first time in many months'. Cardoso's painting methods were highly unorthodox. First he experimented with that most unpromising of materials, shoe polish. He asked to work at Machado da Graça's house: Machado recalls Cardoso working at his painting as if it were a regular job, showing up at a fixed time in the morning, and leaving at an equally fixed time in the afternoon.

Cardoso's designs became far more vivid and interesting when he switched to wax crayons. He was fascinated by the patterns the crayons made when melted. The day Mia visited, he found Cardoso 'with his head in the oven' – not contemplating suicide, but heating up the wax.

> I followed his instructions and saw him, naked to the waist, sweating like an ironsmith, and sticking his head in the oven. When he withdrew from the entrails of that little inferno, he had a sheet of paper in his hands, and was using his nails to draw lines on it, attentive only to the flourishes that the heat was designing on the paper. He stayed there silently for a long time, inhabiting this unformed and magical world. I would not break this spell.

This summary comes from the leaflet Mia wrote for Cardoso's exhibition 'The Residents of the Oven', to which he gave the punning title 'Fornografias' – from the Portuguese *forno* (oven) and *pornografia* (pornography). Mia regarded the painting as a form of self-therapy, and recalls Cardoso admitting he had 'gone to the bottom'. At the exhibition, held from 29 November to 1 December 1991, Cardoso was radiant. I had not seen him so happy in a long time. 'It was as if he had visited hell and come back,' remarked Mia.

PART II

Building an
Independent Media

by Paul Fauvet and
Marcelo Mosse

Carlos Cardoso working on Mediafax.

CHAPTER 17

Birth of a Cooperative

First in his Scandinavian retreat and then engrossed in painting, Cardoso had no input into the 1991 press law. The constitution established the principle of press freedom; the press law put flesh on the bare bones. For once, the ministry of information and the ONJ were more or less in harmony. Producing the draft press law was the last major act of Hunguana as minister. By then he had one foot in the ministry and the other in the peace talks (he was effectively number two on the Mozambican delegation in the long-drawn-out negotiations with Renamo in Rome). Hunguana says he had reached the conclusion that there was no longer a place for a ministry of information in the new political order. The task of the new minister, Rafael Maguni, should be simply to wind the ministry up.

When the law was passed in July 1991, it contained pretty well everything that the petitioners of the previous year had wanted. Right at the start, it declared: 'The freedom of the press shall specifically include journalists' freedom of expression and of creation, access to sources of information, the protection of independence and of professional secrecy, and the right to set up newspapers and other publications.' With that, the state monopoly over the media fell away. Anyone could set up a newspaper. The position with radio and television was not quite so clear: Radio Mozambique, TVE, and AIM would remain in the public sector, but the possibility for private bodies to compete was implicit.

For journalists in state-owned media, the key clause read: 'The mass media in the public sector shall carry out their duties free from interference by any outside interest or influence that may compromise their independence, and shall be guided in their activity by standards of high technical and professional quality.' Free from interference – so no more ministry editorial councils, no more phone calls saying what could or could not be published. The law also gave journalists the rights 'not to be detained, removed, or otherwise prevented from carrying out their duties in places where their presence as media professionals may be necessary, within the limits envisaged by law', and 'not to accept any editorial directive that does not come from the competent authority in their media'. Journalists could not be obliged to reveal their sources, or hand over their notebooks or film. Should journalists be physically attacked or subject to intimidation or attempts at bribery, their employers were obliged to start legal proceedings against those responsible.

The debate in parliament was notable for the self-criticism made by Cabaço, who admitted that journalists 'came under direct pressure from every minister who didn't want his ministry talked about … So we complained that our press didn't say anything, then we phoned the journalists up telling them not to say anything. We rewarded mediocrity and punished those who asked awkward questions.' Albino Magaia, now a deputy, was even more forceful. 'We have lied by omission and by silence,' he declared.

With the press law passed, it became a real possibility to set up papers fully independent of the state. The journalists thinking along these lines were still working on the established media – notably Lima at AIM, Kok Nam on *Tempo*, and Salomão Moyana at *Domingo*. They began talking about setting up a cooperative venture, to be called Mediacoop, whose first task would be to publish a weekly paper. They wanted some big names – Cabaço and Magaia, who both declined; and Cardoso – could he be coaxed back to journalism? According to Gil Lauriciano, he and Alirio Chiziane suggested inviting Cardoso to join the cooperative. At the time Cardoso was still in Scandinavia. Lauriciano dismissed the habitual claims that Cardoso was 'crazy', and said that in reality he was frustrated. 'Our argument was that Cardoso was the kind of person who must always be doing something.'

A further problem was that the cooperative was beginning to look like an offshoot of AIM. Lauriciano, Lima and Chiziane had all worked or were still working at AIM. Add Cardoso and António Gumende (who had been invited to join, although he was then working in Zimbabwe), and there were five cooperative members from AIM. To redress the balance, others were invited: Lourenço Jossias from *Domingo*, António Elias from *Tempo*, and Fernando Veloso (who was working at Electricidade de Moçambique, the state power utility). The cooperative grew slowly; it was not until late 1991 that a Mediacoop delegation went to see Cardoso. According to Moyana, initially he showed no interest in joining, and even told them that he had forgotten how to write. He said that his current life revolved around painting and he no longer bothered to read the papers. He said he was disillusioned with the media and wanted 'to live in my own way'. They did not give up: twice a delegation went to Cardoso's house. His resistance weakened and he agreed to attend a meeting in the provisional Mediacoop offices situated in a garage in Avenida Martires de Machava, a garage that was to loom large in Cardoso's life for the next decade.

By February 1992, Cardoso was a regular and enthusiastic attender at meetings. On 6 February Mediacoop gained legal status as the deeds formally establishing the cooperative were signed at a notary's office. Nina remembered that for Cardoso this was one of the happiest days of his life. He told Nina that the best journalists in the country were working together in the cooperative – and then he wept with joy. Never again would Cardoso abandon journalism. The Mediacoop founders then sat down at Gil Lauriciano's house to discuss the name of the weekly paper. Cardoso wanted to call it *A Região* or *Austral*, but Lima's suggestion, *Savana*, won with seven votes.

So the cooperative now had legal status, and the name for a paper – but no money. A split immediately emerged: Lima had always been the organisation man at AIM, fuming at what he regarded as Cardoso's impulsive behaviour. And so it was at Mediacoop: Lima insisted on feasibility studies for the new paper and lengthy preparations, otherwise it would fail. Cardoso was impatient with this meticulous approach. According to Moyana, he accused Lima of 'complicating things', and claimed that 'to start a paper, you just do it'. Where would the money come from? Lima demanded; the feasibility study indicated that initial capital of 200 000 dollars was required. Cardoso dismissed the feasibility study itself as rubbish and a waste of money. Lima recalls Cardoso suggesting raising funds for just two issues of the paper: then, if it was any good, it would fund itself from the third issue onwards. 'I said, "No way!"' recalls Lima, 'and most of the cooperative members supported me.'

Lima is convinced that Cardoso thought he should be editor of the new paper, a post which eventually went to Moyana. Photo-journalist Naita Ussene recalls Cardoso acting as if he were already editor (but Moyana himself recalls no such ambitions on Cardoso's part). Worries among the cooperative members increased when messages reached them from sources in the new security service, Sise, warning them that it might be 'dangerous' to give Cardoso a position of responsibility. Some Mediacoop members also feared that he would prove incapable of accepting collective discipline. All recall Cardoso's impatience to publish something. According to Gumende, Cardoso declared: 'I don't want any more meetings. I want to start working.' At one point he threatened to start his own wall newspaper, with the help of market vendors. That would cost no more than a blackboard and a few sticks of chalk and would have an instant audience. 'You always want to study and never start work,' Cardoso objected. 'Do something simple that doesn't need a study.'

The cooperative leadership feared that Cardoso might leave Mediacoop and strike out on his own path. At a meeting in Lima's house they decided they should go ahead with some small publication which Cardoso could edit while preparations for the weekly continued. Lima had come across a faxed version of a Brazilian paper. For a cash-strapped organisation, distributing a paper by fax has one enormous advantage. There are no paper costs: or rather, the subscribers pay the paper costs. The disadvantage is that circulation is limited, particularly since, in 1992, there were no more than a couple of hundred fax machines in all of Mozambique. But Cardoso snatched at the idea immediately; for those fax machines were at key positions – in ministries, embassies, large companies – and the material that arrived on them would be read by key political and business figures and opinion makers. No doubt, if the material was good, the fax paper would be widely photocopied and many more than a couple of hundred copies would be in circulation.

What to call the publication? Lima suggested the title *Mediafax*, which was immediately accepted. As for the content, Lima's initial proposal was to make available to people inside Mozambique what media outside were saying about the country. Mediacoop would monitor the BBC, the Voice of America and other foreign media, translate what they said into Portuguese, and distribute it. Cardoso disagreed. Why should they passively reproduce foreigners' views? He thought *Mediafax* should publish news that was an alternative to *Notícias*, and particularly opinion of Mozambicans about events affecting Mozambique. 'We should be the sources for the BBC, AFP, Reuters,' he urged. Lima told Cardoso he 'applauded the principle, but doubted the possibility'.

The cooperative gave Cardoso the green light to prepare the faxsheet. Lima wanted a feasibility study and a plan of action, and predictably Cardoso produced neither. He took the attitude that the best feasibility study was producing the paper; if it didn't work, it would soon die. The capital outlay was minimal, quite possibly less than the cost of hiring someone to do a feasibility study and translate it into English. The immediate requirement was a fax machine that could distribute a paper to a large number of subscribers. But the first machine Cardoso acquired (through Swedish solidarity) proved incompatible with the telecommunication lines. So he turned to Bjorg Leite, the head of the Maputo office of the Norwegian development agency, Norad.

> Early one evening I went to Bjorg Leite's house and told her about the idea. We needed the telefax machine to get the whole thing going.
> 'And when do you need it?' she asked.
> 'Tomorrow,' I said.
> 'And how much do you need?'
> 'Something in the region of US$3000.'
> 'Well, could you come past my office tomorrow

morning with an invoice from the company where you'll buy the machine?'

I did. In a matter of 15 minutes I had the fax cash in my hands. That very same day we got the machine, tested it, and within a week *Mediafax* began publication.

Cardoso's insistence on doing everything himself irritated Lima. 'He didn't tell us he was dealing with Bjorg Leite,' he recalled. Cardoso, however, believed the rest of the cooperative had already given him the green light. He had promised to start *Mediafax* on 25 May, Africa Day – and he did so. But he was entirely alone in the office that night. To get subscribers, Cardoso simply took the public telecommunications company's list of faxes, chose all the most likely and important names, and sent the paper to them, asking them to subscribe. The first three issues were free of charge – after that, subscribers were expected to pay 50 000 meticais (US$21) a month. By the end of the week *Mediafax* had 20 subscribers (Chissano's office was number 6).

As for content, a long interview with the Italian ambassador, Manfredo di Camerana, dominated the first few issues. Di Camerana had become the most important ambassador in Mozambique because of the delicate peace negotiations between the government and Renamo, which had entered their second year in Rome. The frank interview included details that many people – including government members – did not know. The published interview started with a question that had simply not occurred to the rest of the media: how much were the peace talks costing, and who paid for them? Di Camerana replied that the Italians were paying Renamo's costs and the Rome hotel bills for the government negotiating team. So far that came to over 1.5 million dollars. In addition the Italians were funding the Joint Verification Committee set up to monitor a shaky ceasefire in the Limpopo and Beira rail corridors. By May 1992, that had cost another million dollars. How much was the Mozambican government paying? The man authorised to answer such questions was the minister in the presidency, Feliciano Gundana. But when Cardoso asked him for the figures, the minister replied that 'he did not think their publication was yet opportune'.

The founding members of Mediacoop, immediately after the official registration of the cooperative (Cardoso front row, third from the left).

Right from this first number *Mediafax* had a distinctive voice of its own, a voice which certainly had affinities with the AIM of the 1980s but which was now freed of any political constraints. It was a voice located on the left wing of Frelimo, but quite prepared to denounce government blunders or abuses. And it was sharply written. There was none of the leaden and clumsy phrasing that so disfigured much of the Mozambican press. *Mediafax* was not a boring publication: its subscribers read it out of pleasure rather than out of duty.

As the subscriptions continued to trickle in, Mediacoop realised that it was physically impossible for Cardoso to continue doing everything himself. The paper had not flopped: comment was favourable, subscriptions were coming in, and the cooperative could not allow the country's first independent publication to collapse because nobody was supporting its editor. So two other former AIM workers, Oriel Sitoe and Olivia Chiconela, were drafted in to help with the administration. Cardoso was still the only full-time journalist, but other Mediacoop members were beginning to submit articles. The finances were honest but chaotic. Cardoso initially had no formal receipt book; so, as the subscription money came in, he wrote out the receipts on pages of his notebook, keeping a carbon copy for himself.

But, a few weeks into the venture, disaster struck: Cardoso was hospitalised, suffering from the early stages of pneumonia. No doubt this was the result of a combination of overwork, poor diet, and chain-smoking – at this time he was smoking two to three packets of cigarettes a day. Cardoso did not want to admit that he was ill until eventually he was simply unable to get out of bed. Since neither Cardoso or Nina owned a car, they had to ask a friend to drive him to Maputo Central Hospital, where a doctor diagnosed pneumonia and told him that going home was out of the question. Lima went to see him, and Cardoso asked him to take care of the *Mediafax* money: in one pocket of Cardoso's favourite olive-green trousers Lima found the receipts (89, as he recalls) and in the other was the money. Lima checked the receipts against the money, and found a discrepancy of only 15 dollars.

Nina took responsibility for feeding Cardoso; but he refused to eat anything except biscuits and yoghurt, and in mid-1992 there was no yoghurt to be found in any Maputo shop. Nina mobilised members of the Norwegian Embassy staff who were shopping in Swaziland to bring back yoghurt. That is why, for a couple of weeks, 'Norwegian fridges across Maputo were full of yoghurt for Carlos Cardoso,' Nina recalled. Cardoso stayed in hospital for a couple of weeks, and then went to stay with Mia Couto. He refused to go home, on the ground that in his weakened state he would just be a burden on Nina and Ibo. Indeed, in his first days out of hospital he could still scarcely walk unaided. Nina was shocked to see how thin he was – 'like a matchstick'. Cardoso realised that he had been seriously ill, and took a long-overdue decision. He stopped smoking. A bout of pneumonia had succeeded where the sadistic teacher at Witbank had failed, and Cardoso never touched a cigarette again for the rest of his life.

While Cardoso was in hospital, Moyana edited *Mediafax*. The cooperative was now fully involved in the paper and invested all available funds to provide two computers, a laser printer, a photocopier, and a second fax machine. Meanwhile there was no sign of *Savana*. A commission consisting of Kok Nam and Lima was set up, with the optimistic timetable of producing the first copy of the weekly within six months. A year later there was nothing. *Mediafax* was the only public face of the cooperative for over two years. Cardoso had taken the lead in his usual unorthodox fashion, and by sheer force of personality had created a successful publication, dragging the rest of the cooperative along behind him.

CHAPTER 18

Peace, Demobilisation and Elections

Peace negotiations between the government and Renamo had been under way spasmodically in Rome since July 1990, covered by just one reporter, AIM's Lisbon correspondent, Tomás Vieira Mário, on the ground that it was much cheaper to send a reporter to Rome from Lisbon than from Maputo. Mediacoop thought the Mozambican public deserved more than one voice on the peace talks, arranged sponsorship from Sweden and from Italian NGOs, and sent Lourenço Jossias to Rome. Jossias was still employed by *Domingo*, but he cleared his visit to Rome with the *Domingo* management and agreed to write pieces for both *Domingo* and *Mediafax*. He later recalled that *Domingo* never published anything he sent. *Mediafax* published his dispatches, usually as the front-page lead, almost every day for a month.

Jossias made a point of talking repeatedly to all those involved: the government side, the Italian mediators, and the chief Renamo negotiator, Raul Domingos. Nobody in the Mozambican press had published interviews with Domingos before, and initially Renamo was paranoid about the media: one of the mediators, Matteo Zuppi, told Jossias there were no photographs of the first round of talks 'because Renamo refused'. Moyana remarked:

> For two years we never knew what the other side, which was talking to the government, was thinking ... The first time Renamo had the opportunity to explain something in the national media was when we managed to send a *Mediafax* correspondent. For the first time we knew what Raul Domingos was thinking. We

gave instructions to interview these Renamo men:
Who are they? What do they think? The people want
to know what they think of things.[1]

Not that anyone could describe the *Mediafax* coverage as pro-
Renamo. 'Corridors blocked', the paper headlined on 15 July 1992,
as Renamo rejected a proposed truce for the distribution of food aid.
In 1992, southern Africa was in the grip of the worst drought in living memory, and the July talks were centred on ensuring safe corridors
for deliveries of emergency aid. Renamo prevaricated: expensive airlifts
yes, but cheap road convoys no. A UN proposal for a three-month
truce was thrown out. Redraft after redraft was submitted, until
eventually Renamo accepted that all forms of transport could be used
– but would only be immune from attack if they flew the flag of the
International Committee of the Red Cross and had no military escort.

Its coverage of the Rome talks established *Mediafax* as necessary
reading. But initially the paper faced considerable reticence in more
traditional quarters of Frelimo. What was this independent medium?
Wasn't 'independent' just another word for 'opposition'? This attitude was by no means universal. Hunguana regards *Mediafax* as having 'a revolutionary impact. It was not enough to have a press law.
We also needed a private press, outside of the public sector. And it
was important that this was done by Cardoso, because of the professionalism he had always shown. *Mediafax* was not a squib.'

By August Cardoso had recovered from his illness. He was thinking ahead: how could the army be demobilised? He found that the
finance minister, Abdul Magid Osman, had given Chissano a document on demobilisation a year earlier. Magid Osman wanted to start
dismantling the army before the war was over because of the 'astro-
nomical defence costs'. He suggested setting up an autonomous
national reconstruction service, subordinate only to Chissano (which
would cut out the increasingly chaotic defence ministry), to deal
with demobilisation and reintegration of the former soldiers. But
how many people would be demobilised? In mid-1991 the government still dreamed of an army of 50 000, and suggested demobilising just 12 755 men. Not only would Renamo not accept this, but
neither would the troops themselves.

By now signs of military disintegration were clear. Several mutinies broke out in mid-1992. The government hastened to make money available for troops' back wages, but solemnly added that 'it cannot tolerate' more mutinies. 'Cannot tolerate?' asked Cardoso's editorial of 27 August.

> What force does the government have today to repress those behind these acts? Little or none, for the simple reason that most of the rioters come from within its own armed forces. So why this language of force? The real strength of the government would come from else-where: from appearing unequivocally in the eyes of the soldiers as being visibly occupied in solving their prob-lems. The current picture is of a government that only acts when it is under immediate pressure.

On military matters, *Mediafax* was well informed. The reporter who became Cardoso's right-hand man on the paper, Orlando Muchanga, had just come out of the army, where he had done his military service.

❖

On 4 October 1992 Chissano and Dhlakama signed the General Peace Agreement for Mozambique in Rome and shook hands. But for a few weeks it looked as if the Rome agreement would make little or no difference. The war carried on: north of the Zambezi, Renamo launched an ambitious land grab, seizing the towns of Angoche and Memba in Nampula, and Maganja da Costa and Lugela in Zambezia. Ironically, it was now in the dying moments of the war that the FAM general staff suddenly opened up, giving the media information, admitting its losses, and keeping the public informed of the counter-offensive to recover the four towns.

Into this situation stepped the UN. A cheerful Italian UNDP official named Aldo Ajello was supposed to run the peacekeeping mission. Initially Ajello was almost alone, facing the task of imple-menting an agreement that was wildly impractical. Journalists read the Accord in detail and quickly worked out that by midnight on 20 October (five days after its ratification by parliament), all Renamo and government forces were to have moved to 49 designated assembly points, each of which was to be staffed by UN military observers 24 hours a day. Over the next 25 days the troops were supposed to move again to the government's established barracks and bases, and to special centres for Renamo. Despite all the praise heaped on the Rome negotiations, this was sheer nonsense, and betrayed an ignorance of both basic military logistics and how the UN operates.

It was Cardoso and AIM who raised these awkward facts at Ajello's first press conference. The then head of the tiny UN military team, the Indian lieutenant-colonel GP Sinha, tried to sweep this under the carpet, claiming that the initial movement phase in the Accord only meant 'they have to get out of their combat positions'. Ajello was more honest, recognising that 'the timetable is a little unrealistic'. From then on, the UN tactic was to declare that the Accord was being implemented, when in fact it was being continually rewritten. Weeks turned into months and there was no sign of the troops assembling, much less demobilising. A climate of peace was returning, and after the FAM retook all four towns seized by Renamo in October, there were no more major clashes. In December, more than two months after the Peace Accord, the Security Council approved a peacekeeping force of 7500 to assist in implementing the Accord and set up a UN mission for Mozambique (Onumoz) under Ajello's leadership. For an international civil servant, Ajello was remarkably open. He had once been a journalist, made a point of establishing friendly relations with the press, and gave regular press briefings that were sometimes astonishingly frank. Here was an official source of information that did not need to be prised open: Ajello insisted that almost everything about Onumoz was to be in the public domain.

Bit by bit, the machinery envisaged in the Accord swung into action. Several top Renamo figures, led by Raul Domingos, were persuaded to come to Maputo to allow the key Peace Accord commissions to be set up. These were the Supervisory and Control Commission (CSC), which was to oversee the entire transition from war to peace under Ajello's chairmanship, and the Ceasefire Commission (CCF), which was to investigate alleged ceasefire violations. But

Dhlakama himself remained at Renamo headquarters in Maringuè, and in March 1993 intervened to order a Renamo boycott of the commissions. This was openly a move, and a highly successful one, to extort money from the government and the international community. Renamo gave 'lack of logistical support' as the reason for the boycott. It claimed that the government had not provided the Renamo delegates in Maputo with the food it had promised them. This was the first time in history that peace negotiations were broken off because one side claimed the other was not buying it enough meals. The government could prove that it had provided Renamo with more than sufficient food, not to mention transport, fuel, furniture and other services.

It didn't matter: the blackmail worked, and donors eventually agreed to finance Renamo twice over – first as a signatory to the Peace Accord, and second as a political party. Two UN-supervised trust funds were set up: one to fund Renamo's transition from a military organisation to a political party, and the second to provide election campaign funds for all registered Mozambican political parties, including Renamo. The boycott ended on 5 June 1993, and by then the first trust fund had six million dollars provided by Italy, and was expected to reach 10 million. Renamo, of course, wanted much more. Domingos told a press conference that Renamo needed 100 million dollars. Ajello could afford to scoff at this, telling reporters, 'Sure, I need a billion dollars, just for me. But that's nothing to do with the peace process.' Cardoso commented thus:

> A cartoon illustrating what Domingos said would look something like this: Renamo with a gun pointed at a map of the country with the phrase 'Look out, International Community, give us a 100 million, or I'll go on shooting.' Hypothetical reply from the international community: 'Shoot at will. When there are no more Mozambicans, we'll come and occupy your country.' The problem is becoming alarming. The more Renamo opts for ultimatums – either money or more war – the more other forces are invited to adopt the same methodology.

Cardoso now regarded both Renamo and large chunks of Frelimo as lazy and complacent. They were both part of the problem. 'There's no doubt the first political force that seems to give an image of hard work will straight away have the support of a large slice of the electorate.' Renamo accepted the 10-million-dollar fund but, as the months passed, demanded more and more; and Ajello repeatedly took the requests back to the donors. His attitude was that peace would cost a lot of money but in the end would be worth it. By the end of 1994, the trust fund had paid 17 million dollars to Renamo; not a penny of this money has ever been publicly accounted for.

In May 1993 *Mediafax* was a year old. On its first anniversary Cardoso wrote that it now had 400 subscribers – 382 receiving it by fax, and others by mail. 'Number of readers: we don't know,' he said. 'We only know there is a real industry of photocopying *Mediafax*.' Cardoso had some hopes that the minor parties now emerging might provide a 'third force', and their leaders frequently contributed to the *Mediafax* opinion columns. Of the more than a dozen parties that bubbled to the surface of Mozambican politics in those hectic days, Cardoso regarded three as serious: the Mozambique United Front (Fumo) of Domingos Arouca, the Mozambican Nationalist Movement (Monamo) of Maximo Dias, and the National Convention Party (PCN) of Lutero Simango. If these three forces could unite, they might yet become serious electoral players. But personal animosities ruined any such hope, and the politics espoused by Arouca, who had spent the entire post-independence period as a lawyer in Lisbon, were a carbon copy of the Portuguese right. He took advantage of the space offered by *Mediafax* to argue the standard anti-communist line, that Frelimo did not liberate Mozambique, and that the MFA had handed the colonies 'on a plate to the Marxist political movements'.

Cardoso resisted Arouca's anti-communist line that decolonisation would have come anyway, and upheld Frelimo's role in making it happen, commenting on 23 June: 'It was from the jungles of Vietnam to the bush of Cabo Delgado that the blasts came which together formed the winds of history of that epoch.' For Cardoso, the Portuguese officers did not free Mozambique but they saved

Portugal 'from a disaster of terrible proportions'. As for communism, 'horror of horrors, perhaps within a short period, one of the dominant trends will again be the people's struggle against poverty – under the label socialist, Marxist, communist or something similar'.

As the peace process stagnated, it affected the economy, and the devaluation of the metical gathered speed. 'Each time Renamo makes another demand, the metical tightens its belt and falls some more,' Cardoso remarked on 27 July. The exchange rate had fallen from 3000 meticais to the US dollar in January to 4800 by late July, and then over 5000 in early August. Cardoso also became aware of military pressure on Chissano. On 11 August he wrote of senior FAM figures pushing for 'a military option against Renamo'. With Renamo no longer enjoying South African support and quite unable to produce 15 000 men for the planned united army, the FAM was finally in a position to 'liquidate Renamo militarily'. Was there anything in these rumours? Dirk Salomons, executive director of Onumoz, waited until 2000 to reveal that some officers were indeed planning a coup. His version, though, was that officers who had been pocketing a large slice of the military budget regarded a successful peace accord as a blow to opportunities for corruption. They intended to take power – until the US Embassy heard of the plan and warned them through informal channels that any coup would result in the immediate suspension of all foreign aid.[2]

Ajello was convinced that persuading Dhlakama to live in Maputo was key to implementing the Accord. Only on 21 August did Dhlakama come to the capital and meet with Chissano. Among his targets was the Mozambican media: in his pocket he had a proposal to set up a commission 'to verify the impartiality of the press'. The entire press regarded this as just another attempt to reinstate control over the media. Cardoso thought it might be worse than the control once exercised by the ministry of information. 'Instead of one interference, from the ruling party, we would have two, sometimes working together, and sometimes contradictory – a recipe to bring total discredit on the press,' Cardoso warned. Renamo refined its idea into a proposal for a 'High Authority for the Mass Media' consisting of representatives of the government, Renamo and Onumoz, which would supervise the entire public sector of the media and sack any editor who refused to take its orders. Renamo backed down when this received no support from any quarter.

Despite his hostility to the public media, Dhlakama was in fact given an easy ride. In a TV interview on 3 September there were no hostile questions, and the obsequious style of the interviewer allowed Dhlakama to evade anything that might embarrass Renamo – such as its creation by the Rhodesian secret services, its use by the apartheid regime, and the systematic practice of massacre, rape and mutilation. Cardoso could not forget the past so easily. When Dhlakama visited Maputo Central Hospital in October, he expressed shock at the shortages of basic equipment such as bed linen. This inspired Cardoso to write an indignant response:

> The destruction of the tea industries in Zambezia, the suspension of coal exports from Moatize, the destruction of Caia and Marromeu, the fall in exports from 250 million to 90 million US dollars, the disintegration of the roads, the destruction of bridges and railways, the transfer of the country's few financial resources to the war, the generalised dependence on the outside world, the systematic destruction of social sectors such as health and education, the physical and psychological exhaustion of workers in the state apparatus, etc., etc. – for Dhlakama does none of this have any relationship of cause and effect with the lack of sheets in the Central Hospital? Reconciliation, yes – hypocrisy, no.[3]

By mid-1993, *Mediafax* still had just one other permanent reporter, Orlando Muchanga. Other members of the cooperative – Moyana, Lima, Jossias – chipped in with articles, but their minds turned increasingly to the preparations to launch *Savana*. Out of the blue a young former teacher named Arnaldo Abilio turned up on the doorstep and asked to work on the paper. For him, Cardoso created a weekly column entitled 'Youth Trend'. Abilio recalled that when he submitted his first piece Cardoso 'was annoyed. He said it was no good. Then he explained how it should be written.' Abilio stuck with his demanding editor, who sent him to find out what young Mozambicans were thinking. Abilio surveyed a sample of 206 Maputo secondary school students and asked awkward questions about corruption in schools. At Maputo's Josina Machel Secondary School, the largest in the country, he found pupils resigned to paying 'parallel costs' – bribes for enrolment, bribes to pass exams, or payments to their own teachers for 'additional explanations' outside the classroom. Out of 255 students, only 47 said they had not made extralegal payments. The picture was similar in Francisco Manyanga, the other major secondary school in central Maputo. This was the road to ruin. 'How many companies, if they are able to choose, will give a job to a recent graduate from Francisco Manyanga?' asked Cardoso. 'They will tell us it's not like that, other students really did study, they didn't buy their final marks. And that's true, but how are companies to know who is who in this sea of disrepute into which the schools are sinking?'

Since the jettisoning of socialist ideology and the embrace of free market economics from 1987 onwards, the decay in the moral fabric of Mozambican society had become all too evident. 'Theft, extortion and bribery are today part of our life to such an extent that they are perhaps among the principal means of the social distribution of money,' commented Cardoso. 'They are part of the economic system.'

In December 1993, Abilio was taken on as the third full-time journalist, coinciding with Mediacoop's move to much larger premises, acquired for the launch of *Savana*. The first issue of the weekly appeared on 21 January 1994 with an initial print run of 15 000. With two publications, financial issues began to loom much larger. Mediacoop had to employ more people: *Savana* was suddenly overflowing with journalists, while the full-time reporting staff of *Mediafax* still consisted of just Cardoso, Muchanga and Abilio. *Savana* was supposed to the cooperative's flagship publication. This was the paper that would carry independent journalism all over the country. The cooperative's priorities switched to *Savana* – so much so that sometimes all four vehicles the cooperative owned were being used by *Savana* journalists. When that happened, the *Mediafax* journalists, Cardoso included, would go on foot. Since he had left the post of AIM director, Cardoso had become used to walking and expected his subordinates to do likewise. But Muchanga and Abilio became uneasy at the slack discipline in the cooperative. 'Cardoso didn't want to know about problems with cars,' recalled Abilio. 'But people from *Savana* were using the cars, not just for work, but to go out on their drinking sprees. There was no control.'

Despite Cardoso's admiration for Ajello, in January 1994 he had no hesitation in exposing an ugly little scandal involving the Italian troops serving with Onumoz and child prostitutes. It was *Mediafax* that published parts of a letter sent by the International Save the Children Alliance to Ajello, alerting him to the problem. Among the allegations were that Italian soldiers based in Chimoio used street children 'to arrange contacts with female children to be used for sexual services. The majority of these children are between 12 and 14 years old.' It was even said that a former security building had been turned into a brothel, with rooms rented out to girls who were then visited by Italian soldiers. 'The Catholic bishop of Chimoio has complained that condoms are thrown out of the windows of the brothel in question into the yard of his adjacent residence,' wrote Ernst Schade of the Norwegian Save the Children organisation, Redd Barna. Ajello ordered an investigation and found the claims well attested. The offenders were repatriated, and they were not all Italians (but Onumoz refused to name them or even say how many were repatriated).

❖

The first assembly points for the troops finally opened on 30 November 1993 (over a year behind schedule). Quartering of the troops occurred at a leisurely pace, and demobilisation did not start until mid-March 1994. Progress was agonisingly slow – partly because nobody knew how many men were in either army. The government had told Onumoz that 61 638 troops would trek to the assembly points, while another 14 768 or so would register at 'unassembled points' (fixed units such as air and naval bases, military hospitals, and the general staff). When, after five months, nowhere near 61 000 troops had turned up at the centres, the government lopped 12 000 off the size of its army. It told Onumoz that it was now planning to garrison 49 630 troops at the assembly points and

14 480 at the 'unassembled points'. This confirmed what Cardoso and others had long suspected – that the army contained thousands of 'ghost soldiers' who never existed (or had died) and whose wages were pocketed by corrupt officers.

The matter was repeatedly discussed in meetings of the CCF, until its chairperson, the Italian colonel Giorgio Segala, lost patience and wrote a long memorandum to the CSC, giving a blow-by-blow account of government attempts to explain how it was 12 000 soldiers short. This memo was leaked and, to the government's embarrassment, Cardoso published it virtually in full. Segala said that the government delegation on the CCF, led by Brigadier Aleixo Malunga, explained the discrepancy

> by referring to the difficulty in keeping the number of soldiers on active duty updated during the war in a country of such precarious logistics. He noted that the total number of government troops was being constantly reassessed. The reasons for the discrepancy, he said, include the lapse of time between events on the ground (e.g. the death of a soldier) and the time the event was registered; the tendency of FAM field commanders to declare a larger number of soldiers under their command than they actually have in order to acquire more rations for the troops who do exist; the tendency of some officers to declare more soldiers under their command than they really have in order to pocket the wages of the non-existent soldiers; the practice of not removing the names of soldiers from the wages sheet even after they have left the FAM ...

Here was a brigadier admitting massive corruption inside the army (but never expecting that his words would find their way into the press). When Segala suggested checking the figures of the defence ministry against those of the finance ministry to see if these would shed light on the discrepancies, Malunga refused, claiming that 'the differences in numbers were a mere question of interpretation'.

Mediafax could witness military corruption in broad daylight. At the Maputo air base, fuel was stolen quite openly – not a few litres here and there, but tonnes of fuel. Air force officers came to *Mediafax* with the story, and reporters simply went and watched. They could see soldiers 'rolling 200 litre drums from inside to outside the base. They left the drums there and went back for more. Some of the drums were immediately taken to houses on the outskirts. Others stayed there until the fuel was transferred into 20–25 litre containers.' Nothing was hidden, and the theft was perfectly visible from the Maputo airport control tower. The petrol and diesel were sold on the black market, as was the jet fuel, as a substitute for kerosene. One soldier told *Mediafax*: 'There are planes that receive two to three tonnes of fuel every day, but they are not operational.' Six weeks later, in early July, *Mediafax* returned to the air base to find the looting continuing. 'With or without public denunciation, the business carries on,' Cardoso remarked.

While the Peace Accord commissions argued about numbers, troops at the assembly points, on both sides, were restless. Incidents ranging from soldiers going AWOL to full-scale riots became increasingly common. Most of the soldiers wanted to go home. They had no intention of joining the new unified army, the Mozambican Defence Force (FADM). This reality caught up with Renamo first: Renamo suggested cutting the size of the FADM from the projected 30 000 to just 15 000. The government scoffed. Even 30 000 was 'ridiculous', given the size of Mozambique. *Mediafax* found this position perplexing: the government seemed to prefer to have 15 000 Renamo members in the army rather than 7500. There was even talk of eventually boosting the FADM from 30 000 to 60 000 troops. Cardoso asked: '60 000 men or 60 000 problems? Perhaps it would be useful to start asking whether there is some relation between the fact that Costa Rica is one of the most stable countries in the Americas, and the fact that it has no army.'

In the end both armies just disintegrated, in what Sérgio Vieira aptly labelled 'demobilisation by riot'. Even elite units mutinied. Thus in late June 1994 the third commando battalion at Bobole on the outskirts of Maputo threw up barricades on the main north–south road, demanding immediate demobilisation. The chief of staff, António Hama Thai, claimed that 'somebody must have spread agitation among the soldiers'. But Cardoso sent Muchanga to Bobole, and he found that what had once been a skilled unit (trained by the British in Zimbabwe) had degenerated into a gang of undisciplined and drunken thugs. A mutineer boasted, 'For the past year our main activity has been getting drunk.' In July discipline on both sides collapsed. Mutinies were breaking out all over the country: almost every day a new unit would demand demobilisation. Some of the mutinies were huge; thus, in Dombe in Manica province about 1000 Renamo soldiers threw up barricades on a main road and took 70 vehicles and 150 people hostage. One of the hostages was a jurist, Abdul Carimo, who was able to contact Cardoso by radio, telling him what was going on. The Renamo men had not the slightest intention of joining the FADM. 'They just want to be demobilised, they want their wages, they want food, blankets, shoes, and they want to go home,' Carimo told Cardoso. Even in the largest government barracks, at Boane, soldiers threatened: 'Demobilise us, or we march on Maputo.'

Cardoso asked Ajello, 'Are you sure that the government and Renamo are finally prepared to demobilise their troops?' Ajello replied frankly, 'If they aren't, the men will demobilise themselves.' The FAM and Renamo leaderships had no choice. The troops were hastily demobilised, and the FADM was formed out of just 11 579 troops, with more officers than enlisted soldiers.

As the elections approached, Cardoso was worried at what seemed a political drift within the cooperative towards opposition parties. It was one thing to interview leaders of Renamo and of the newly formed parties; but it was quite another to turn Mediacoop publications into partisan mouthpieces. Cardoso wanted it made quite clear that the cooperative was not in the pocket of any politician. His own politics were quite clear: for all his criticisms of Chissano's government, he remained within the Frelimo intellectual sphere, and would vote for Frelimo in October. Lauriciano recalls that, shortly before the elections, Cardoso met with other Mediacoop members, 'closed the door and asked people to identify themselves politically. "I'm Frelimo," he said.' But few of his colleagues were prepared to put their cards on the table. 'Cardoso was annoyed,' recalled Lauriciano. 'We were suspicious that some forces wanted to use the Mediacoop publications. They wanted *Savana* to adopt certain political ideas and lose its independence.'

One incident on the eve of the elections bore out Cardoso's fears, when *Savana* published a forged document purporting to come from the Brazilian PR firm Vox Populi, which Frelimo had hired for professional advice during the election campaign. The document appeared to show Vox Populi advising Chissano how to win the election by fraudulent means. Such a document should never have been published without a thorough investigation of where it had come from. It was clearly intended to damage Frelimo's chances and throw a shadow over the results if Frelimo won. Not that Cardoso uncritically endorsed the Frelimo campaign. He was practically the only journalist who did not merely report the Frelimo election manifesto but analysed it, pointing out that Frelimo was promising the electorate a higher growth rate than that agreed in discussions with the IMF. There were 'two different undertakings, one with the IMF and one with the electorate – possibly both wrong, given the highly unpredictable behaviour of our economy'.

There were ugly scenes when some Frelimo supporters disrupted rallies of minor parties, sometimes even using children. On 3 October Cardoso attacked these abuses:

> To herd children together to wreck the meeting of a party does nobody any favours. Particularly if it is a ruling party that uses children in this way … So far of the top leaders of Frelimo, only Graça Machel and Sérgio Vieira have distanced themselves from the aggression against the leader of FAP [Patriotic Action Front] a few days ago.

He urged Frelimo candidates 'to educate your followers in the spirit of tolerance and respect for those who have a different viewpoint'.

The results of the elections, held on 27–29 October, came as a shock for both sides: for Renamo, because it lost; and for Frelimo, because its margin of victory was much smaller than expected. In the presidential election Chissano had a fairly easy victory with 53.3 per cent of the valid votes, to 33.7 per cent for Dhlakama. Ten minor candidates shared the other 13 per cent between them. But it was much closer in the parliamentary elections, where Frelimo took 44.3 per cent of the vote to 37.8 per cent for Renamo. In terms of seats, Frelimo had 129, Renamo 112, and the Democratic Union, a coalition of three minor parties, took nine. Frelimo had an overall majority of just eight. The vote split along ominous regional lines: Frelimo had crushing majorities in the four southern provinces (Maputo City, Maputo Province, Gaza and Inhambane), and somewhat smaller majorities in the far north (Cabo Delgado and Niassa). Renamo dominated a huge swathe of central Mozambique (Sofala, Manica, Tete and Zambezia), while the largest province, Nampula, divided roughly 60–40 in Renamo's favour. This was a long way from the confident Frelimo predictions of a few weeks earlier. The head of the Frelimo election office, Mariano Matsinha, in a *Mediafax* interview on 28 September declared, 'We are relying on a victory of between 60 and 66 per cent.'

Although Ajello declared the elections 'the best ever held in Africa', Renamo shouted fraud; indeed, on the first day of the voting Dhlakama announced a boycott, which was ignored by most Renamo supporters. Ajello and the CSC ambassadors offered him a face-saving formula, and he rapidly backed down. Cardoso noted, 'Accusations of fraud, on Renamo's part, began in 1993, before the electoral law had even been passed.' The accusations continued, even though Renamo members sat on all the electoral bodies. 'One part of Renamo became jointly responsible for organising the elections, while another part stayed outside, throwing stones,' Cardoso wrote immediately following the vote.

> The irregularities, the organisational inadequacies, any problem no matter how small, it was all the fault of somebody else – the government, Ajello, Frelimo, the National Elections Commission, the press: never did the leaders of Renamo admit that Renamo was at the centre of organising the elections.
>
> Dhlakama used fraud that didn't exist to destabilise the elections. Threats were his main electoral propa-

ganda, and therein lies the real fraud of these elections. Regularly Dhlakama said he would never go back to war. But at the same time he played on the ambiguity of a possible slide back to conflict.

While the country was still waiting for the official results, on 13 November *Domingo* splashed the banner headline 'Renamo prepares for war' across its front page. The story consisted of extracts from a document purporting to be minutes of a meeting of the Renamo leadership held to discuss preparations for resuming the war. The document not only outlined a strategy for seizing power, it seemed to implicate the US ambassador, Dennis Jett. There was just one problem with this scoop: the document was a forgery. Ajello did not believe a word of it, regarding it as the latest in a series of forged documents, including the fake Vox Populi document and a letter, allegedly from Prime Minister Mário Machungo's office, giving orders that a bomb be placed in Dhlakama's house. Ajello thought that somebody 'is interested in creating panic and tension'. He accurately predicted that Renamo, despite all its cries of fraud, would accept the results. 'Dhlakama is very comfortable in Maputo, and so is the rest of the Renamo leadership,' he said.

But Jett and other ambassadors (from Britain, Germany and Portugal) whose countries were named in the document were annoyed enough to hold a joint press conference with Ajello the following day, at which *Domingo* was denounced for its 'unethical' and 'unprofessional' behaviour. Jett was not content with a mere denial. 'If there were a Nobel prize for stupidity, this article would win it. If there were a Nobel prize for hypocrisy, *Domingo* would win it.' But he then fired a broadside at the rest of the media. *Domingo* was not the only guilty party, he said. 'There are others among you who are equally unprofessional. Perhaps you were communists at university and have never grown up.' He claimed that these reporters were using journalism to propagate 'your own discredited ideology'.

Communists at university? Most of the senior Mozambican journalists, including Cardoso, could qualify for this description, if by 'communist' is meant adherence to some form or other of Marxism. And Cardoso hit back the following day. 'If there were a Nobel prize for arrogance, the American ambassador would win it,' his editorial declared. 'His behaviour is once again characterised by exaggeration, insults and the debasement of his diplomatic functions.' Certainly *Domingo* merited criticism for publishing a forgery at a delicate moment: but Cardoso noted the double standard in the diplomats' response. There had been no such 'orgy of repudiation' when the forged Vox Populi document appeared in *Savana* on the eve of the elections. The press conference, Cardoso concluded, 'was a disagreeable spectacle that came close to an attempt to intimidate the Mozambican press'.[4]

Ajello quietly but firmly dissociated himself from Jett's remarks. When he bade farewell to the Mozambican press at a final briefing on 12 December, he declared: 'I don't believe in neutrality. There's no such thing. People always have their own opinions. But I do believe in intellectual honesty and professionalism, and I found a lot of these qualities in the Mozambican press.'

CHAPTER 19

The Battle for the Cashew Industry

In early 1995, Cardoso accompanied Nina and Ibo to Norway. Nina was pregnant with their second child, but there were complications – the baby was overdue. Leaving Nina in the hands of the Norwegian health service, Cardoso took Ibo back to Maputo so that he could return to school.

Once back in Mozambique, Cardoso found himself at the centre of a growing storm over the behaviour of the minister of the interior, Manuel António, and his deputy, Edmundo Alberto. One investigation by *Mediafax* pointed to police involvement in a stolen-car racket. An article in the paper claimed that Alberto had intervened to allow a stolen vehicle to be returned, not to its rightful owner but to the Mozambican who had benefited from the theft. According to this report, police twice returned a BMW saloon, stolen in South Africa, to its illegal 'owner', Mohamed Kolia, even though both the police and customs had been informed of the theft. *Mediafax* claimed that Alberto intervened on behalf of Kolia to get the car released from customs. It also quoted a South African official as saying this was not an isolated case. Alberto refused to comment, and *Mediafax* called for a full inquiry by the attorney-general's office.

The initial sources cited were anonymous, but later a named source – Fernando Saete, head of the Maputo city police command – confirmed that Alberto had ordered the release of the car to Kolia because the warrant under which it had been seized was allegedly 'illegal'. Without success, *Mediafax* asked about the precise nature of this 'illegality' and why the police had given the car back despite explicit warnings from the South African Embassy that this was a stolen vehicle. On 13 March, Manuel António announced that Saete was being transferred to Niassa. *Mediafax* asked whether the transfer had anything to do with the BMW or with the fact that Saete had dared to speak to the paper. Alberto threatened to sue for libel, and so Cardoso and his lawyer appeared before a Maputo city attorney, Afonso Antunes, on 14 March. Cardoso denied that there was any libel involved. At no stage had *Mediafax* actually accused Alberto of complicity in the robbery. Furthermore, the paper had given Alberto every chance to put his side of the story, but he had refused to comment.

These were difficult days for Cardoso. His wife was thousands of kilometres away, about to give birth, and he was under immense political pressure: for at this stage, it was not at all clear how the new government that had emerged from the elections would behave towards the press. The *Mediafax* clash with the ministry of the interior was the first litmus test. Furthermore, once out of Nina's sight, Cardoso had neglected his health and was scarcely eating anything. He also had housing problems. Cardoso and Nina had moved to a larger flat, which was being sublet to them. This practice was common but may have been technically illegal; and in March, Apie officials appeared on the doorstep to evict Cardoso. The rest of Mediacoop mobilised to reverse the eviction. Fearing the adverse publicity, Apie rescinded the order later in the day; so in the morning all Cardoso's property was dumped on the pavement outside the flat, and in the afternoon the bailiffs threw it all back inside.

On 15 March, staff at an Oslo hospital finally induced Nina into labour. 'It was a horrible experience, I was 10 months pregnant,' she recalled. Nina's father rang Maputo to tell Cardoso he had a beautiful baby daughter. The child was named Milena (after Cardoso's sister-in-law). On the phone Cardoso sounded very happy at the news. But he was also very ill. The next news Nina received was that he was in the private Sommerschield Clinic. Cardoso had let his health deteriorate to the point where he was scarcely able to move. Friends found him in dire pain and almost prostrate in the flat. They took Ibo into their care and rushed Cardoso to the clinic. When Nina arrived a few days later, she went straight to the clinic and showed him Milena. 'He smiled, but did not have the strength to hold her. He was swollen up like a balloon because of a urinary infection,' she recalled.

On medical advice, Cardoso was sent for further treatment in South Africa, where he deteriorated alarmingly. When Cardoso realised he might be dying, he summoned the willpower to demand another doctor. This determination may have saved his life, for the second doctor found that the treatment Cardoso was receiving was poisoning him, and he ordered an immediate stop to all medication. Cardoso then recovered without further medicines, and when he felt strong enough to leave hospital he went to stay at José Caetano's house for a couple of weeks. He was still too weak to do more than gaze at television for most of the day. When he returned to Maputo, Cardoso told Nina, 'Never let me be treated in South Africa again. They don't care about patients from outside.'

In the months following the elections, most of the media were fixated on the new parliament. Cardoso soon concluded that the Assembly was largely irrelevant: most of its first sitting of 1995 was devoted to debating its own standing orders. *Mediafax* switched its attention to the economy. There was precious little economic journalism in Mozambique, and Cardoso decided to fill the gap. He received help from António Souto, who now worked for Gapi, a company promoting small-scale investment, and from an economics lecturer, Rui Baltazar, who both contributed to the paper and gave Cardoso a crash course in economics. The key issue was: how to revive the Mozambican productive sector in the post-war situation? The government felt it had no option but to accept the ideologically driven recipes handed down by the World Bank and the IMF. In 1995, the Bretton Woods institutions assumed that free trade led automatically to poverty reduction. This was the belief underlying the World Bank's 1995 country assistance strategy (CAS).

Essentially this document was an ultimatum: it set forth four conditions that Mozambique had to satisfy to qualify for 400 million dollars' worth of loans. The most outrageous was that the Mozambican government should end its protection of the cashew processing industry. This demand followed the privatisation of the nine factories of the dismantled state cashew company, Cajú de Moçambique. Businessmen who had bought factories in the belief that the industry was protected suddenly found the rug pulled from under their feet. The purpose of protection was to ensure that the processing factories had sufficient raw materials and that the raw nuts were not all exported (to the Indian hand-shelling industry). Under World Bank pressure the government abandoned attempts to restrict the export of unprocessed nuts, and in early 1995 adopted a surtax. Businesses could export as many raw nuts as they liked – but they would have to pay a 25 per cent tax on sales of up to 600 dollars a tonne, and then 70 per cent on each dollar after that.

The World Bank was far from satisfied. It wanted to eliminate the surtax altogether, and even presented a set of specious statistics at a June 1995 seminar, claiming that export restrictions harmed the interests of peasant farmers and actually reduced the country's foreign exchange earnings. It is a basic of economic theory that processing raw materials adds value to them: but here the World Bank was claiming that Mozambique's processed cashew kernels were worth less than the unprocessed nuts. The Mozambican factories, the story went, were so inefficient that, by processing the nuts, value was being subtracted, not added. The unstated conclusion was clear enough: the country would lose nothing by shutting the entire industry down and shipping every nut off to India.

The Cashew Industry Association (Aicajú) made short work of the World Bank's paper, demolishing all its claims. Aicajú believed that the World Bank was simply dancing to the tune of powerful Indian cashew interests that wished to destroy competitors. Aicajú and the Cashew Workers Union (Sintic) put up a united front against World Bank efforts to strip the industry of protection. They found a ready ally in Cardoso, who, even before the 1994 elections, had been fascinated by the conflict between cashew processors and exporters. Cardoso believed that Mozambique could advance only through industrialisation. The World Bank recipe was a way to guarantee that the country would be an eternal exporter of raw materials. It was in the pages of *Mediafax* that Aicajú could be sure its position would receive a hearing, at a time when most of the media had not woken up to the cashew issue.

Cardoso noted at the June seminar 'the virulence of the Bank against our industry'. He thought the Bank's basic solidarity ought to be with the war-battered processing industries, and it could express that solidarity 'without abandoning its criticism of the companies' current inefficiency'. In the very recent past the Bank and Mozambique's main creditors had demanded privatisation. 'The Mozambican government obeyed,' wrote Cardoso.

> National and foreign businesses bought up the state-owned factories, some of which had been paralysed for years. Scarcely had they reopened their doors, when along comes the World Bank proposing a radical rupture with the previous rules of the game, a rupture that the Bank recognises may lead all the industries to close their doors again. If things go badly, who will give these businesses back the rivers of money they have poured into re-equipping the factories, and paying wages to thousands of workers?

Cardoso had seen this sort of thing before. In his youth, some white Mozambican capitalists (including his father) had favoured local processing 'but faced pressure from the colonial metropolis, which wanted the colony to export its raw materials to Portugal, and Portugal would then supply Mozambique with the finished product.' Something similar was now happening, with the World Bank using 'the same type of discourse as colonial Portugal imposed on my father's generation'.

Mediafax strongly supported an attempt in September 1995 to reconcile the interests of the industry and the exporters. In negotiations between the government, Aicajú and the exporters, it was agreed to set the 1995/96 surtax at 26 per cent, and the local industry would have the right to step in and buy up any nuts that would otherwise be exported. The surtax would then drop by 4 per cent a year until it reached zero. The minister of industry and trade, Oldemiro Baloi, took this consensus to the World Bank – who tore it up. The Bank wanted to slash the surtax to 15 per cent at once and reduce it to zero by 1999. Baloi negotiated for 20 per cent in the 1995/96 season, 12 per cent the following year, and a decrease to zero in 2000.

At a press conference on 7 December, Cardoso challenged Chissano about the Bank's offensive against the cashew industry. Chissano hinted that the government had little choice. 'We are re-habilitating other industries, not just cashew, and this money has to come from outside,' he said. The government had to decide which measures would not 'prejudice us still further'. At the end of the con-ference, Chissano noted the scowl on Cardoso's face, and asked why he was so angry. A conversation between the two men ensued when Cardoso replied that he was deeply concerned at the fate of the cashew industry. 'What's the alternative?' the president asked him. Was this really the right time 'to say goodbye to the World Bank'? – for Chissano feared that, if the government rejected the Bank's cashew diktat, then it would be 'saying goodbye' not only to the Bank but to the European Union and Mozambique's other major western partners.

Cardoso argued that the government should not allow 40 years of investment in cashew processing to be destroyed, and claimed that 'the World Bank is on its own over cashew'. Chissano retorted that in order to discover whether the Bank really was alone the govern-ment would first of all have to take the risk of 'saying goodbye' to the Bank. Disappointed at the president's timidity, Cardoso wrote an editorial urging the government to call the World Bank's bluff. He did not believe that the United States, when one of its major corpo-rations, Enron, had just agreed to invest 700 million dollars in exploiting Mozambican natural gas, would abandon the country merely because the World Bank was obsessed with closing cashew factories.

Kekobad Patel, who chaired Aicajú, recalled how Cardoso was quick to realise that the World Bank's demands would lead the industry to ruin. He was a researcher, and he listened to the entire sector – to the industry, the traders, the trade unions. He understood the policy would be a disaster. He understood the industry's arguments, confirmed them with Sintic, and understood that Aicajú was defending national interests. He knew that the declarations of the exporters were false – it was just a way of exporting capital.

More than just defending the Aicajú cause, Cardoso immediately understood that, should the cashew industry go bankrupt, if nuts could no longer be processed in Mozambique, then other industries might follow the same path. It would be the beginning of the end. Cardoso was looking to the future.

Cardoso became a frequent visitor to Patel's home, discussing strategies to save the industry. 'He was a nationalist and he was defending the Mozambican cause,' recalls Patel. 'We passed the information on to Cardoso, he published it, and he ensured that it was republished in other papers.'

The battle now went beyond Mozambique's borders. Energetic lobbying, in which Cardoso and Joe Hanlon, now working freelance in London, played a prominent role, ensured that articles appeared in the European and American press, and that World Bank officials found themselves asked awkward questions about Mozambican cashews in meeting after meeting. Aicajú hoped that the government would at least maintain the 20 per cent surtax, and even the exporters of unprocessed nuts accepted this. But Cardoso's sources told him of further World Bank tactics: either the government reduced the surtax, or a recently agreed credit of 100 million dollars would be cancelled. The government's sole resistance was to reduce the surtax for the 1996/97 season to 14 per cent, rather than the 12 per cent initially demanded by the Bank.

But in February 1997 the World Bank's president, James Wolfensohn, personally stepped into the cashew dispute to overrule the hostile Phyllis Pomerantz, the Bank's country director for Mozambique. At an airport press conference before departing after a short visit to Mozambique, Wolfensohn made a point of asking if either Cardoso or Hanlon was among the reporters (they weren't). He then announced a major climb-down. The Bank would not insist on any further reduction in protection. The surtax would be left at 14 per cent while awaiting a study on the impact of liberalisation. He regretted that he could not start all over again from scratch – but he could not 'unscramble the omelette'. 'We are open to any solution. We are not insisting on anything prearranged,' he said. 'We will weigh the advantages to the peasant farmers, and the need to have a thriving processing industry.'

This was radically different from the contemptuous line taken by the Bank's officials in 1995. Indeed Wolfensohn even congratulated Hanlon, whose latest book, *Peace without Profit*, had been a scathing indictment of IMF and World Bank operations. 'Some of Hanlon's criticisms I have taken to heart,' he said. 'I think the Bank should recognise that governments run countries. I was not elected President of Mozambique. I was elected President of the World Bank.' Wolfensohn declared that the Bank wanted to change its methods, and that in future World Bank projects would not be approved without consulting the relevant institutions of civil society.

But the Bank's change of line came too late: one by one the processing plants were closing down, forced out of business by what they regarded as unfair competition from the exporters of unprocessed nuts. A 14 per cent surtax might be an improvement on 12 per cent, but Aicajú still regarded it as ruinous. Mass redundancies in the industry began in early 1997. This was a bad year for the cashew harvest anyway, and Patel told *Mediafax*: 'In difficult years, liberalisation just makes matters worse.' Cardoso commented that the World Bank's interference seemed designed 'to destroy the formal sector of our economy'.

> Democratic rules dictate that, in order to change national policies, a party must win an elections. But these rules don't apply to the World Bank. No Mozambican political party, hypothetically in favour of dismantling the cashew industry, was elected. There was no need. The World Bank is destroying our industries without needing any democratic process first.

❖

Meanwhile, the Mediacoop publications had spearheaded a drive to remove the minister of the interior, Manuel António. *Savana* called for an inquiry into the minister's alleged links with car theft rackets, while *Mediafax* published an opinion poll indicating that António was deeply unpopular. Cardoso also recruited his old friend Leite Vasconcelos as a regular *Mediafax* columnist, and his columns returned over and over again to the corruption and incompetence ensconced within that ministry. António was given to diatribes against the press – particularly when the media called for his resignation. In April 1995 he thundered, 'The press is infiltrated with journalists determined to libel me.' Vasconcelos replied, 'Manuel António behaves towards those calling for his resignation as a hungry puppy behaves towards the threat that the bone he is gnawing will be removed.'

Mozambique was now becoming notorious as a corridor for illicit drugs (usually on their way to the South African market). The police scored what looked like a major success with the seizure of 40 tonnes of hashish in two trucks. Manuel António accused a prominent businessman, Mohamed Iqbal, of being the trafficker. António headed a public campaign against Iqbal, thus usurping the role of the courts. This would have been bad enough if Iqbal really had been a drug baron; in fact he was innocent, and when journalists probed, the case against him fell apart. (It was weeks after the first public accusation before the police bothered to arrest Iqbal – had he been guilty, he would have had plenty of time to flee the country.) What was the purpose of the campaign against Iqbal? 'What is being covered up? The identity of the real traffickers in heavy drugs?' Cardoso asked. 'Faced with this assault on the most elementary ethics of ministerial and police conduct, the country's entire judiciary should have risen up in protest.' But there was only silence.

'The continued presence of Manuel António as minister of the interior is ever more incomprehensible,' Vasconcelos wrote a few days later. 'The present team leading the police has committed so many illegalities, violations of elementary rights, and blunders, and has shown that it is not really committed to fighting crime.' Shortly afterwards Vasconcelos returned to the question of drug trafficking. 'Bearing in mind the total impunity of those who traffic in hard drugs, and the zero performance of the police and the public prosecutor's office in this area, it is legitimate to suppose that we have reached the inertia required by this traffic and those who promote it,' he wrote.

Some within Frelimo read and appreciated the *Mediafax* campaign against Manuel António. In a parliamentary debate, Teodato Hunguana quoted word for word the Vasconcelos paragraph cited above. Yet the Frelimo parliamentary group had little impact on the government, and Chissano, while not endorsing António, refused to sack him either. But the minister became an extraordinary liability for the government when, on 22 January 1996, he gave an interview to *Notícias* blaming deaths in prison on the prisoners themselves. The ministry of the interior had no food for the prisoners, and so they died. The police weren't maltreating them, he claimed. 'Is it the ministry that should give them food?' he asked. 'Who told these detainees to commit misdeeds?' António concluded: 'A man has to die, he has his limits. When his time's up, it's over. He goes. It's not because they've been maltreated by the police' – remarks that raised doubts as to his sanity, let alone his fitness to hold high office.

Outrage rippled through Mozambican society, so that, when António called a press conference on 1 February (the day after he had been summoned by the prime minister, Pascoal Mocumbi, to explain himself), journalists assumed he would announce his resignation. Instead he declared, 'This idea that I'm going to resign – you can get that out of your heads. I'm one of those who liberated the country. Why should I submit my resignation?' António ended the press conference with a defiant quote from a popular song: '*Daqui não saio, daqui ninguem me tira*' – 'I'm not leaving, nobody takes me from here.' It sounded very much like a direct challenge to Chissano. But it took 10 months of further relentless pressure before Chissano finally sacked Manuel António. Meanwhile, a suspected thief, Frenque Tchembene, was tortured to death in front of his wife and three-month-old child in a Maputo police station. The publicity was such that five policemen were arrested and charged with murder. Manuel António brushed the matter aside, even when he received a summons to appear before a parliamentary commission. Challenged by *Mediafax* he declared, over a month after Tchembene's death, 'I can't blame the police. The autopsy will say whether he was tortured.' Before the parliamentary legal affairs commission, António admitted that the methods used on Tchembene were 'not appropriate', and that beating up prisoners was not official policy. His performance angered the entire commission, though the Frelimo members refrained from calling for his resignation.

The government found how much of a liability António was when it asked donors to support a project to retrain the police. The money was to be channelled through the UN, but *Mediafax* quoted the outgoing UNDP representative, Eric de Mul, as warning that any investment in the police should be treated with great caution to ensure that the money did not end up in the hands of crime syndicates. The bottom line was simple: donors would not put money into the police while António was minister. Violent crime in Maputo was spiralling out of control, in the face of police complicity or incompetence. In broad daylight, on 1 October, gunmen shot a Swiss anthropologist, Nicole Besenczon, dead in an outlying Maputo suburb, and stole her car. A week later there was no sign of any police investigation, and the heads of several diplomatic missions met at the Swedish Embassy to discuss the government's lack of response. One of the participants told *Mediafax* that one purpose of the meeting was to demand 'a political signal' indicating that the government was committed to fighting crime. The Swiss government threatened to cut off its aid programme, running at about 34 million dollars a year. António's reaction was to blame the public for not denouncing criminals to the police.

'Manuel António has presided over the almost total destruction of the state's capacity to punish crime,' Cardoso declared on 11 October. 'Today the criminals don't need any courage to do what they do; any coward can become a criminal today with the greatest peace of mind because he knows he will enjoy total impunity.' Vasconcelos turned his anger against the president's inaction on 22 October. 'It is impossible for the president not to know the situation in the police,' he said;

> the corruption that flourishes there, the daily evidence
> of extortion, the collaboration with criminals and net-

works of thieves and traffickers, the blatant indiscipline, the carelessness and degradation on view in any Maputo police station. It is impossible that the president does not know ... One day, sooner or later, Joaquim Chissano will have to face seriously a reality which he is allowing to become ever more explosive. When that happens, I don't think Chissano will be able to sack the people.

Cardoso returned to this theme on 6 November. The president 'has allowed corruption to go much too far among the country's political leaders, he has allowed the breakdown of institutions such as the police, and he has allowed Frelimo to wither,' he wrote. He warned that this risked 'giving the initiative to the gangsters'. The country could never tell when Chissano 'would take the side of the honest sectors of society, and when he would leave the door open to illegality'.

The following day, Chissano at last sacked António, replacing him with a former air force pilot, Almerino Manhenje. Cardoso's editorial was unlikely to have had much influence on this decision, but neither can one accept Chissano's routine denial that he had acted under any foreign or domestic pressure. Less than a week later Switzerland announced that it would not carry out its threatened cuts in aid. Cardoso had no doubt that the media campaign against António over many months had indeed played a significant role in the outcome.

❖

Cardoso came to consider Manuel António as the most visible aspect of the illegality tolerated, if not encouraged, by Frelimo. He was sure that the government knew of four exports of hashish (disguised as tea) from the port of Nacala in 1993, and of illicit imports, with no duties paid, of Toyota vehicles (which led to a strong protest from the licensed Toyota dealer in Maputo). And these two examples (involving the same business figure in Nampula) were just the tip of the iceberg.

'After the first years of protestant honesty in the governance of the socialist Frelimo, and particularly after the death of Samora Machel, Frelimo has been taking on board an enormous dose of illegality,' Cardoso wrote on 12 July 1995.

We have even heard the argument among the leaders that capital accumulation can only occur as in the rest of Africa – that is, by illegal means, by personal appropriation of public property. When they were asked 'But don't you see the rest of Africa is in misery precisely because of this?', they replied that this was an inevitable phase, and nothing could be done about it.

Corruption was now spreading, and two major cases threatened relations with key donors. In September 1995, Sweden and Norway demanded to know exactly what had happened to funds channelled in 1993/94 to the emergency seeds and tools programme (Pesu), designed to provide basic agricultural inputs to peasant households. About 2.3 million US dollars had gone missing, and Norway demanded the money be returned. It turned out that some of this money was still lying, unused, in ministry of agriculture bank accounts. But over a million dollars had been misused – in paying for goods not approved of by donors, or paying companies for goods they never delivered, or for 'purposes not envisaged in the programme' (a polite Nordic euphemism for theft). Interviews in *Mediafax* with Ann Stodberg, Maputo representative of the Swedish aid agency Sida, showed how angry the Scandinavians, Mozambique's firmest friends in Europe, were. She accused agriculture ministry officials of 'deliberate deceit'.

Equally serious was the theft of US-donated maize from Maputo port in October. Two ships carrying market food aid (for distribution via the normal commercial channels) had been raided, and a total of 2000 tonnes of maize disappeared. This was not the petty pilfering that all ports suffer from, but organised looting. After weeks of fruitless investigation, the donor, USAID, issued an ultimatum: it would not fund any more commercial food aid through Mozambican ports unless those involved in the theft were identified and prosecuted. Mozambique would now pay 'the price of theft and corruption', *Mediafax* warned. The Americans were threatening to cut food supply, and the Swedes might end their support for the agricultural sector and for the balance of payments.

But in the event both donors retreated. It was enough to repay the donors for business as usual to be restored. The government dipped into taxpayers' money to pay for the thefts – the state budget had to find 1.4 million dollars for the Scandinavians and 247 000 dollars for USAID. The donor demands for prosecutions were quietly dropped: not a single senior figure ever stood trial for either case, even though the finance minister, Tomáz Salomão, told *Mediafax* he believed that two provincial governors were involved in the Pesu scandal. These were perhaps the first clear cases of donor complicity with corruption: the culprits were allowed to go unpunished, since the most important thing was not to shake the Mozambican success story.

❖

Among Cardoso's more idiosyncratic campaigns was for the legalisation of cannabis. This was not merely the nostalgia of a former Wits student. Cardoso argued that the plant *Cannabis sativa*, known in Mozambique as *suruma*, was not just a drug: it could be used to produce clothing, rope, even paper. It was a valuable resource that flourished readily in the Mozambican climate, but was criminalised merely because it produced a soft drug. Cardoso cited examples across the globe of cannabis being used for legitimate purposes. 'Portugal is now making clothing from *suruma*,' he announced on 30 June 1995. He asked the environment minister, Bernardo Ferraz: 'How much of the doubtless meagre budget of your ministry do you intend to earmark for serious research into the *suruma* sub-species that exist in Mozambique and the variety of markets they could reach?' There was no reply.

The war on drugs waged by the police was largely a war on cannabis. Regularly the police would announce the destruction of fields of cannabis, but rare indeed were reports of seizures of cocaine or heroin. And when the police stumbled upon a factory manufacturing the drug Mandrax, an attorney was easily corrupted to set free the Indians and Pakistanis arrested there before they could reveal who was employing them. Cardoso noted that, in the past, local alcoholic drinks had been suppressed by the colonial rulers in order to guarantee a market for poor-quality Portuguese wine. Was something similar happening now, with a local inoffensive drug criminalised while powerful Mozambicans profited from trafficking in hard drugs?

He did not doubt the need to combat 'the drugs that kill', but argued that this combat was made difficult by the inclusion of cannabis. 'Right now, since everything is illegal, those who traffic in hard drugs enjoy the solidarity of those who sell the so-called soft drugs,' Cardoso wrote. Perhaps the government needed more time to study the matter, but 'at least let's stop arresting our peasants and informal rural traders,' he urged. At a meeting between the president and senior journalists in March 1996, Cardoso even suggested to Chissano that the government should legalise cannabis. The president seemed stumped for an answer: it was something completely off the government's horizons.

The mentality of a 'war on drugs' had penetrated Mozambican politicians so deeply that parliamentarians were absolutely amazed, in late 1996 during a debate on a bill to tighten penalties for drug trafficking, to find two deputies, Lina Magaia and Abdul Carimo, suggesting that cannabis was actually a useful plant. Magaia thought it would be a source of revenue when used to manufacture paper. Carimo was a little more daring, suggesting that it was less dangerous than tobacco and could be considered 'the plant of the century in ecological terms'. But on this issue there was a conservative majority in parliament which ignored warnings that, if cannabis was treated as equivalent to hard drugs, then it would be impossible to apply the law. Against the intentions of the original drafters, the bill was amended so that the final law equated cannabis with the entire modern range of narcotics and hallucinogenics. A field of *suruma* and a laboratory producing heroin were exactly the same in the eyes of this law.

❖

The number of *Mediafax* staff increased. Marcelo Mosse, the paper's correspondent in Inhambane, came to Maputo in 1993 to work full-time for *Mediafax*. Cardoso also recruited Zacarias Couto, a former worker on Mozambique Airports, who had been one of Cardoso's sources on aviation matters, and Victor Matsinha, who came from an abortive project to set up a paper that was never published: he

Carlos Cardoso and his son Ibo, at the Piri-Piri restaurant in central Maputo.

asked for an apprenticeship on *Mediafax* and stayed. With *Mediafax* prospering and paying better wages than the public sector media, other workers from AIM went knocking on Cardoso's door – a secretary and a driver, for instance. 'He's even taken our cleaner!' exclaimed Ricardo Malate one day, when a modest woman who swept and polished the AIM premises went to work at Mediacoop.

Tragedy struck on 6 April 1996, when Orlando Muchanga died in hospital after a motorbike accident. Cardoso was determined to find out how the accident had happened: he and Abilio retraced Muchanga's final journey, and found that his death was caused by a lethal combination of alcohol and police indifference. Muchanga had been to a reception, drunk too much, and ignored advice not to ride his bike. He gave a lift to a *Notícias* journalist, who said that plain-clothes policemen stopped the bike and demanded he accompany them to the station. Despite his obvious drunkenness, the police let him and the bike go – in effect, the police sent him to his death.

Inside Mediacoop, this coverage of a colleague's death was criticised. 'They didn't like us going into such detail,' Abilio recalled. 'But Cardoso thought people should know how he had died.' Cardoso took responsibility for the education of Muchanga's only son, 11-year-old Zito. Until his own death, he was paying for the boy's education.

CHAPTER 20

The Split in Mediacoop

Cardoso's break with Mediacoop was provoked by money. *Mediafax* was subsidising *Savana*. By the end of 1996 there were 350 paying subscribers to *Mediafax*, plus a bit of advertising: the paper was the financial bulwark of the cooperative. Both *Savana* and the cooperative's fortnightly English publication, *Mozambique Inview*, were losing money.

Cardoso wanted to increase the wages of the *Mediafax* workers, but found the rest of the cooperative distinctly cool to the idea. They feared the possible consequences of paying *Mediafax* workers much more than *Savana* ones. On 6 September 1996 Cardoso wrote a letter to the management council:

> I want to repeat what I said at last week's meeting. I did not come into the private sector in order to pay miserable wages, and to exploit people's work in an immoral fashion. The wages paid to the *Mediafax* staff are an injustice, and for me, as co-owner of this company, they are a disgrace. These workers produce income that is 15 times greater than their wages. In terms of profits the ratio is five or six times their wages.

He found this 'morally intolerable'.

But the meeting Cardoso mentioned had made it clear that, for the time being, the other Mediacoop publications would need the money generated by *Mediafax*. Cardoso's first proposal was to generate more money that would be used exclusively to raise *Mediafax* wages. He thought that a classified ads column in *Mediafax* called 'Publifactos' could raise between 12 and 15 million meticais a month, earmarked to increase wages. But the idea was not followed up, months passed and there was no improvement. Meanwhile, discontent was building up over the general handling of Mediacoop funds. Cardoso believed that large sums of money were going astray: at one point, he objected to the transfer of money held in a New York account to Maputo, for fear that it would be 'assaulted'. Certainly money was being funnelled into *Savana* to keep the weekly afloat, and Cardoso did not see why this should continue indefinitely. 'Cardoso was right. The financial management of Mediacoop was always disorganised,' said Moyana, blaming the problem on dishonest accountants and the failure of the Criminal Investigation Police to follow up complaints against them. The management council whose term of office ended in 1997 never verified the accounts.

Cardoso was also unhappy with the cooperative's loans policy. There was an understanding at Mediacoop that the organisation's funds could be used to improve members' living conditions – particularly to provide them with decent houses – but they would have to guarantee repayment of the money. The practice soon snowballed as more cooperative members took out loans. They were supposed to pay interest on the loans at 10 per cent of the US dollar equivalent. António Gumende admits that the members found it 'easy to take the money, but difficult to repay. I don't think the problem was so serious,' he says. 'But it gave the impression we were dishing out money.' Gumende estimates the loans at perhaps 4–5 per cent of Mediacoop's gross annual income. They were not taken from the money for current operations but from the 'cushion' of the New York account.

Cardoso did not see why Mediacoop should use its money in this way, and was sceptical about the chances of repayment. He told Nina that a loans policy he regarded as reckless was 'decapitalising' the cooperative. Cardoso also felt it impossible to justify paying miserably low wages to *Mediafax* workers when their employers – the cooperative members – were helping themselves to large sums in the form of loans. The matter added to growing tension within the cooperative. At the start of 1997, with no improvement to the wages of *Mediafax* staff in sight, Cardoso adopted a much more radical stance. He wrote a brief letter to the other founding members of Mediacoop on 26 January 1997 with a proposal that they found breathtaking. 'It's a simple matter,' he wrote. 'I would like to buy *Mediafax*. If, in the next two or three weeks, you tell me you're interested in discussing the matter, I'll continue.'

An extraordinary general meeting of Mediacoop to consider Cardoso's request was held on 22 February, and had to be continued on 8 March. By then Cardoso's proposal was no longer that of buying the paper. His new position, summarised in a statement issued on 12 March by the Mediacoop management council, was: 'Mediacoop grants me *Mediafax* in a regime of lifetime rent' and 'ceases to have any power of decision over anything to do with *Mediafax*. Monthly, quarterly, every six months, every year, I will pay Mediacoop 5 per cent of the entire *Mediafax* gross turnover.' He later wrote that he dropped the idea of purchase 'because I did not feel entirely comfortable with the idea of keeping a title which is, in all regards, the property of Mediacoop … The idea which prevailed was always that of my total control over the *Mediafax* income, give it whatever name you like. I never shifted from that position.'

But the very mention of purchase had fatally prejudiced Cardoso's case: most of his Mediacoop colleagues believed that this was an attempt to privatise cooperative property, and they found it unacceptable. The meeting discussed whether it could accept the principle of 'autonomy' for any of the Mediacoop publications, but could not agree. So the meeting was suspended for a fortnight, and when it resumed Cardoso submitted a revised proposal. He no longer spoke of buying the paper, though most of Mediacoop thought the revised proposal amounted to the same thing. He wrote, in a letter to Mediacoop workers of 10 March, that he had wanted

> total management autonomy, on my part, over *Mediafax*, and delivery of 5 per cent of turnover to the company's Management Council (this figure was negotiable, it depended on the short and medium term needs of *Savana*, but it could not be more than 10 per cent, so that I could restore justice at *Mediafax*); 2.5 per cent of

turnover would be for me and 1 per cent for the person
I chose as manager of the paper (these rates would be
renegotiable every year).

In addition, 'all the equipment used by *Mediafax* would be valued
and the money delivered to the Management Council' and 'all
money would continue to belong to Mediacoop. There would be no
distribution of profits within *Mediafax*.' Cardoso put in a safeguard:
'At any time the company could suspend this arrangement with me;
that is, if it should be shown that I was failing, the company would
step in at once to correct the situation.'

The atmosphere in the cooperative was tense and acrimonious.
Moyana recalls telling Cardoso, '*Mediafax* is not for sale,' and when
Cardoso threatened to resign, he retorted: 'Then you can go.' Lima
believed agreement was within reach but in the end there was no
contract, partly because Cardoso did not bring the detailed document Lima had wanted that would show exactly how much money
Mediafax was making. But this was no easy undertaking – the
accounts of the three publications were not separate. It was fairly
clear that *Mediafax* was making money and *Savana* was not, but
exactly what were the sums involved? Eventually the meeting
decided a vote must be taken. On what? somebody asked – and since
it was the only specific proposal on the table, the meeting voted, by
secret ballot, on 'autonomy in the exact terms in which Carlos Cardoso posed the question'. Of the 11 members present, seven voted
against autonomy, three in favour, and one abstained. 'Cardoso lost
because he did not have the tactical sense to convince his colleagues
that his proposal would work,' Lima later concluded.

Immediately after the result was announced, Cardoso asked to be
excused for the rest of the meeting and left the room. Two days later,
the management council received his letter resigning as editor of
Mediafax. He proposed leaving *Mediafax* on 15 April at the latest,
and promised 'to try to continue *Mediafax* elsewhere and, naturally,
with another name. In all other aspects, the new paper will be the
Mediafax which the readers are used to.' Since Cardoso was about to
set up a rival publication, he also had to cease his membership of the
cooperative. He told the other Mediacoop members: 'I have had

great pleasure in working with some of the journalists who have done most for Mozambican journalism. Our deep differences of today in no way alter my respect for the contribution they have made, and will certainly continue making, for a press that is increasingly free and useful for the country.'

In fact, it took time for the wounds left by this bruising dispute to heal – at first it was not clear whether *Mediafax* could survive without Cardoso, or whether Cardoso would be able, in short order, to found another publication. Cardoso told Lima he was certain that both *Mediafax* and the cooperative itself were doomed. But the market for faxsheets proved larger than anyone had imagined. Although no one could seriously doubt that there was a decline in the quality of *Mediafax*, it did not lose many subscribers to Cardoso's new paper, *Metical*. Instead, institutions and companies simply bought both. The financial crisis at Mediacoop was largely resolved when a new management council, chaired by Gumende and with Chiziane as treasurer, realising that the cooperative was on the brink of disaster, imposed tight controls.

To start his new paper, Cardoso needed premises and money. Neither proved much of a problem. He set up in the garage where *Mediafax* had been born. It needed some renovation, but it provided adequate space for a faxsheet. As for finance, Cardoso now enjoyed such prestige that he found people were ringing him and offering him money. *Mediafax* had started with an investment of 6 000 dollars: *Metical* was rather better off, with initial funding of 30 000 dollars. Work on making the garage once again the home of a publication took longer than expected, and so *Metical* could not launch itself on 16 June as Cardoso had hoped. 'But on that day,' wrote Cardoso, 'we improvised a reception to mark the birth of the paper. One of the workers "blessed" the outside of the newsroom rapidly with a little champagne,[1] we ate some chicken piri-piri and we regarded *Metical* as born. 16 June will thus be the paper's birthday.'

Cardoso deliberately used the name of the country's currency for his new paper, indicating that it planned to concentrate on the economy and would take a strong line of economic nationalism. The first issue came out on 25 June, the anniversary of Mozambique's inde-

José Cabral

Carlos Cardoso and his staff at the founding of Metical, *June 1997.*

pendence, with an editorial declaring that the new paper was *Media-fax* under another name. 'The editor and his team are the same, and they could hardly learn to make an entirely different paper in just two months.' Such was the loyalty Cardoso inspired that the entire staff of *Mediafax* – not just the reporters, but also the secretarial staff and the cleaner – accompanied him to *Metical*. One journalist from *Savana* also joined them. Nina recalls Cardoso's surprise at this. He had intended to start *Metical* with a smaller staff, but found it impossible to turn down anyone who had come from *Mediafax*. Indeed, before leaving *Mediafax* he had called a staff meeting, and announced his intention to set up a new paper. They could come with him, or they could stay with Mediacoop: he did not expect them all to follow him, but the staff trusted him and they all handed in their notice to Mediacoop. Cardoso told Nina that other workers from *Savana* came knocking on the *Metical* door, and he had to reject them.

There were 15 staff (including Cardoso himself) on *Metical*. They were earning what were, by Mozambican media standards, generous wages, plus 10 per cent of any profits. Cardoso also encouraged them to study, and every single reporter on the paper took this opportunity. Cardoso gave his reporters great freedom. There were no fixed working hours, recalls Marcelo Mosse. 'But when he felt that my productivity was falling, he would look at me as if I were in pain. In that look I caught a mixture of questioning and compassion.' Even more than at *Mediafax*, everything revolved at *Metical* around Cardoso and his ideas and hunches. He did not hold lengthy meetings with the staff; instead, he distributed tasks in accordance with the areas where the journalists had shown an interest. There was often no hurry. 'We didn't have to rush to finish an article,' Mosse remembers. 'Sometime we would spend a week or two researching a particular theme ... This was good, but it wore out the editor, though he never complained. It wore him out, because he was writing some 70 per cent of the paper.'

In a society deeply marked by a culture of secrecy, journalists faced a dilemma: the people who had key information about sensitive issues did not want their names mentioned for fear of reprisals. Even in simple labour disputes, citizens took refuge in anonymity. But was it ethically correct for a paper to rely heavily on anonymous sources? Cardoso argued that this was acceptable: the credibility of the paper would solve the dilemma. He had shown this at AIM; his reliance on anonymous Angolan and Cuban sources was vindicated when everything they told him turned out to be correct. At AIM, *Mediafax* and *Metical*, Cardoso cultivated a rigorous approach, the imperative of crosschecking sources, and the importance of numbers, statistics, as a crucial representation of reality. 'Only thus would we win the respect of our sources,' Cardoso argued. If investment in credibility worked, then the paper would have no difficulty in using anonymous sources.

At *Metical* the paper's accounts were made public every month. Cardoso had them fixed on the noticeboard so that everyone would know all the figures – everything above board. As *Metical*'s owner he put into practice the transparency that he demanded from Mozambique's rulers. 'Over the years we established bonds of steel with our editor,' Mosse recalls. 'He was courteous, transparent, honest, and genuine. We embraced the *Metical* project because we believed in him. And he believed in us.'

CHAPTER 21

Together for the City!

An immediate challenge for the new paper was the forthcoming municipal elections. Cardoso never agreed with the model for local elections chosen by the government. In *Mediafax* he had suggested that local elections could be carried out at low cost, with the direct involvement of the churches (or of civil society in the broad sense) in organising them. In his insistence that democratic politics had to be cheap, at one point he even suggested that voters might pay 'two or three thousand meticais in the act of casting their ballots' – an idea which, fortunately, he quickly abandoned.

In mid-1997 the government announced the cost of the elections in the 33 towns and cities chosen for the first directly elected mayors and municipal assemblies: 21 million US dollars. Cardoso argued that this sort of democratisation, bearing in mind the cost of the 1994 elections and now the predicted cost of local elections, would prove extremely burdensome for the country. The fact that launching a multi-party system cost so much, and was in addition so dependent on foreign donors, 'might open the path to repressive alternatives, resting on the following rationale: since we don't have the money for this type of representative democracy, then we can't have any democracy at all'.

Cardoso had long criticised the inertia and corruption that characterised the Maputo city council under the 10-year reign of Mayor João Baptista Cosme. The mayor (who frankly admitted never liking the job) always complained that the city was starved of funds, and took no initiatives of his own. Municipal organisation, once quite strong in the city, withered. An inert, bureaucratic machine governed an atomised capital, where solidarity among its citizens had been allowed to decay. A raging cholera epidemic in November 1997 forced Chissano to sack Baptista Cosme. The mounting death toll was a stark indictment of Cosme's stewardship of the city. Cholera is a disease caused by poor sanitation; and anyone who, in the months prior to the outbreak, cast a glance at the festering heaps of rubbish in the streets, or at the nauseating state of the city's drainage channels, converted into open sewers, would have had no difficulty in predicting a public health disaster. More than a hundred people died of cholera before the city council belatedly imposed rules of hygiene on the selling of foodstuffs. It seemed equally inept about (or complicit in) other problems threatening Maputo: coastal erosion, the illegal sale of land, buildings springing up in inappropriate places (including hillsides, where they were liable to be washed away in the heavy rains), the desperate shortage of public transport, and the conversion of many areas after nightfall into no-go areas for honest citizens.

Chissano replaced Cosme with Artur Canana, who was believed to have done a reasonable job in his previous posting as governor of Manica. This was the last time the head of state could appoint a mayor; as from 1998, all city mayors would be directly elected. The local election law also made it possible for independent candidates to run for office. Whereas in national elections all candidates for the presidency and for parliament had to be proposed by registered political parties, in local elections 'groups of citizens' could put up their own candidates. This became of vital importance when Renamo and most of the minor opposition parties boycotted the 1998 municipal elections. The only serious opposition to Frelimo would come from the independent 'groups of citizens'.

In Maputo, Cardoso attended the first meeting of an embryonic slate of independents. Indeed, *Metical* played an active role by publishing, free of charge, the announcement of the first meeting of 'a group of residents of this city who are inviting civil society to think of an independent candidate for mayor, and a list of councillors, for the Maputo municipal council'. The moving spirit was Philippe Gagnaux, the Mozambican son of a much-loved Swiss doctor, René Gagnaux, murdered by Renamo in 1990. Also in the core group were a former deputy agriculture minister, Paulo Zucula; a former secretary of state under Machel, Maria dos Anjos Rosario; and the chairperson of the Commercial Association, Mário Ussene. They described themselves as 'citizens concerned with the gradual environmental deterioration, the poor quality of life, and the maintenance of this city'. When Gagnaux said he wanted to stand for mayor but would only do so 'if people want me to', the meeting burst into spontaneous applause. He did not yet have a list of candidates for the municipal assembly, any programme or any money, 'but his candidature can rely on what may perhaps prove a trump card: an electorate tired of parties,' Cardoso wrote.

Cardoso had not initially imagined he would become an active municipal politician, nor had he wanted to become one of the driving forces behind the independent ticket. But his contribution to the political thinking of the independents was so great that there was a certain inevitability that he would be high up on Gagnaux's list for the municipal assembly. In February 1998, for the first time since his student days, Carlos Cardoso was running for elected office. Explaining his decision to *Metical* readers on 11 February, Cardoso said he intended to fight for 'a transparent governance for the city that serves to counterbalance the shadowy governance of the central government and of many of its international partners; public works that will give jobs to thousands of the unemployed, enlarge the informal trading sector and reduce crime; and the regularisation of titles for urban land'. He warned that nobody could take his vote for granted: 'independence' meant precisely that. Should Gagnaux win, 'sometimes I will support the positions and acts of the city government headed by Dr Gagnaux, at other times I will oppose them. And I shall always take my decisions publicly ... This means I do not accept any voting discipline. A group of independents is just that – a group of independents and not a party.'

The group took the name 'Juntos pela Cidade' (JPC – Together for the City). It suffered a blow when Paulo Zucula dropped out, but most of the initial group stayed firm, and were joined by such figures as the photographer Ricardo Rangel and the coordinator of the National Peasants' Union, Ismail Ossman. Cardoso brought with him into JPC friends and colleagues from *Metical*. But his direct involvement in politics, first as a candidate and then as a municipal deputy, raised a serious dilemma. Could you be, at one and the same time, the editor of an independent daily paper and also a candidate for, and then a member of, the municipal assembly? Cardoso saw no problem, and frequently used *Metical* to publicise his views and those of JPC on how the municipality should be run. Although an effort was made to differentiate the views of *Metical* from those of JPC, it was often hard to spot the difference, for Cardoso never did anything by halves: he threw himself passionately into municipal politics and believed that, as long as he was not deceiving his readers, he could use the pages of *Metical* to publicise the positions of JPC. The role of *Metical* as an unofficial (but quite open) mouthpiece of JPC was clear during the election campaign, and even clearer after the election when JPC became the opposition in the municipal assembly.

Cardoso dismissed the calls of 'fraud!' from Renamo, and its appeals for an election boycott. 'What you are doing with this nonsense of an election boycott', he told Renamo, 'is giving Frelimo the right to turn to the world and say, "Look – we want democracy in Mozambique; it's the opposition that doesn't want it."' JPC strongly resisted pressure for the independents to drop out. Furthermore, Cardoso wrote, the elections should be held on time, in June 1998. 'If we delay the elections over and over again, we shall only worsen the degraded state of our municipalities.' Unlike opposition parties, which habitually demanded that the state or foreign donors fund their election campaigns, JPC relied on its own meagre resources.

But whereas the National Elections Commission of 1994 had worked competently and efficiently, the same could not be said of the 1998 electoral bodies. Polling day, much to the delight of Renamo, was a shambles. Even in Maputo, every polling station opened at least an hour late, and some of them six hours late. Many trunks containing the ballot papers and other essential electoral materials were sent to polling stations without keys; and when, hours later, nobody had showed up with the keys, polling station staff smashed open the padlocks. In many cases, basic items such as glue (for sticking sample ballot papers on the walls) or kerosene lamps (to ensure that counting could take place at night in places without electricity) were missing.

No doubt this organisational mess contributed to the appallingly low turnout. Just 14.58 per cent of the municipal electorate cast their votes: in Maputo the figure was even lower, at 13.12 per cent. In this admittedly small pool of votes, JPC made a strong showing. Canana won the mayorship for Frelimo with 65.01 per cent, but Gagnaux made an excellent showing in second position (out of four candidates) on 28.82 per cent. In the second ballot, for the municipal assembly, Frelimo took 70.3 per cent, and the JPC 25.58 per cent. This gave the JPC 15 seats in the assembly, one of them for Carlos Cardoso.

The results were a serious warning to Frelimo, Cardoso observed.

> If, over the next five years, Chissano's party continues the kleptocratic behaviour that the electorate believes is its calling card nowadays, the city halls, in Maputo and in many other places, will escape its control. Given that everything indicates that kleptocracy will continue, that the parties will continue to suck from the common good, and that Frelimo will continue to hand the management of public property over to foreigners, we can see every reason for the independents to persevere on the difficult path they have chosen, that of restoring dignity and competence to governance ... Someone has to take Mozambique away from the process of degeneration.

He was optimistic that there was a fertile space for municipal independents: 'perhaps, under pressure from the independents, Frelimo will refrain a bit from its current expropriating and anti-patriotic drive. This consideration leads to the following: the independents must not interrupt the process that they have started.'

Cardoso immediately became one of the most active members of the assembly, and at its very first meeting he parted company with the rest of JPC. In order to save money, he wanted to reduce drastically the number of city councillors: the assembly could decide what posts on the council were needed 'but let us not fill those posts for as long as municipal revenue has not increased'. José Chichava of Frelimo said this suggestion was 'the same as setting up a government without any ministers', while for JPC Maria dos Anjos Rosario said that Cardoso's proposal would lead to 'a power vacuum'. On 30 August 1998, Cardoso was the only member of the assembly to vote against a proposal for 14 city councillors – he regarded this as 'an increase in expenditure without an increase in revenue, and therefore an increase in municipal dependence on central government'.

❖

Given the success of JPC, Cardoso began to dream about the possibility of expanding the group nationally, from 'Together for the City' to 'Together for Mozambique', so that civil society might obtain seats in the Assembly of the Republic itself. This idea was also pushed by Machado da Graça, now a regular columnist for *Metical*. He wrote that the local elections

> showed that the Mozambican people are fed up with people who are shameless, corrupt and incompetent. I seriously doubt whether it is possible to cure Frelimo's ills from within. I don't believe that there is enough strength of will for this. My proposal to the honest people still inside Frelimo is that they abandon the rotting ship and join all of those who, while not wanting to fall into the arms of parties like some of those we have, do want to drag the country out of the swamp into which it is sinking. With 'Together for the City' we shook the system. Perhaps in 1999, we can be a credible alternative in 'Together for Mozambique'. What do our readers think?

Cardoso brushed aside the objections that only political parties could stand in national elections, and that they faced a barrier clause: to win any parliamentary seats at all, a party had to score at least 5 per cent of the national vote. If necessary the independents could register as a party and, given hard work such as that which had characterised JPC, he was sure that the 5 per cent would only be a 'virtual' barrier.

Cardoso threw himself into his new role as municipal deputy with the same enthusiasm that he showed for his journalism. The problems he faced were not new; but in the past he had just written about them. Now he was in a body which would take decisions that were, in theory, binding on the city council. At *Mediafax* Cardoso had addressed the most evident problem of urban management – how to collect the garbage. He then proposed decentralising the job down to neighbourhood level: citizens in each of the city neighbourhoods should organise themselves to collect a garbage disposal fee with which they would pay a private company to take away the rubbish. Cardoso organised a meeting at which dozens of people turned up to debate the city's garbage problem. His proposals were listened to politely, and he received promises of collaboration. But the promises remained on paper, and the periodic garbage crises in Maputo worsened while the council complained it had no money.

Cardoso would never give up, and now he was in a position where his persistence might pay off. When he gave a TV interview in August 1998, shortly after the assembly was sworn into office, he said he had agreed to be a candidate so that later nobody could accuse him of not having tried to contribute to the process of turning the city into a municipality, with elected bodies, through the formal channels of democracy. Those channels were time-consuming, and there were times when his municipal tasks seemed to threaten the survival of *Metical*. But the paper still reached its subscribers' fax machines every day – even if it meant that Cardoso had had to work deep into the previous night. And if anyone wanted to know what was happening in municipal politics, they would turn to the pages of *Metical*. Although all sessions of the municipal assembly were public, the other media, notably radio and television, did not show much interest. Cardoso made some effort to separate his function as a deputy from that of a journalist – but it proved an almost impossible task, for he was writing many of the JPC speeches and documents: he was not going to write anything substantially different in the paper.

Cardoso was elected a member of the assembly's economic affairs commission, chaired by José Chichava, later to become minister of state administration. Cardoso sometimes invited Chichava back to the paper, where they would discuss the ugly facts and figures proving that the city was virtually bankrupt. The commission was told to look at the financial reality of the municipality, and the potential for raising more money. What it found was depressing. On 4 December Cardoso wrote: 'I was convinced that the municipal revenue was about 30 billion meticais a year. A pretty miserable sum, but at least 30 billion meticais. It was a lie. Neither I nor my colleagues had yet understood properly the difference between own revenue and earmarked revenue.' In reality, the municipality's own revenue, that which it really collected from taxpayers for its own use, was no more than 2.5 billion meticais per year in 1997 and 1998. 'That doesn't even cover 25 per cent of the municipality's monthly wage costs,' Cardoso wrote. 'The municipal budget is running a deficit of about 99 per cent. In financial terms, Maputo municipal council scarcely exists.'

What to do? Cardoso argued that in 1999 there had to be two municipal revolutions – one in the tax rates charged, and another in methods of collection, so as to broaden the tax base. The city would only be viable with greatly increased efficiency in collecting taxes and improvements in the way the money was used. To increase revenue, the citizens of Maputo had to pay for services. Through the pages of *Metical*, Cardoso stressed: 'All those of you who use municipal services – markets, car parks, billboards, places to sell on the streets – get ready: your costs are going to increase and, in some cases, substantially.' But the first move to increase revenue was to squeeze more money out of registered market traders. These were the people who were already paying (though it was doubtful how much of their fees found a way into the city coffers). Cardoso objected to increasing the rates charged to people who were already contributing before extending the tax net to cover those who paid nothing, and before improving controls on collection. So he voted against the increase in market fees even though everybody else in JPC voted with Frelimo, in favour.

It turned out that the major municipal battles were not fought along party political lines: the split was not between Frelimo and

JPC. Much more important were the increasingly frequent clashes between the city council, and particularly Mayor Artur Canana, and the entire municipal assembly. One of the earliest of these clashes arose from Canana's attempt to hand over the historic Maputo central market to foreign interests without any debate in the assembly and without taking precautions to ensure that the 400 vendors whose lives depended on the market could survive. In August 1998, Canana presented his plans for 'modernising' the central market, which must have been drawn up before the municipal elections. The vendors saw the plan as just an attempt to turn the market into a supermarket run by South African companies. Canana was assumed to be turning it over to South African interests. The vendors knew that the council was proposing major building work inside and around the market – but the details of any deals struck with potential investors were absolutely secret.

The published document said that Canana's aims were to provide better hygiene and security, and to renovate the building 'so that it continues to shine as one of the most important parts of the cultural and architectural heritage of Maputo'. The council assured the vendors that they would 'continue to carry out their social and economic function in a modern environment' – but not in the existing market: the document spoke of a 'new area', to which the vendors would be transferred. The vendors had other ideas. They wanted the council to upgrade the stalls, restore the power supply, and clear out the gangs of petty criminals who infested the area. They had no wish to be squeezed out of the prime selling area by South Africans. Challenged by reporters, Canana insisted that the project would 'take care of all interests'. But he refused to say whom he was negotiating with. There would be foreign and local investment in the market 'but I cannot reveal the names of those who will do this'.

Thanks to the publicity generated by Cardoso and JPC, the idea was dropped, and no South African supermarket opened in the heart of the central market. Canana retreated because it was becoming a political risk: the operation was alienating the market stallholders and their clients, to whom Frelimo had appealed in the elections. JPC chalked this up as its first victory. It also clearly signalled the growing chasm between Canana and Teodoro Waty, who chaired the municipal assembly. Canana was governing the city as if the assembly was a show, and this the Frelimo group could not tolerate. The first sign of this clash was when Canana authorised the building of a wooden hut in the middle of a city avenue. It was to serve as the offices for a company selling expensive flats in a new apartment block, but the location violated by-laws and the assembly had not even been consulted. The assembly struck back and, much to Canana's annoyance, ordered the removal of the hut.

In the early months Canana did not always attend the weekly meetings of the assembly or send any representative there, although this was a legal requirement. It was clear to JPC and Frelimo members alike that Canana regarded the assembly as a piece of window-dressing that could safely be ignored while he continued to rule the city directly with the help of council department heads. In December 1998, Frelimo and JPC members joined hands to throw out the budget Canana submitted to the assembly. Only then did Canana suggest closer collaboration between council and assembly. The assembly accepted – but Waty made it clear that any collaboration would have to respect the assembly's independence. It was not going to be a fig leaf for the mayor. For Cardoso, this represented a significant, albeit still timid, change within Frelimo.

Another serious problem facing Maputo was where to bury the dead. Lhanguene cemetery was fast running out of space for more graves, and matters worsened when people displaced by the war occupied areas reserved for cemetery expansion. The city needed a new cemetery, and the plan inherited by Canana was to build one on waste land in the suburb of Hulene. But the area had problems, notably the height of the water table. Studies were made, and they recommended that there should be no cemetery in Hulene. The city council ignored the recommendation and began fencing off an area for the new cemetery. In 1999 Canana appeared to yield to JPC pressure and promised to stop work on the cemetery until further studies were done. Then he changed his mind and a few weeks later the work continued. In December 1999, a furious Cardoso wrote: 'Canana must change his behaviour. There are heavy political and moral costs to be paid for his systematic recourse to a form of governance that is ambiguous, from the point of view of legality, and clandestine, from the point of view of method.' Canana was acting without regard for the assembly and its decisions, and this was discrediting both the council and the assembly. 'Only somebody on the inside can know how much we have fought within the assembly to drag Maputo out of chaos and to bring Canana to respect assembly decisions,' Cardoso declared.

Canana's cavalier attitude to assembly decisions led JPC to propose a vote of no confidence in the mayor in 1999. Cardoso warned that if Canana 'insists on making this assembly irrelevant, and continuing governance that is so often illegal, I would feel obliged to resign so that nobody could accuse me of conniving at a coup by the mayor'. The motion failed since, despite its misgivings about Canana's behaviour, the Frelimo group was not prepared to throw him out of office. Cardoso reconsidered his threat to resign – since it was still possible to complain against the mayor to the central government or to the courts.

Canana was not only at odds with the energetic opposition in the assembly. Indeed he was usually out of step with his own Frelimo comrades. Perhaps he believed he could get away with it because he was on the Frelimo political committee and Waty was just a mid-level party member. 'Canana and Waty don't get on,' Cardoso wrote in December 1999.

> We all know that. We knew it long before Canana said
> so openly a few days ago at the meeting with the Fre-
> limo group after the secret ballot vote on the JPC
> motion in which his party, with great dignity, defended
> him en bloc. It's up to him to make an effort to deserve
> that loyalty. But at least he had the frankness to tell the
> Frelimo group he doesn't get on with Waty. That's a
> step forwards.

Cardoso had come to admire Waty greatly, as he chaired the assembly in a democratic fashion and always defended the rights of the assembly against the mayor and the council. 'Whether Canana likes the chairman of the assembly or not, it's he, Waty, who has the correct legal and political interpretation of the local authority legislation, approved by parliament. It's as simple as this: the assembly is in charge. Full stop.'

❖

Cardoso could claim much of the credit for halting in its tracks a project to incinerate hundreds of tonnes of obsolete pesticides in the furnace of the Matola cement factory. Without any public discussion the government had negotiated the acquisition of Danish incineration technology to be installed in the factory. The official Danish aid agency, Danida, would fund the collection of the obsolete pesticides; those containing heavy metals would go into a landfill, while the rest would be burnt.

This plan leaked out in Denmark before the Mozambican public knew about it, and it was foreign NGOs (such as Greenpeace and the South African Environmental Justice Networking Forum) that raised the matter in Maputo. They brought over an American expert, Dr Paul Connet, whose fears were given prominent coverage in *Metical*. Connet regarded the Danida environmental impact study as a shoddy piece of work, noting that it paid scant attention to the emission of dioxins during incineration: these substances are highly toxic. 'This is a project that would not be implemented in the United States, and not even in Denmark,' Connet declared. Furthermore, Danida had not informed the local community: the relevant documents were obtained by the Danish branch of Greenpeace and were all in English – nothing in Mozambique's official language.

Government officials brushed aside all concerns and insisted on incineration. The national agriculture director, Sérgio Gouveia, declared: 'The project will go ahead as it is, though there may be some alterations, if justified ... But, if someone comes and offers us financial and technical assistance, and shows us an alternative, then we may retreat.' Francisco Mabjaia, the general secretary of the environment ministry (Micoa), admitted he did not know what level of dioxin emission would be caused by burning the pesticides, but 'it's guaranteed that pollution will be minimal ... We're not going to stop the project. We're open to discussion, but we're not going to stop.' Faced with government intransigence, and informed of an impending threat by *Metical*, a couple of dozen people, supported by over a thousand signatures collected in Matola and Maputo, decided to set up an environmental NGO, which they called Livaningo. Its first task was to present a formal protest against incineration to the government.

Cardoso helped mobilise people to join the ranks of Livaningo, which soon became one of the main voices for environmental conservation in the country. He sent Marcelo Mosse to follow Livaningo's meetings closely, and Mosse signed the initial Livaningo petition against incineration in the name of *Metical*. The Livaningo coordinator, Aurelio Gomes, recalls with gratitude the role played by Cardoso and his staff. 'It was thanks to the commitment of Cardoso and of *Metical* that Livaningo was born,' he says. 'When the other media criticised us, but then closed their doors to us when they demanded that we buy space to advertise our position, the only journalist who opened doors to us was Carlos Cardoso.'

Metical had a major scoop on 9 October 1998: Cardoso discovered that two members of the government, finance minister Tomáz Salomão and environment minister Bernardo Ferraz, had signed authorisations for the import and export of toxic waste. The authorisation from Ferraz was for an Argentinian–Mozambican joint venture for the international trade in, and local treatment of, toxic waste. His excuse was that, at the time he signed this, Mozambique was not a member of the relevant conventions against this type of trade and did not even have an environment framework law. Salomão said he could not remember ever signing such an authorisation. But it bore his signature, and Cardoso published it. It was only after publication in *Metical* that the two authorisations were revoked. Naturally, this discovery raised strong suspicions that the idea behind installing new incineration technology in the Matola factory was not merely to deal with pesticides. Perhaps the intention was to have a permanent facility to destroy toxic waste imported from all over the world.

The struggle against incinerating the pesticides was also taken to the municipal assembly. Cardoso convinced his JPC colleagues that the struggle waged by Livaningo and Matola residents was entirely legitimate. So JPC issued a statement on 14 October 1998 in which it supported the collection and storage of the obsolete chemicals but called for 'an informed public debate to choose the most appropriate way to treat this waste, in accordance with norms of transparency'. Cardoso thought it important that JPC should put itself on the side of civil society in the search for alternatives to government policies and decisions. Solidarity, he would say, was a key part of Mozambican identity. Frelimo backed the JPC motion and so it was passed unanimously.

The Danish government could not claim innocence in this affair. Cardoso wrote, on 15 October:

> If the incinerator is indeed installed, and if things go badly with the pesticide operation, if the incinerator is then used to burn imported toxic waste, and if things go even worse for the health of people and of the environment, and if Mozambique, because of this capacity installed in Matola, joins clandestinely in the criminal international trade in toxic waste, Denmark cannot pretend that it has nothing to do with it.

In the event of any disaster, Cardoso warned, those who had supported incineration

> will be the first to point accusing fingers at the Danes and demand many millions of dollars from them in compensation.

> The Danish government knows that it is funding the capacity to incinerate toxic waste in a country characterised by high levels of domestic corruption and of links with the world of organised crime. It knows that this technology requires local technical capacity and a social discipline that Mozambique does not have ... It knows that the project was conceived and designed in a climate of secrecy that violates the most basic norms for projects of this sort.

Also in October, Aurelio Gomes visited Denmark on behalf of Livaningo and tried to awaken Danish public interest, pointing out that a project funded by the Copenhagen government had been slipped into Mozambique furtively, without any public consultation. Gomes recalls that Cardoso was among those pushing Livaningo to send somebody to Denmark: he thought Livaningo could probably win only if it brought its side of the story to Danish public attention. Gomes managed to speak to senior Danida officials. He not only demanded that an alternative be found to incineration but warned Danida that Waste-Tech, a South African company hired to collect and store the pesticides, gave no guarantees that these dangerous chemicals would be safely stored in accordance with international standards. Gomes thought that Danida's hands were tied by the contracts it had signed with the Danish companies providing the incineration technology. Danida also told Livaningo that the Mozambican government had promised that the Matola incinerator would never be used to destroy imported waste. But it had no answer to the authorisations signed by Ferraz and Salomão.

Mixed signals came from the government. Micoa accused 'some people and groups who have been waging campaigns against the project' of having 'commercial interests' in ensuring that the obsolete pesticides should be 'sold to European countries'. It accused Livaningo of being a creation of Greenpeace. But at the same time, the government was on the retreat, and expressed a willingness to revise the environmental impact assessment. Mabjaia even declared, on 21 October: 'We've learnt our lesson. Henceforth we will hold public consultations.' The government promised to translate the assessment into Portuguese, and accepted Livaningo's suggestion for the creation of a forum to monitor the project. In February 1999 the government signed a contract to review the assessment, with a team headed by the Mozambican company Impacto. The preliminary findings of this review in March vindicated the position taken by *Metical* and Livaningo. It warned that 'the technical and management conditions that would make it possible to authorise the incineration process responsibly have not been met.' The cement factory management did not show 'the profound understanding or the level of commitment normally required in this sort of project'.

Furthermore, the factory violated basic safety procedures: the Impacto specialists watched as workers went about their duties without any protective equipment. They detected ways in which substances could leak out from the furnace during incineration, particularly during the frequent power cuts. This could contaminate maize milled in a nearby food-processing factory. But perhaps the most damaging finding was that the Matola factory, before a single gram of pesticides had been placed in the furnaces, was already issuing harmful particles into the atmosphere at a level three times that recommended by the World Bank.

So it was no surprise that the final report, in April 1999, opposed incineration and came down in favour of re-exporting the pesticides. On 25 May the Danish government suspended the project, and promised to finance a viable alternative. Micoa proved more obdurate and said it would re-export those pesticides whose origin could be identified; but about 130 tonnes would still be incinerated in Matola. Livaningo demanded that not a gram of pesticides should be incinerated – and eventually the government backed down. Victory came on 27 September 2000 when the new environment minister, John Kachamila, announced that all the pesticides would be re-exported.

Of all the causes that Cardoso championed at *Metical*, this was the one for which total success could be claimed. In a campaign lasting for about two years a government policy, backed by one of the country's main donors, had been turned on its head, and a possible environmental disaster in the densely populated area of Matola had been avoided.

CHAPTER 22

In Pursuit of the Powerful

By 1997 Mozambique had been through 10 years of structural adjustment, and one of the things that had been adjusted was Frelimo itself. The words 'democratic socialism' appeared in its statutes, but there was no sign of socialism in the actions of the Frelimo government. A capitalist order was being built. The question was: would this be a humane, welfare version, akin to Scandinavia, or just another variant of the savage lawless accumulation so prevalent in other parts of the third world? Could the Mozambican elite possibly degenerate into a kleptocracy not fundamentally different from the ones that had ruined Zaire or Nigeria?

Gone were the days when Frelimo insisted that party militants were the first to make sacrifices and the last to enjoy benefits. Now capitalists were welcomed into the party, and members of the leadership became shareholders and partners in one company after another. For Cardoso, there was nothing wrong with this as long as it was above board. But was the growing wealth of senior Frelimo figures all the result of their own hard work? Or had it leaked from the state in one form or another of corruption? The struggle against corruption, promised by the attorney-general, was nowhere to be seen. Cardoso never left Frelimo, the Frelimo that refused to admit him to membership; as far as he was concerned, it was Frelimo that had drifted away. He would sometimes say, 'I belong to the other Frelimo' – the Frelimo of Samora Machel, where there was no place for robbery, corruption and lies.

In the new Frelimo there was no room for the worker–peasant alliance: the stress was now on forming the national bourgeoisie as a key to winning economic independence. Hundreds of state-owned companies were privatised. A few of the large ones where foreign capital moved in (such as the breweries and the cement factories) proved highly successful. But many of the smaller ones collapsed: funds drained from the state went towards buying cars and other superfluous goods rather than improving production. Building a bourgeoisie through denationalisation proved an expensive failure. The person at the top, just as he could take credit for success, could not be exempted from responsibility for failure. And so *Mediafax*, and particularly *Metical*, took a highly critical view of Joaquim Chissano. This went beyond politics: Cardoso asked whether the president and his family were not among those becoming unduly rich, and began looking into their business affairs.

The problem was a lack of transparency. Nowhere was it clearly stated how much the president (and members of the government) earned, and what their assets were. Cardoso applauded a law passed by the Assembly under which leading figures in the state would have to declare their assets; but disillusion set in when it became clear that these declarations were not public. Leaders would list their property and turn the lists over to the ministry of state administration (and later to the administrative tribunal). The public had no access. How much wealth was being accumulated almost clandestinely, hidden by such useless laws? On 15 June 1997, Cardoso wrote that Chissano's refusal to declare his property publicly was unacceptable.

> This weakens the president because it grants a privi-
> leged – and obscure – type of citizenship. If the assets
> of business people are a public matter and are inspected
> in detail by the finance ministry, why should state lead-
> ers be treated differently? How can we know whether
> the president and other leaders pay taxes as we do?

Cardoso had hoped that Chissano would set an example in transparency – and that maybe, under civil society pressure, he still would. But until he did so, *Metical* warned, 'much of this society will continue to believe – perhaps wrongly – that he and his wife are accumulating enormous wealth, such as thousands of hectares of land'. From then on, *Metical* repeatedly investigated the business activities of the Chissano family, an area which no other journalist had touched upon.

In September 1997, the People's Development Bank (BPD) was privatised, and suspicions were aroused that the Chissano family was among the new shareholders. The private consortium that took 60 per cent of BPD shares was led by the Southern Bank Berhard of Malaysia in partnership with Invester, a group of Mozambican companies. The new chairman of the BPD board was Octavio Muthemba, a former minister of industry known to be close to the Chissano family. Cardoso believed that in reality he represented the president's family on the BPD board. Chissano's refusal to publish any list of assets added to these suspicions, as did the appearance of the president's oldest son, Nyimpine, alongside the Malaysian investors at the ceremony where the share certificates were handed over, on 3 September 1997. 'Is Chissano a banker?' asked *Metical* on 12 September. Initially the paper could not even discover who the members of Invester were, and a public notary simply refused to let *Metical* see the deed constituting the new BPD. But Cardoso was scrupulous enough to check further, and a week later published a full list of shareholders. The Chissano family was not among them; but the fact that no Chissano appeared among the shareholders was not enough to convince Cardoso. He suspected that Muthemba was a front man for the presidential family, and wondered why Nyimpine Chissano had been present at the signing at all if he had no link with the bank.[1] Muthemba had been silent when asked about the deed founding the new BPD, and the public notary had been downright obstructive. All this was indicative of 'the heavy burden of secrecy with which the government undertakes state business,' Cardoso wrote.

In October 1997, *Metical* switched its attention to the interests of the first lady, Marcelina Chissano. In a lengthy article on 27 October, the paper revealed that Marcelina had just acquired title to 4000 hectares of land in Bilene, Gaza province, for livestock purposes. Cardoso said he had written to Marcelina, asking if she had other property in the far south of the country between Ponta Dobela and Ponta do Ouro. There is no record of any reply. The same article reported claims that the first lady had been personally involved in an eviction, in an attempt to acquire a desirable flat in central Maputo.

In November, Cardoso revealed another presidential acquisition: a house in Ponta do Ouro which had once belonged to Radio Mozambique had been sold to Marcelina. Furthermore, in addition to Marcelina's 4000 hectares in Bilene, another 168 hectares had been registered in the president's name in his home locality of Malehice, and *Metical* reported another livestock farm (of unknown size) that had gone to Marcelina. In Maputo, *Metical* went back to the building where the first lady had allegedly evicted a tenant, to report further expropriation. 'The tenants are asking: does the Chissano family want this block all for itself?' the paper remarked. Cardoso sent reporters to Malehice with instructions to investigate the president's land holdings in depth. The initial article made the bold claim that land expropriation was making Malehice feel like Maringuè, the fear-laden redoubt of Renamo in Sofala. The main claim – that Chissano was grabbing land 'that does not belong to him' – was investigated over six pages. Fear was said to stalk the Eduardo Mondlane village, and the Human Rights League had a list of 25 peasant families who complained that the president was usurping their land, including land on which their ancestors' graves were located.

This time Chissano reacted, through his press attaché, António Matonse (a former colleague of Cardoso on *Tempo*), who denied that the land with graves had anything to do with Chissano. He said the president had requested land which had once belonged to a Portuguese settler. The local authorities had investigated to see if the land was occupied 'and they granted it to the citizen Joaquim Chissano. If there's any controversy, the local authorities can clarify the matter.' Alberto Langane, the administrator of Chibuto district where Malehice is situated, dismissed the complaints. He told *Metical* they were the work of Renamo members, of 'scoundrels' and of 'agitators'. But Chissano himself took the matter more seriously: in parliament in April 1998, when Raul Domingos asked him about the alleged land grab, the president replied,

> I never usurped land from anybody. As a citizen, Joaquim Chissano asked the state for some land for an

agricultural undertaking. I did not participate in choosing the land. Through the normal channels land was given to me which had not been used for many years. Two years later people came and demanded nine hectares, where some of them had been, and which had been overlooked when the land had been demarcated.

Chissano solved the problem by handing over the nine hectares. 'The land law is to be complied with, even when it refers to the head of state,' he said. The incident showed the gulf between the president and local officials, who regarded peasants claiming their rights as 'agitators'. The *Metical* reports did not seem to anger Chissano, who never behaved less than correctly towards Cardoso and his staff.

The same could not be said of his son. Shortly after returning from studies in the United States, Nyimpine Chissano threw himself into the world of business, becoming a partner in the travel agency and car-hire firm Expresso Tours, which landed plenty of contracts for government business. *Metical* kept an eye out for Nyimpine's business ventures, but his attitude towards press investigations was usually hostile. The first reported conversation between the paper and Nyimpine was in late 1997, when the paper asked whether he had any links with wealthy businessman Momad Bachir Suleman, owner of the MBS chain of stores. Cardoso had it from 'an impeccable source' that Nyimpine too was part of the MBS group. He wanted to find out, in particular, whether Nyimpine had any connection with the MBS shop Zeinab Textiles, which sold the cheapest cloth in Maputo. Nyimpine denied the story: 'I've got nothing to do with them,' he said. But he added, 'Don't play with me, I'm not a public figure. You can play with members of the government, or with the president. I'm Nyimpine.'

In February 1998, *Metical* published a story that Nyimpine Chissano wanted to take over management of the state lottery in partnership with Malaysian businessmen. The idea of handing over the financially healthy lottery company to private management irritated Cardoso – particularly because there had been no public tender. A government official, António Sumburane, told *Metical* there was no need for a tender 'since it's just a transfer of know-how.

They're offering to manage the company, and we're going to think about it.' Cardoso remarked, 'As far as we know, the lottery always made a profit. So why privatise its management? ... We don't agree with this non-transparent kind of handover to anybody, and particularly when everything points to the involvement of a relative of the president.' This time *Metical* did not contact Nyimpine. Cardoso explained to his readers that, since Nyimpine had very clearly said he had no wish to speak to *Metical*, 'we are freed from our obligation to hear his version of the facts. If, in future, Nyimpine changes his mind, we will naturally register what he has to say.'

But in May 1999 the paper did contact Nyimpine, this time to hear his version of a brawl in a police station. The weekly paper *Demos* had printed a story alleging that Nyimpine, when called into a police station because of a minor traffic accident involving an Expresso Tours car, assaulted a policeman named Arlindo Nota and threw a police typewriter to the floor. The local commander, Bernardo Egidio, confirmed that Nyimpine had been in the police station, and that the matter was under investigation. A violent outburst inside a police station seemed highly newsworthy. But was it true? *Metical* rang Nyimpine up, and instead of defending his good name he said he had no comment and hung up. There the matter might have rested had it not been for Cardoso's professionalism. *Metical* followed the matter up, and a few days later Egidio gave the definitive police version. Yes, there had been a scuffle – but it was Arlindo Nota's fault. Egidio said there was an accident outside the station, but the two drivers agreed there was no need for police intervention. Nota thought differently and demanded that they come into the station. So the Expresso Tours driver rang Nyimpine Chissano on his mobile phone, and when he arrived Nota insisted that he enter the police station. According to Egidio, Nota said Chissano had drunk too much, which precipitated the conflict in which the typewriter was thrown to the floor. Egidio claimed the clash was provoked by Nota, and said he even offered to start proceedings against Nota for insulting Nyimpine, but the last-mentioned dropped the case.

Nyimpine ought to have been grateful to Cardoso – for, while Egidio had confirmed a bad-tempered outburst by Nyimpine, the version of the incident in *Metical* was much more favourable towards the president's son than the original story in *Demos*. Cardoso was certainly not pursuing Chissano's family out of any personal animosity. Indeed, he continued to praise the president's commitment to freedom of expression. Nor was there any suggestion that the Chissano family could be compared to the grotesque charlatans and thieves – the Mobutus or the Abachas – who had plundered their countries. But the Frelimo of Samora Machel had set certain standards for people in high office, and Cardoso thought journalists had the duty to see that the traditions of the recent past were being respected. And since it was the public who paid the salaries of state leaders, they had the right to know about their business interests.

❖

As predicted, the cashew-processing industry went into steep decline. The 14 per cent surtax on raw nut exports was not enough. Struggling to acquire their raw materials and deeply in debt to the banks, the processing plants closed one by one. The study on liberalisation, carried out by the respected consultancy firm Deloitte & Touche, recommended unequivocally that Mozambique should adopt a policy of cashew industrialisation. It could find no significant benefits to peasant farmers from liberalisation; instead the benefits had gone to the middlemen, the traders. The World Bank had paid for the study, but since the Bank's bureaucrats found the conclusions unpalatable, they just ignored or distorted them. Aicajú and Sintic now thought the only way that the cashew industry could be saved was by an outright ban on the export of unprocessed nuts. They had supporters in parliament as, finally, Frelimo deputies woke up to the scale of the disaster. A bill drafted by Sérgio Vieira and Abdul Carimo proposed a prohibition on the export of raw nuts for 10 years (unless all the processing plants were fully supplied with raw materials). The bill also ordered the government to provide incentives to businesses to reopen cashew factories that had closed, and to pay compensation to cashew workers made redundant.

This horrified both the government and the IMF. An IMF document was leaked to Cardoso, who promptly published it in April 1999. This document, intended for the IMF board, described the

Frelimo bill as 'worrying' and claimed that, if it were approved, it 'would annul the government's efforts to raise the level of rural incomes and to liberalise trade'. These claims rested on the old argument that liberalisation lifted peasants' incomes, an argument demolished by the Deloitte & Touche study. The IMF 'urged' the government to 'resist' the Frelimo bill: thus, a foreign institution was telling a Frelimo government to oppose a measure proposed by Frelimo in parliament. And the government did precisely that, working hard to convince the Assembly's commissions to water down the Bill. These efforts were successful. An amendment was moved replacing the ban on exports with a higher export surtax (of between 18 and 22 per cent). Patel dismissed this as 'just playing about': four years earlier, the industry would have accepted a 20 per cent surtax, but now much more drastic measures were required.

Cardoso was furious at the compromise reached by the Frelimo group with the government, which simply gutted the bill. Shortly before the bill went before the Assembly plenary for debate, Patel, Carimo, Sintic general secretary Boaventura Mandlate and Cardoso met to discuss future strategy. Cardoso surprised the meeting by announcing that he intended to go on a hunger strike. He said he was 'preparing his family' for this dangerous step. Nina, however, refused to go along with what she regarded as a useless gesture. 'I threatened to leave him,' she recalled, 'for I knew that, if he did it, it would be serious, and he would die. They wouldn't change the law just because Carlos Cardoso was prepared to die for the cashew industry.' Patel and Carimo also persuaded him to drop the idea. 'With the kind of people we have in Mozambican politics, I didn't think a hunger strike could possibly work,' recalled Patel. 'Cardoso's main responsibility was to his family, to his children, who needed their father. It was obvious there was no political will in the government to do anything for the industry, and I doubted that a hunger strike would change their minds.' Patel was impressed that Cardoso was prepared to sacrifice his life – but between them he, Carimo and Nina persuaded him he was more valuable alive than dead.

By late 2000 most of the cashew factories were paralysed and some 8000 of their workers were unemployed. Cardoso pursued the subject right up to the month of his death. On 21 November 2000 *Metical* reported that traders were buying raw nuts for as little as 3000 meticais a kilo; the price was expected to rise later in the buying season, but to no more than 4000 meticais (24 US cents). In 1996 the price had been 40 cents a kilo. In one of his last editorials, Cardoso remarked that, whenever the cashew issue was raised, the government and the World Bank proclaimed, 'Yes, the factories have closed, 8000 workers have lost their jobs, some towns have come to a standstill, the balance of payments has suffered substantially, indiscipline has entered the sector and ruined the quality of our nuts, yes, all this is true – but liberalisation produced an ever higher price for the peasant farmer.' And this, declared Cardoso, was simply 'an enormous lie'.

❖

Cardoso was greatly disappointed by government fiscal policy. He had initially welcomed the appointment of Tomáz Salomão as finance minister and Luísa Diogo as his deputy, believing that they would embark on a serious debate about taxes. Cardoso strongly believed that the best way of collecting taxes was to cut tax rates but ensure that more people paid them. He consistently argued that a key reason for tax evasion was that the rates were too high: an importer would prefer to bribe officials because the bribe would be less than the combined duty and taxes on the goods. The government could lower taxes, more people would pay, and in the end the state would not lose.

Initially, he believed the government was talking seriously to businesses about revising customs duties downwards. But, under pressure from the IMF to slash evasion, the government farmed out customs management to the Crown Agents, a British firm. *Metical* regarded this as an outrageous violation of Mozambican sovereignty. Much worse, in Cardoso's view, was the hasty adoption of value-added tax (VAT), a move strongly opposed by almost all the country's businesses. In theory, VAT is a much fairer tax than the old sales tax. Unlike sales tax, VAT is not cumulative. With sales tax, the taxes paid at an earlier stage in the sales chain are added to the value of the goods and taxed again, thus artificially inflating the consumer price.

With VAT, the cumulative nature of sales tax disappears: only the value added at each stage is taxed. But this depends on proper accounting systems and the use of invoices, so that when, for instance, a manufacturer sells an item to a wholesaler, he can deduct from his VAT bill the tax already paid by the importer on the raw materials used. The government argued that, with sales tax paid at every stage from importer onwards, the snowball effect meant the consumer ended up paying a final tax of about 27 per cent. Cardoso contested this figure, since it assumed that all wholesalers and retailers were very scrupulous about paying their taxes. But the finance ministry itself had frequently complained of massive evasion of sales tax.

In the fight against VAT Cardoso found an ally in a former finance ministry tax expert, João Coutinho, who became a regular columnist for *Metical*. Throughout much of 1997 and 1998, he and Cardoso waged a losing battle against VAT. Essentially they lost because the government had promised the IMF and the World Bank it would introduce VAT. This was part of the quid pro quo for debt relief under the Heavily Indebted Poor Countries (HIPC) initiative. The deal was very simple: no VAT, no HIPC relief. Against that, all the arguments of Mozambican businesses counted for very little. The main argument against VAT hinged on the risk of introducing a tax typical of a modern economy into the 'completely disorganised' economy of Mozambique. *Metical* argued that the prerequisites for VAT simply did not exist; for the tax to be successful, the country required 'properly organised commercial links from the producer through to the retailer, and the generalised practice of keeping organised accounts, and these do not exist'.

Cardoso was deeply disappointed by government intransigence: in practice, the introduction of VAT was a complete break with the government's promise to hold a meaningful dialogue with the private sector. 'We knew that VAT was lurking in the catacombs of government and IMF intentions,' he wrote in early 1999, 'but both the government and the IMF fed perceptions that it was something that could be put off indefinitely, and that tax reform would result from a prolonged debate'. VAT looked like another episode in making it impossible for Mozambicans to control their own development. Cardoso recalled other impositions, such as the World Bank-funded Rocs (Roads and Coastal Shipping) programme involving massive road construction and upgrading, often with wildly inappropriate technologies, and carried out overwhelmingly by foreign rather than local contractors. Such programmes, with rules weighted against local businesses and with armies of foreign consultants, were not 'development' at all, but a way of ensuring that Mozambican companies could not develop. Cardoso recalled the bitter experience of Rocs, and the failure of projects such as Fare (Economic Rehabilitation Support Fund), which were supposed to build up local businesses. 'With VAT, the small Mozambican formal sector will become still more fragile, suffering a considerable contraction in business and a heavier tax burden,' he predicted.

In March 1999 Chissano announced that VAT would take effect on 1 April. Businesses had just a fortnight to complete their preparations. Chissano, wrote Cardoso,

> has ended the wearying ambiguity with which the government has treated its main economic partner – the business class. VAT, the president says, takes effect on the date chosen by the government. This must be the only country in the world where the date for VAT to take effect is announced just 15 days in advance. Clear-sighted citizens of this country have tried to persuade the government not to impose VAT by force on Mozambique. They did their duty. And the government did not listen.

With VAT now a *fait accompli*, Cardoso and Coutinho switched their focus to the tax rate, fighting against the 17 per cent announced by the government. Coutinho wrote in March 1999 that there were 'more than enough reasons to establish VAT rates so that the maximum is no higher than the South African rate (14 per cent)'. This was particularly important for tourist concerns, which were already subject to a 3 per cent tourism tax. What was to stop such companies simply running their businesses from South Africa rather than Mozambique?

What irritated Cardoso most was that the government, despite all its promises, did not enter into any real dialogue over the issue. A 17 per cent VAT had been promised to the World Bank and IMF, and it would be imposed regardless of what anybody in Mozambique might think. On this issue Cardoso was certainly in line with popular feeling. It was not only businesses that protested at the hasty introduction of VAT. So did the main trade union federation, the OTM, which feared that VAT would lead to a general increase in prices and thus reduce workers' purchasing power. The protests did wring one minor concession out of the government. Full implementation of VAT was postponed by two months, to 1 June 1999 – although most businesses wanted a postponement until at least January 2000. *Metical* thought the delay was just a public relations exercise, and that 1 June had always been the real date, agreed months in advance with the IMF; 1 April was simply impossible since key decrees (such as how companies should deal with stocks) had not been published.

The government called VAT 'the tax that benefits everybody', implying that taxes would decrease. *Metical* predicted a wave of price rises. Using finance ministry figures, it suggested that the real average sales tax paid by consumers was about 10 per cent; so, if the government made a serious attempt to collect VAT at 17 per cent, prices were bound to rise. In fact neither scenario was fully borne out. There was no sharp rise in inflation, but there were very few price cuts either. There was, however, plenty of profiteering: prices of basic foods should have fallen since they were exempt from VAT – but, apart from a few large supermarkets, in most shops there was no sign of any change in the price of bread, maize or rice. The VAT exemption just filled shopkeepers' pockets.[2]

Sometimes Cardoso carried his economic nationalism to extremes. In August 1997 the government decreed a list of tax exemptions for Shoprite, the first major South African retail chain to set up branches in Mozambique. Shoprite was planning to invest 63 million dollars in building a series of shopping centres in Mozambique, the first of which would be in a run-down area beside an abandoned bullring in

Maputo. A report from Salomão confirmed that the government was granting a 50 per cent reduction in corporate tax for the first two years of operation, and exemption from customs duties not only for the import of equipment but also for the 'first consignment' of goods for sale (this referred to everything on the shelves the day the shops opened).

Mozambican traders woke up to these exemptions only when *Metical* published Salomão's report on 7 August. They railed against the customs exemptions, and Cardoso backed them. The government had not consulted Mozambican businesses, he said, instead confronting them with a *fait accompli*. Was this not a stab in the back, 'an absolutely unnecessary political risk'? He regarded it as 'a blow against the culture of paying taxes, which is already feeble'. He complained that the South African retailers and the Mozambicans allied to them already enjoyed comparative advantages, including export subsidies, cheaper transport and easy bank credit. He predicted that 'if Shoprite goes for a policy of low prices, it will knock out of business hundreds of Mozambican importers, as well as a considerable proportion of the shops and stalls of Maputo'. And, once its competitors were out of the way, Shoprite would raise its prices, he warned.

Cardoso claimed that the Shoprite exemptions would damage the chances of the government reaching its 1997 fiscal targets. Salomão, however, argued that the state would make, not lose, money on the Shoprite deal; for Shoprite was not exempt from sales tax (and later from VAT), and it was simplicity itself to calculate the tax, since all sales were properly receipted and registered in computerised form. This was quite unlike what happened in most Maputo shops, where receipts were the exception rather than the rule and where the finance ministry, given the lack of proper records, had to estimate how much tax they should pay – leaving the door wide open to evasion.

The battle was bitter but futile: the Maputo public paid no heed to arguments that the government was discriminating against local shopkeepers of Asian origin. Cardoso's calls for boycotts and tax strikes fell on deaf ears. The enormous pre-opening publicity (much of it generated by the anti-Shoprite lobby) ensured huge crowds when the centre opened on 28 August 1997. Some even queued for hours, fearing that the announced bargains might run out. Both the ACM – the Mozambican Commercial Association, the main grouping of shopkeepers and traders – and Cardoso would have to live with the fact that consumers voted with their pockets for Shoprite. By and large Shoprite was cheap, and it introduced an element of competition that had been sorely lacking in the Maputo retail trade. And despite the dire predictions, there were no mass sackings of shop workers, and not a single shop can be said to have closed its doors because of Shoprite.

❖

Mozambique's second multi-party general elections proved more difficult than the first. Right from the voter registration in July 1999 through to the count and the results in mid-December, Renamo was claiming fraud. *Metical*, however, tended to keep its focus on the economy, leaving the rest of the media to cover the election campaign. Frelimo's attitude was triumphalist: this time there would be no problem, and Renamo would be hammered. Some party spokesmen boasted that Frelimo would secure the two-thirds majority in parliament needed to change the constitution on its own. Even Chissano threw caution to the winds and declared at the end of the campaign: 'We in Frelimo expect a great victory. Our number of parliamentary seats will increase substantially, and I will be elected by a very large margin.' He believed that Frelimo would make a strong recovery in the provinces where it did badly in 1994. Some analysts explained away the 1994 results as a 'vote for peace'. According to this theory, the electorate had, in some mysterious way, decided to distribute the votes so that neither side would have an overwhelming majority. Logically, now that there was no fear of a return to war, the real feeling of the public would be felt, and there would be a massive swing to Frelimo. But nobody who had watched the huge turnout for Dhlakama rallies in what was supposed to be a Frelimo heartland, the northern province of Cabo Delgado, could possibly believe this.

Voting on 3–5 December was orderly, but then came the long wait for the official results as the votes from each polling station were counted. *Metical* and the other media published partial results as and when they got them. But, had they had the commitment, the political parties could have mounted their own system for a parallel count. Nothing in the electoral law prevented this. Since each party could have observers at every polling station, and the count occurred at the polling stations immediately after the end of voting, this was the simplest way of halting any attempt at fraud. Frelimo came nearest to having a proper parallel count, but Renamo scarcely bothered. The previous year JPC, which had been set up only three months before, set up a parallel count in Maputo, which proved very accurate. A few hours after the count had begun, JPC could predict that it would win 25–26 per cent of the votes. And so it did: 25 per cent was the final official result.

At very low cost (plus enthusiasm and a few sandwiches), JPC was able to ensure that no fraud was possible. So how was it that Renamo did not follow suit? Cardoso asked.

> It is not acceptable that a national party such as Renamo, five years after the first general elections, still claims it has difficulty doing the same. If there is any anti-fraud mechanism in this country, it's the electoral law. Any party that is prepared to put in a little work can control the entire electoral process, from the vote to the count. They don't need anyone inside STAE [the electoral branch of the civil service].

But the problem for Renamo, for the minor parties and even for Frelimo was that the time of enthusiasm and unpaid militancy had passed. Now members and supporters tended to demand payment for their electoral work – hence the difficulty in arranging an effective parallel counting system.

By 13 December, Cardoso was convinced that Frelimo had won the parliamentary elections, but by a much smaller margin than predicted: some circles in the party were whispering of a victory 'tasting of defeat'. The key moment came on 14 December, while the count was still under way. That night Renamo suddenly claimed victory. Speaking for Renamo, Gulamo Jafar gave reporters what he called 'official results and projections', supposedly showing that Dhlakama would win the presidency and Renamo would be the largest party in the new parliament. Lazy Portuguese journalists rushed to give Lisbon the news: Renamo had won! The Frelimo era was over! Some of the Mozambican press parroted this line, while others, like Frelimo itself, fumed in rage. How dared Renamo pre-empt the official announcement of the results!

Just two media – the AIM English service, and Cardoso at *Metical* – scrutinised the Renamo figures closely. Independently, they both concluded that Jafar's figures suggested the exact opposite of what he had proclaimed: the Renamo figures in fact told of a Frelimo victory. Anyone who understood the system of proportional representation used in Mozambique could convert the provincial percentages given by Renamo into seats: by taking Jafar's percentages, the final result would be around 130 seats for Frelimo and 120 for Renamo. Even by making assumptions favourable to Renamo, Cardoso could not bring the Frelimo tally down to less than 127 seats. When *Metical* challenged Jafar about this, he admitted that he had 'not done his sums'. The projections for the presidency were rather more complicated, since this was not a matter of winning seats but an absolute number of votes. Assumptions about turnout had to be made in order to turn the Renamo percentages into votes. Cardoso used two sets of assumptions, both favourable to Renamo, and they both gave Chissano victory (albeit by narrow margins – 33 000 and 15 000 votes). 'For us, the main story of these elections was certainly the Frelimo and Chissano victory announced by Renamo,' wrote Cardoso. 'But it was precisely this story that the Mozambican press and foreign correspondents did not give to the world.'

Renamo appealed against the results, but the Supreme Court could find no virtue in the Renamo arguments, and on 4 January 2000 validated the results. Cardoso agreed with the court that the Renamo arguments were empty: Renamo 'still wants to be able to attack everybody and everything without the requirement of proof'. Nonetheless, he thought the court had missed an opportunity by failing to order a recount; there was a suspicion (shared by Cardoso) that the margin of Chissano's victory had been inflated, and that it was rather less than the 200 000 votes officially announced. All doubts could be set at rest by a recount. The Supreme Court took the practical view that since no conceivable set of circumstances could reverse the results, a recount would not be worth the time or money.

Renamo continued to insist that the results were fraudulent, that Dhlakama was the real president, and that Frelimo's parliamentary majority was fictitious. It threatened to boycott parliament and to set up a parallel government. *Metical* had no time for these antics. 'We have to understand Renamo,' Cardoso wrote.

> Yesterday, it was generalised killing and destruction. Today, it is boycotts and threats. Behind this lies the attempt to grab concessions from Frelimo. This is a classic case of a disintegrating feudalism. Over the past five years in parliament, Renamo was unable to join a single one of the causes that civil society took up ... Threatening the country remains the only way Renamo understands so as to make society, fearing the worst, push Frelimo into making the concessions Renamo wants.

Cardoso regarded the election results as a severe rebuke for IMF and World Bank recipes imposed on Mozambique. 'If Mozambique is the economic miracle that the IMF and World Bank proclaim, then why did 50 per cent of the Mozambican population vote against Frelimo?' he mused. 'Where is the famous "trickle-down effect" that the Bretton Woods institutions invoke when it is argued that large jumps in GDP in small pockets of the economy are not felt in the rest of the system?' The warning Frelimo had received from the electorate 'is also a warning against the economic policy of increasing foreign domination that Frelimo has been applying', with its train of industrial closures, growing corruption and 'subservience to international financial bodies'.

Blood Banks

Perhaps the shoddiest privatisations of all were in the banking sector. Under heavy World Bank and IMF pressure the two state-owned commercial banks were sold off – the Commercial Bank of Mozambique (BCM) in 1996, and the People's Development Bank (BPD) in 1997. In neither case was a proper 'due diligence' audit undertaken. People who buy banks without having them properly audited first are either fools or knaves. In the Mozambican case, the evidence points to an intention to loot the banks. The BCM went to a consortium which, though theoretically headed by the Portuguese Mello Bank, had been put together by António Simões, a businessman whose other interests in Mozambique were in engineering. As mentioned in the previous chapter, the BPD was bought by a Malaysian–Mozambican consortium and chaired by the former industry minister, Octavio Muthemba.

Cardoso's main concern was the BCM: where had Simões got the money for his share in the bank? The Simões group was known to be in debt to the BPD. Had it paid those debts off? Did Simões obtain concessional loans from the Mozambican treasury? 'Not in 1995,' was the rather evasive reply from the deputy finance minister, Luísa Diogo. A little further digging revealed the truth. Simões's companies – the steel-rolling mill CSM and the wire-drawing company Trefil – obtained over 17 million dollars of concessional loans from the treasury between 1992 and 1994. The money was to be repaid over 12 years in meticais. The money used was foreign aid – from Norway, France, Germany, Switzerland and Sweden – and Cardoso could cite the dates and numbers of all the agreements. The loans for

CSM were 'exclusively' to finance the import of equipment, or for goods and services needed to revive the factories. But there was no sign of any revival of CSM or Trefil, and Cardoso wondered whether Simões had not used the money to purchase his share of the BCM. Repeatedly Cardoso asked the government and the donors whether these loans were being repaid. He never received a straight answer.[1] Later, Simões sold on his share in the BCM to the Mello Bank.

Immediately prior to privatisation, the BCM suffered a major fraud. Vicente Ramaya, manager of the BCM branch in the Maputo suburb of Sommerschield, allowed several members and associates of the Abdul Satar family to open accounts. The Satars, who were of Pakistani origin, had come from the northern Mozambican city of Pemba, as had Ramaya. Within a few months, their accounts were used to drain 144 billion meticais (14 million dollars at the exchange rate of the time) from the bank. The mechanism of the fraud was simple. Dud cheques were deposited: Ramaya allowed them to be treated as good cheques, and so the Satars were able to withdraw, from other branches, perfectly real money. When the fraud was detected, some members of the Satar family fled the country, but others stayed. Ramaya lost his job but set himself up as a consultant. The investigation ground to a halt because some of the attorneys and police involved were allegedly on the fraudsters' payroll.

Momad Assife Abdul Satar (known as 'Nini') felt confident enough to return from Dubai in 1997. He spent a brief period in detention, and then the friendly attorneys released him. He set up an office for illegal money-lending operations in Unicambios, the foreign exchange bureau owned by his brother, Ayob. It looked as though the Satars and Ramaya were entirely immune from prosecution. The fraud might have been forgotten had it not been for the determination of the BCM's lawyer, Albano Silva, and the growing sense of outrage felt by Cardoso – for it was not the new owners of the BCM who lost the money; it was the Mozambican taxpayer, since the government felt obliged to replace the lost money before privatisation. When Cardoso asked her in March 1998 if this was true, Diogo confirmed it with the exclamation, 'What can we do!'

Cardoso was revolted at the way the state handled the matter.

More than anything else, the BCM case shows the degree of corruption we have reached. 14 million dollars are stolen from a bank, and the government replaces all the money ... The matter becomes more repugnant as we watch the government fold its arms. Neither prosecutors, nor courts, nor the president are putting any pressure on the attorney-general's office [PGR].[2] Complicity in the theft is generalised.

But the privatised banks seemed to be doing nicely. The BCM announced profits, the BPD changed its name to Austral and computerised – but both banks were engaged in reckless lending. On 16 March 1998, Cardoso demanded, 'There must be an official investigation into the privatisations of the BCM and BPD. Once we add up the non-performing loans in the two banks, plus the 14 million dollars of the BCM fraud, how much will in fact be torn from the pockets of the taxpayers?'

The stakes were raised when, on 29 November 1999, gunmen tried to put a bullet through Albano Silva's brain. They missed by a couple of centimetres. After this brush with death, Silva took Cardoso fully into his confidence. He was convinced that the gunmen had been hired by the Satars, and he explained to Cardoso the BCM fraud and the complicity of top attorneys. On 1 December, Cardoso wrote that the attempted murder was 'just the tip of an iceberg', and when the whole story came out it would shake the country's entire legal and financial apparatus. He pointed out that Silva was demanding investigations not only into the Satars and Ramaya, but into a dozen others, including Pic (criminal investigation) agents and attorneys. On Silva's list of people suspected of involvement in the fraud were the current attorney-general, António Namburete, and his predecessor, Sinai Nhatitima.

Cardoso was more and more convinced that Ramaya and the Satar family would do all in their power to obstruct justice. He and Silva believed that their strategy was just to buy off anyone who might get in their way – in the first place, police officers investigating the case, and the prosecutors who were supposed to press charges. They ensured that the investigation made no headway:

according to Silva they had spent about two million dollars on bribes. Cardoso sought the reaction of the Satars, and Ayob categorically denied any connection with the shooting. 'Dr Albano Silva is the bank's lawyer, as everybody knows,' he said. 'But that doesn't mean he's our enemy. We regret what happened.'

In a strong editorial Cardoso wrote that Silva was 'one of the few lawyers in Mozambique, if not the only one, who takes on difficult cases, those which involve personal danger'. It was Silva who had defended Mohamed Iqbal against Manuel António in the hashish case, and in 1999 defended the South African official, Robert McBride,[3] who faced a ludicrous charge of espionage when he investigated the smuggling of guns from Mozambique to South Africa. In such cases Silva had faced, 'often entirely alone, the institutionalised cowardice of our legal system'. Unless something was done quickly to find and arrest those responsible for the attack, 'no lawyer will believe in the possibility of institutional solidarity on the part of the executive', Cardoso wrote. Law in Mozambique 'is one step away from irrelevance', he warned. But matters could improve – just as Chissano had eventually been forced to sack Manuel António, so it was possible for the country's leaders to summon up the courage to solve this case and 'restore credibility to the system'. The Bar Association demanded that the authorities take action to arrest those behind the attempted murder, but even three days after the incident no government body had come out in solidarity with Silva – even though he was married to Luísa Diogo, a senior government member.

A few days later, Cardoso returned to the government's decision to repay the money stolen from the BCM. 'It is the firm conviction of people who have followed this case closely that the government has not yet shown any interest in recovering the money from the thieves,' he wrote. Why not? Cardoso's sources told him the BCM board had discovered that something was seriously wrong in August 1996.

> The fraud happened between March and August, with a clear acceleration in July, before privatisation was achieved. So the new shareholders ended up buying a basket with fewer eggs than they were promised. Natur-

ally they complained. To ensure that the bank could operate, the treasury injected 10 million dollars immediately. Later, the whole amount stolen was replaced. Now sources close to the BCM allege that the bank, with all the money replaced, is not putting pressure on the government to arrest the criminals. For its part the government has not pressed the judicial apparatus to take action.

Cardoso could only assume that the government was not interested in the case coming to court, because if it did so 'it is likely that many alleged irregularities in the BCM privatisation will bubble to the surface'.

❖

When Chissano announced his new government in January 2000, Cardoso was unpleasantly surprised to find that he had kept José Abudo as minister of justice. It was a surprise, Cardoso wrote, because leaving Abudo to head the justice ministry 'clashes openly with the most elementary expectations of society, and with Chissano's own promise, reiterated when he took the oath of office, to reform the legal system'. The criticism of Abudo was that, over the previous five years, he had done virtually nothing: he was the least visible member of the government. Cardoso held the minister's inaction as partly responsible for the rampant corruption within the judicial apparatus. 'Out of respect for the truth, it should be said that Abudo inherited a situation of growing corruption in the sector,' wrote Cardoso.

> But out of respect for the same truth it should be said that under his leadership, the ministry has allowed what little capacity of its own it possessed to die. More important still, Abudo gave no impetus at all to the sector. Chissano's decision in justice thus spreads a thick blanket of discredit across the promises he made to reform the legal sector.

Cardoso warned that, with Abudo still running the ministry, companies would feel that Chissano did not want a clean and efficient justice system. 'Changing Abudo was the least that could be expected in order to take seriously Frelimo's promise to build the rule of law. Not because Abudo has become notorious for personally corrupt practices or for incorrect policies in the sector. No. But because he has been the most absent minister in the last five years.'

Cardoso did not argue that Abudo, as minister of justice, should have intervened in the BCM fraud case; that would have been to usurp the role of the courts. But he had a responsibility, as a political leader, to ensure that the case did not gather dust and fall into oblivion. 'The critics of the minister – and I stress, the minister, not the citizen José Abudo – know perfectly well that the executive cannot interfere in the decisions of the prosecutors and the courts,' he wrote.

> That's not the criticism. But one expects that a minister of justice will fight politically for justice. When the courts fall ever deeper into disgrace, when the PGR shows a stony passivity towards organised crime, as in the BCM case, then it's up to a minister of justice to use all the legal influence of the executive to demand responsibility from the system. And this the minister has never done.

With no change of minister, who could defend the state against the corrupt prosecutors in league with those who plundered the banks? Perhaps the press could.

❖

Cardoso rarely attended parliamentary sessions. But he was there on 14 March 2000 to hear the Frelimo deputy Eneas Comiche plant the bomb that would bring the rotten structure of the attorney-general's office to the ground. Attorney-general António Namburete delivered an offhand, shoddy report to the Assembly that day, which devoted just five laconic lines to the BCM fraud. Even those few lines attempted to blame Albano Silva for the delay in the case coming to court. Those attorneys who had enjoyed proceeds from the fraud clearly believed they had arranged matters so that it could never come to trial. They had not counted on the tenacity of Albano Silva, or on the fact that the BCM had chosen as chairperson of its board Comiche, a former minister and now a prominent parliamentarian.

So Comiche demolished Namburete's dishonest report, and explained in detail how the fraud worked. He pointed out that by the end of 1996, Silva and Pic had collected pretty well all the evidence needed. But in 1997 the attorney in charge of the case, Diamantino dos Santos, 'used his influence and fomented intrigues to get rid of the entire investigating team who had been working on the case since the beginning'. When the attorneys did finally present a charge sheet, it was deliberately flawed and could never have formed the basis for a successful court case. The case papers had been disorganised, accused Comiche. 'Important documents that the BCM handed over are missing. The case is in no condition to be charged and submitted to trial. Evidence is being concealed and documents misdirected.'

Silva and Comiche found in Cardoso a firm ally. Cardoso insistently demanded that the case come to trial – and since the attorneys had done such an appalling job, the state would be better off using the charge sheet drawn up by Silva. Cardoso was now convinced that Namburete was no improvement on Nhatitima, dismissed thanks to pressure from parliament and the media in 1997. Since senior attorneys were involved in the BCM fraud, the whole edifice had to be brought down if there was to be any chance of reviving the judicial system. In an editorial entitled 'Society defenceless' on 10 May 2000, Cardoso wrote:

> It seems obvious that the PGR does not want to investigate anything. The state thus has two lines of defence. The president can dismiss the current attorney-general, and appoint someone else, who clears out all the attorneys allegedly complicit in crime and starts a serious investigation of the fraud. Alternatively, the Assembly of the Republic can set up a parliamentary commission of inquiry. If neither the president nor the Assembly acts, that will be a terrible sign that at this level too the state has abdicated from its job of defending society.

As Cardoso continued to investigate the fraud, he became aware of a range of other illegal activities undertaken by the Satars, with the supine passivity or active complicity of state agents. The Satars had used at least some of the money stolen from the BCM as the basis for loan-sharking – they offered money to people, often other members of the Asian, Muslim community, who for whatever reasons could not obtain bank loans, but at scandalously high interest rates. They then used their contacts among the police and prosecutors to force their clients to pay up. They gave the orders to arrest and release debtors, and Pic agents carried them out. Citizens in conflict with the Satars thus lacked any protection from the state, which seemed to be at the service of the Satar family rather than of law and order.

On 9 May, Cardoso dedicated an entire issue of *Metical*, five pages long, to the illicit activities of the Satars. He published evidence that the two brothers not only extorted money from other businessmen but also enjoyed sufficient influence to put private wiretaps on the lines of the public telecommunications company, TDM. One of the victims, the Abdul Magid family, owners of the company Bazar Central, provided Cardoso with a cassette that apparently proved the allegations of illegal wiretapping, as well as the insults and threats the Satars used against their debtors. Cardoso wrote that the Satar brothers 'have, in recent years, been Mozambique's main loan sharks, with monthly interest rates ranging from 5 to 20 per cent, depending on how desperate the potential debtors are. They have enormous influence in the police and legal system, and resort to extreme methods in debt collection.'

To pay off other debts resulting from disastrous business deals, Abdul Magid Hussein borrowed 600 000 dollars from Nini Satar. Part of the debt bore an interest rate of 5 per cent a month (60 per cent a year), and the rest 10 per cent a month (120 per cent a year). Satar waited until May 1998, when the debt stood at 1.125 million dollars. A meeting then took place between Magid and his two sons and the Satar brothers at Unicambios, where the Satars threatened Magid with imprisonment and, in Magid's words to Cardoso, 'invoked names of relatives of the president, attorneys and police officers as guarantees that they could carry out this threat'. They forced Magid to hand over two luxury houses, which the Satars valued at 500 000 dollars (Magid said the true value was 660 000).

The debt now stood at 635 000 dollars and the interest continued to mount. Magid was obliged to sell off other properties to satisfy the appetites of the Satars, and by May 2000 he had paid the equivalent of 1.6 million dollars. 'Usury in this case', Cardoso wrote, 'resulted in accumulated interest of a million dollars on a loan of 600 000 dollars in about three years.' He also confirmed that the Satars used public prosecutors and Pic agents to detain their 'clients'. One of these prosecutors, Rui Seuane, was also involved in the BCM fraud, and serious allegations of corruption were made against him. He signed an initial charge sheet in the case which the BCM and Silva regarded as laughably inadequate. It was also Seuane who declined to press charges against Nini and Ayob Satar's parents, Abdul Satar Abdul Karim and Hawbay Abdul Latife, leaving them out of the investigation, when the BCM regarded both as among the principal suspects.

Metical heard the other side of the story, and asked both Satars for their reactions. Nini declared it was 'absolutely false' that he had ever lent money to Magid, and described his statements as 'delirious'. But he did not stop there – instead he launched a venomous personal attack on the Magid family.

> Their whole fury against me derives from the fact that I was once the boyfriend of Magid's daughter, who became pregnant. The parents wanted to force me to marry her, and I refused because I wasn't sure I was the father. Later I was told the girl got an abortion in South Africa. That's one of the causes of this agitation against me.

Ayob likewise denied all the allegations, and insulted Magid and his wife, calling them 'real swindlers'. He took a swipe at Albano Silva, claiming the lawyer 'invents everything to damage our image as successful foreign currency traders. There's a campaign waged by Albano Silva and his lackey Abdul Magid to put the BCM case in the papers in order to influence the judicial decision.'

The more he understood the activities and character of the two brothers, the more angered Cardoso became. The private wiretaps were particularly alarming:

Anyone who can get into the TDM network to listen to the conversations of businessmen can also listen to any other citizens, including members of the government. And when those who do this make no attempt to hide it, it's because they think they enjoy impunity. This level of parallel power should frighten the politicians. This is the level of debasement to which we have sunk. It's the raw material from which coups d'état are later manufactured.

A lengthy article followed on 12 May. Entitled 'Biographical notes on the first cheque of the fraud', it was exactly that: a minutely detailed examination of the first fraudulent cheque deposited in a Satar account at Ramaya's branch. This combined Albano Silva's work with further details researched by *Metical* itself. The article indicated that Vicente Ramaya was the key figure, the internal architect, of the fraud. Cardoso recalled that the state still held 49 per cent of the BCM's shares. So it was the state that had been robbed, but the state, through the PGR, was doing nothing to punish the thieves. Who should be held responsible? For Cardoso 'the constitution holds the president responsible for this matter. He has the power to sack the PGR.' But the Assembly was also responsible for failing to set up a commission of inquiry, as were other judicial bodies who had the power to take the detailed charge sheet drawn up by the BCM as their own but failed to do so. On 15 May came the article 'Satar methods' containing further confirmation of the Satar brothers' wiretapping activities. The tapes that *Metical* had heard could lead the Satars to lengthy prison terms, for they confirmed the illegal wiretaps, and the Satars could also be heard making kidnapping threats and boasting of theft, which in the context could only refer to the BCM fraud.

Ramaya reacted on 16 May to the 'Biographical notes' article. He started with a series of insults, claiming that Comiche and *Metical* were being manipulated by outside forces. Then he gave his version of the fraud, claiming he had 'carried out scrupulously the instructions of my superiors' – so the true mentors of the fraud were these 'superiors'. For the first time he claimed there were other frauds, through which the BCM had lost 80 million dollars. 'In due time I will send *Metical* the list of the inquiries which I deem indispensable for discovering the truth,' he said. He declared his readiness to take part 'at any time in an open and transparent debate on the BCM, where you can choose the moderator, and with banking experts chosen by both sides'. Cardoso immediately accepted this proposal, which he regarded as not very different from the call for a commission of inquiry. It could look at such questions as 'whether the public prosecutor's office has hidden evidence as Eneas Comiche alleges, whether the charge sheet sent by the public prosecutor to the court, and rejected by the Bank's lawyer, was or was not deliberately vague, intended to be summarily rejected by the court, and whether allegations that prosecutors have been bribed are true'.

If, as Ramaya and others were claiming, 'there are "sharks" responsible for this and other major frauds, we are sure that an informed debate on the 144 billion meticais fraud will lead us to clues and conclusions about the others'. Furthermore, such a debate 'might throw up answers to the questions this paper has raised about the privatisation of the BCM'. Cardoso pledged that whatever it found out, *Metical* would publish. This was not the reply Ramaya had expected. He never sent Cardoso any list of 'indispensable' inquiries, and when Cardoso faxed him a series of questions he did not reply. Perhaps it was at this point that those who orchestrated the BCM fraud decided that Carlos Cardoso was too dangerous to remain alive.

❖

Rifts began to appear in the attorney-general's office. One of the six assistant attorney-generals, Afonso Antunes, was deeply worried by the BCM scandal and wrote a letter to the technical council of the PGR with a stinging attack on his fellow attorneys. To Namburete's fury, the letter was published in *Metical* on 25 and 26 May. Namburete suspended Antunes, accusing him of undermining the 'prestige' of the attorney-general's office. 'Prestige? What prestige?' editorialised Cardoso.

> For years, the PGR has had no prestige at all. The irrelevance of the PGR as an instrument to defend and pro-

mote legality is longstanding … Now we have the BCM case. Why does the PGR not investigate the case? Why does it not answer Comiche's questions? And all this is just the tip of the iceberg. For a long time public opinion has been asking if the problem with the PGR is just one of incompetence, or a lack of culture in terms of attachment to the rule of law, or if it is more serious … And the president knows all this, but so far has decided not to exercise the corrective powers he enjoys under the constitution.

Cardoso was summoned to appear at Namburete's office. Despite legal advice that he was under no obligation to obey the summons, he went there 'as a matter of courtesy' on 2 June. He found his interrogators asking the absurd question: Who sent *Metical* the open letter signed by Antunes? He refused to tell them; in this, he was protected by the clause in the 1991 press law allowing journalists to respect the confidentiality of their sources. He explained to *Metical* readers: 'I told them all I had to say was this: I thought it very odd that they were asking an editor how his paper received a document whose very author described it as an "open letter." If the letter is open, then how can it be important to know who sent it?' He went on to argue: 'The fundamental problems of the attorney-general's office cannot be solved with inquiries into the intentions of this or that individual. The problem is political and has to be solved politically. This PGR does not defend the interests of the state, and does not comply with its political duty to defend society against crime.'

The pressure on Namburete was such that he yielded and ordered an inquiry into the behaviour of the prosecutors who had supposedly investigated the BCM case. The inquiry was chaired by the Supreme Court judge Luís Sacramento, and it confirmed Comiche's main accusations: the case file was indeed disorganised in an attempt 'deliberately to hinder the course of justice'. The inquiry blamed three attorneys directly (Diamantino dos Santos, Rui Seuane and João Júlio Mutisse), and a fourth, Manuel Duarte, one of the assistant attorneys-general, for failing to supervise the case properly. But by the time the inquiry was completed, on 15 March 2001, Carlos

Cardoso was already dead. Setting up the inquiry was one of Namburete's last acts as attorney-general. With Namburete and Antunes swapping insults and threats in the press, the credibility of attorneys had collapsed. Chissano stepped in on 3 July to sack Namburete and all six assistant attorney-generals, appointing as the new PGR Joaquim Madeira, a Supreme Court judge with a reputation for integrity.

In retrospect, this can be seen as one of the highest points in Cardoso's career. Together with outspoken Frelimo parliamentarians such as Comiche, he had brought down the whole corrupt and complacent structure of the attorney-general's office, opening the path for rebuilding a credible legal system. But this also earned him implacable enemies who blamed him for the disappearance of their shield of immunity.

❖

Cardoso went on his last holiday in August 2000, taking the family to visit his parents in Guimarães. His younger brother, Nuno, recalled that during those holidays 'Carlos, who hadn't removed his beard for 30 years, decided to shave it off. When I asked him why, he replied it was so that his children could see him without a beard before he died.' His family was full of foreboding. Maria Luísa told

Carlos Cardoso, Nina Berg, Ibo and Milena.

her son, 'Take care, or somebody's going to shoot you.' Cardoso replied, 'If that happens, I'm ready for it.' 'He was calm and full of energy. He knew he might be killed, since he had already been threatened several times,' Nuno told the Portuguese news agency Lusa two years after the assassination.[4]

Cardoso's way of relaxing was to take long Turkish baths (Nuno had installed the necessary equipment) and sit in front of the television watching football. Ever since his days at Witbank, Cardoso had been a sports enthusiast. He once told Nina, 'If I wasn't this sort of journalist, I'd be a sports writer.' 'He knew about all the money paid for any player in European soccer,' said Nina. When he visited Scandinavia regularly, he took an interest in Scandinavian football 'and knew more about the Norwegian game than my brother did'. So Cardoso spent much of his final weeks of rest observing and discussing the finer points of Portuguese football teams. It was a sharp contrast to what awaited him back home.

When Cardoso returned to Maputo in September, the beard had grown back, and almost immediately he resumed the battle over the privatised banks. They were not suffering merely from fraud: on 4 October, a shareholders' meeting of the BCM revealed losses for 1999 of a staggering 1987 billion meticais (equivalent to 127 million dollars). The shareholding structure had changed, with the largest Portuguese bank, the BCP, taking a majority holding. The BCP set about investigating the true state of the BCM and discovered that it was catastrophic. The shareholders agreed to rescue the bank by mobilising the equivalent of 107 million dollars over the next six months. The state still owned 49 per cent of the BCM, and 49 per cent of 107 million is more than 52 million. Where, Cardoso wondered, would the state find a spare 52 million dollars?

It soon became clear that the government would issue domestic debt (high-interest-bearing treasury bonds) to pay for the recapitalisation of the BCM. Much of what had been gained in foreign debt relief under the HIPC (Highly Indebted Poor Countries) initiative, which the government had fought so hard for, was annulled at a stroke. 'It is painful to see a country as poor as ours a victim of so much injustice,' commented a Cardoso editorial.

It is painful to see that there is no money to pay teachers and nurses decent wages, or for moderate subsidies for agriculture, but there are rivers of cash to cover the disastrous private management of the commercial banks. It is painful to watch the spectacle of the IMF and World Bank preaching sermons about transparency, but keeping their mouths shut about the information they certainly have on all of this.

Cardoso's banking sources were warning him that the situation in the Austral Bank might be as bad, or even worse. Austral's executive director, the Malaysian K Muganthan, brushed aside the claim, putting the Austral losses for 1999 at 'only' 10 million dollars (and the state, owning 40 per cent of the bank, covered four million dollars of these losses). Cardoso feared that the Austral losses were on a much vaster scale. He was proved right after his death, in April 2001, when Austral came close to collapse, with the private shareholders withdrawing and handing their shares back to the state.

Where did the BCM's losses come from? One of Cardoso's banking sources noted that the BCM handled most of the World Bank loans for the private sector, and businesses had simply not repaid the money. About 80 per cent of the World Bank money channelled through the BCM was now in the category of non-performing loans. But that amounted to only about 30 million dollars. Where had the other 97 million gone? Was this not organised looting of the bank? Clearly there had been a massive drain of BCM funds post-privatisation. The bank's position had steadily deteriorated, but the BCM management had lied about it. The losses could not have accumulated in a single year – they were the result of bad debt for which no provision had been made in the past. This allowed the BCM to announce fictitious profits until, under new ownership, all the provisioning had to be done at once.

Had the Bank of Mozambique been asleep through all this? The economists whom Cardoso contacted asked why the central bank had not intervened. Was it really unaware of the BCM's huge losses? António Pinto de Abreu, of the Bank of Mozambique's board, tried to explain its inactivity thus: 'Commercial banks are very special companies. The role of the central bank is not to go onto the rooftops and make a noise, but to seek all means of ensuring the stability of the financial system, the income of the depositors, and their trust in the system.' Laudable goals – but the near-collapse of the BCM threatened all of them.

Cardoso certainly planned to write much more about the ailing privatised banks, but the bloody clashes between Renamo and the police on 9 November took priority. Cardoso declined to take either the government or the Renamo version of these events at face value. From business sources in Montepuez, *Metical* concluded that the violence in this town was the responsibility of Renamo, which had indeed staged an insurrection. But in other towns – notably Nampula, Nacala and Beira – it was the police that had moved first. Cardoso concluded that there was no uniform pattern of behaviour on either side of the conflict. The long-term solution, he suggested, was 'a third force', which would be able to stand against both Frelimo and Renamo in general elections. But in the meantime *Metical* urged civil society 'to begin expressing itself in favour of maintaining the peace, and against the logic of permanent instability which prevents Mozambique from developing'.

Cardoso criticised Mozambican Television for its coverage, which stressed the crimes of Renamo in Montepuez but passed over police violence elsewhere. The press could only claim legitimacy, he stressed, 'if it tells the truth, case by case'. He warned that

> the members and leaders of Renamo who have much to lose with the destruction of the peace that has prevailed for the past eight years don't want the madness that Dhlakama's wing seems prepared to unleash, but the absolutely unnecessary police repression in some places will make these same Renamo members feel they must support the antics of Dhlakama.

He feared that the violent clashes would push other matters off the national agenda. 'With the Renamo demonstrations, we enter a political climate propitious for still further delays in bringing the BCM fraud to court,' he wrote. 'Once again Dhlakama has proved very useful to the gangsterised wings of Frelimo.'

Meanwhile, as from early October *Metical* was visited by an unusual client – someone who wanted to buy a single copy of the paper but never had the right change. While the *Metical* staff sought for change for inconveniently large banknotes, the stranger took close note of the office layout and routines. Occasionally he was accompanied by a short stocky man of mixed race, who once asked, 'Is that white guy Carlos Cardoso?' *Metical* staff asked for their new client's name and where he worked. He told them he was Carlitos Rachid, and in quick succession named two workplaces; the journalists checked them out, and neither place employed a Carlitos Rachid. A *Metical* security guard became alarmed one evening when Rachid and his colleague were seen in a red Citi-Golf apparently pursuing the *Metical* Toyota as it took Cardoso to a meeting at the Maputo General Union of Cooperatives. But nothing happened. The office manager, Zacarias Couto, insisted that Rachid should take out a proper subscription to the paper like any client. He did not do so, and 17 November was the last day on which he bought the paper.

The aftermath of the demonstrations, the death throes of the cashew industry, the disasters in the privatised banks – all these matters vied for space on Cardoso's editorial agenda as November drew on. All were to prove unfinished business. As Cardoso busied himself on the afternoon of 22 November, discussing with Machado da Graça and Salomão Moyana an appropriate response to the violence, writing his editorial in defence of the vegetable oil industry, ringing up Teodoro Waty about municipal rubbish collection – on the other side of the road, the three men in a red Citi-Golf bided their time. At the driver's wheel sat Anibal dos Santos Junior, the man who had wanted to know if 'that white guy' was Cardoso. In the back sat the lookout, his friend Manuel Fernandes. And in the front passenger seat Carlitos Rachid cradled an AK-47. At 18.40, that gun rang out five times and carried Carlos Cardoso out of Mozambican journalism and into Mozambican history.

❖

Marcelo Mosse returned from his university class to the *Metical* newsroom shortly after 19.00.

I opened the door and switched on the lights. I saw the editor's chair empty, but bearing marks on its arms made by his movements, signs of an extremely active human presence that was suddenly an absence. I could still imagine I was seeing him, his eyes staring intently at the computer screen, his fingers tapping on the keyboard.

Tears dampened my face. I switched on the computers, and began to write the saddest story of my life. What words would suffice to announce the death of our editor? Or rather, not just this stark death, but the life and the man, his struggles and his passions?

People began to arrive at the paper. Was it true? they asked. Some had already seen the grim images of Cardoso's shattered body on the television news. His close friend, the lawyer Lucinda Cruz, asked me: 'Did he suffer?' I did not know what to say.

I had no strength to write. Machado da Graça arrived, and I asked him to work my notes into an obituary. He did so, and our short text declared that, though they had murdered Cardoso, his pen would not fall. I was afraid. What now? How could we preserve his work?

CHAPTER 24

Aftermath: Investigation and Trial

18 November 2002. The trial of six men charged with the murder of Carlos Cardoso begins before the Maputo city court. For security reasons, the accused are not moved from the prison to the court; instead the court has come to the Maputo top security prison, and is sitting inside a giant air-conditioned tent erected on the prison's football field.

The accused, though handcuffed, stride in jauntily, smiling and exchanging pleasantries with their lawyers, much to the annoyance of the judge and the prosecution.

A long, hard road was travelled to reach this court in a tent. Two years earlier, we feared that there would be no arrests, no trial. Two of the Pic agents put in charge of investigating the murder were men accused of working on behalf of the Satar brothers, issuing arrest warrants against their opponents in the Asian community. So initially the police investigation barely existed, despite promises from Chissano and Mocumbi. A month after the murder, *Metical's* patience snapped, and it revealed that the police case file on the murder was just four or five pages long 'and nobody is taking the case seriously'. But this was one crime that would not be forgotten. Candlelight vigils were held on the 22nd of every month at the murder site. An international petition gathered many thousands of signatures. The matter was raised when Chissano or other government figures travelled abroad. Prominent foreign writers, headed by the Nobel Laureate Günter Grass, issued an appeal demanding to know

'Who killed Carlos Cardoso?' On 2 February 2001, when she received the Index on Censorship's prize for 'Courage in Journalism' awarded posthumously to Cardoso, Nina took the opportunity to attack the 'non-investigation' into her husband's death.

Under public pressure – and also because some police professionals, notably the head of the Maputo Pic, António Frangoulis, took their job seriously – the first arrests were made in late February. With Frangoulis now in charge of the case, the police tracked down the man they believed had driven the Citi-Golf, Anibal António dos Santos Junior (better known as 'Anibalzinho'). He and an accomplice, Manuel Fernandes, were picked up in Swaziland. *Metical* staff positively identified Anibalzinho as one of the mysterious clients who had visited the paper in October and November 2000. It turned out that he was well known as a trafficker in luxury vehicles, with excellent contacts among high-ranking police officers. No doubt this explained why he had never been arrested before – even though a warrant for his arrest in connection with an armed robbery had been issued in 1991. The South African police were also looking for him, and had alerted their Mozambican counterparts.

In March 2000 the net closed on the Abdul Satar brothers. The police arrested Ayob and Momad Assife Abdul Satar, and Vicente Ramaya. The sixth arrest was that of Carlitos Rachid Cassamo. He was the man who had regularly visited the *Metical* offices, never had the right change to buy the paper, and had lied about his workplace. This arrest was thanks to cooperation between *Metical* and Pic. A *Metical* worker spotted Rachid at a bus stop, alerted a colleague, and kept in contact with Pic by mobile phone. Eventually the *Metical* workers grabbed Rachid on a crowded bus. This citizens' arrest enjoyed the cooperation of the ticket inspector and the passengers, and the bus drove Rachid to the nearest police station, where Pic was waiting.

19 November 2002. Manuel Fernandes confesses that he was recruited to the death squad by Anibalzinho and sat in the back seat of the car as a lookout.

20 November 2002. Nini Satar half-confesses. He admits to paying the equivalent of 50 000 dollars to

Anibalzinho, but says this was at the request of Nyimpine Chissano. As evidence, he produces seven cheques signed by Nyimpine.

25 November 2002. Carlitos Rashid Cassamo confesses that he fired the fatal shots at point-blank range into Cardoso's body. He claims that he witnessed three meetings between Anibalzinho and Nyimpine Chissano.

Months of investigation followed the arrests, and in September 2001 the investigating magistrate formally charged the six suspects with the murder. They immediately appealed against the case going to trial, but the Supreme Court did not hear, and reject, the appeal until May 2002.

By then *Metical* no longer existed. Nina closed the paper down at the end of December 2001, because legal ownership of *Metical* had become a nightmare. With Cardoso dead, responsibility for what appeared in its pages fell on the shoulders of Ibo and Milena. Nobody came up with a feasible solution (such as setting up a new company to run the paper); and the ownership issue became a direct threat to Cardoso's family when Nyimpine Chissano sued *Metical* for libel over articles published in February 2001, when Marcelo Mosse was editing the paper. The criminal libel suit meant that Mosse was threatened with jail, and the inheritance Cardoso had left his children, plus Nina's own savings, would be devoured in the libel damages of 78 000 dollars demanded by the president's son.

The *Metical* staff were paid their redundancy money, and Abilio, Couto and Matsinha set up a new paper, *Vertical*, clearly hoping to inherit the *Metical* subscription base.

5 December 2002. Nyimpine Chissano is obliged to testify. He denies any knowledge of Anibalzinho and says he met Nini Satar only once in his life. As for Carlitos Rashid: 'I don't know this wretched individual.'

6 December 2002. The court confronts Nini Satar and Nyimpine Chissano, who call each other liars.

> 9 December 2002. One of Chissano's associates, the wealthy entrepreneur Candida Cossa, testifies to a long-standing relationship between Expresso Tours and the Satars.

Mediacoop had some difficulty in coming to terms with the Cardoso legacy. On 25 May 2001, the editorial marking the ninth anniversary of *Mediafax* did not even mention Cardoso's name. In the pages of *Savana*, letters from those accused of murdering Cardoso appeared regularly, week after week, published as huge adverts and insulting judges, attorneys, police officers and witnesses. Albano Silva openly accused the *Savana* head of reporting, Paulo Machava, of working for the Satars. But in 2002 Mediacoop changed its structure from a cooperative to a limited company, and the general meeting elected Lima chairperson of the board. On the tenth anniversary of the foundation of *Mediafax*, a plaque in honour of Cardoso was unveiled at the Mediacoop offices. Later that year, men trained under Cardoso became the editors of the two main Mediacoop publications – Fernando Gonçalves at *Savana* and Marcelo Mosse at *Mediafax*. The pages of *Savana* were closed to lengthy diatribes from people accused of murder.

Lawyers for the six accused used and abused every device available under Mozambican law to prevent the case from coming to trial. But eventually all the avenues of appeal had been used, and Judge Augusto Paulino was all set to fix a trial date (he was believed to have late September 2002 in mind). Then Anibalzinho disappeared. During the night of 1 September, someone opened the three padlocks on his cell, and he walked out of the Maputo top-security jail. There were immediate calls for the resignation of the interior minister, Almerino Manhenje – even from the most pro-Frelimo of all the papers, *Domingo*.

> 11 December 2002. The prosecution witness Vasco Matavele says he has received a phone call from Anibalzinho warning him not to make any statement in court.

> 19 December 2002. Judge Augusto Paulino refuses to accept a tape from Anibalzinho as evidence, and

demands that if Anibalzinho wants to speak to the court he must do so in person.

20 December 2002. The attorney-general, Joaquim Madeira, announces he does not believe that only low-level officers were involved in Anibalzinho's release.

The escape of Anibalzinho delayed the trial for 60 days, the statutory period allowed for a fugitive to surrender before he is tried in absentia. It was during this period that allegations were published that others besides the Satars and Ramaya had ordered the elimination of Cardoso. One witness, Gerry Opa Manganhela, came forward with stories of conversations in prison with Nini Satar. According to Opa, Satar admitted his role in the killing but claimed he was only a middle-man, carrying out instructions from 'the son of the rooster'. Who was this mysterious personage? the court asked. 'Nyimpine Chissano, the son of the president,' came the immediate reply. A second case file was opened, in which the main suspect was Nyimpine Chissano.

Within the ministry of the interior, the alleged connection with Nyimpine was already known. In his prison cell, Nini Satar had told Frangoulis back in November 2001 of meetings at the house of Candida Cossa, attended by Nyimpine Chissano, at which the murder of Cardoso was supposedly plotted. Frangoulis put it all in his notebook, and informed his superiors. They took no action. In July 2002 Frangoulis was sacked – for doing his job too well. He was also stripped of protection: even his bodyguard was disarmed. The gun was returned only after Frangoulis protested loudly through the press. From his South African hide-out, Anibalzinho sent death threats to Frangoulis's mobile phone and boasted that he still wielded great influence within the police.

There were two other high-profile murders – of António Siba-Siba Macuacua, interim chairperson of the Austral Bank, on 11 August 2001, and of the popular musician Pedro Langa, on 20 November 2001. One witness came forward suggesting that those who had ordered Cardoso's assassination were behind the Siba-Siba and Langa murders too. It was said that, the day after Siba-Siba's assassination, Nini Satar celebrated in his prison cell.

Like the BCM, Austral had been driven to ruin by a huge burden of bad debts. Unlike the BCM, the Austral management under Siba-Siba made a serious attempt to recover the debts, and even printed a list of over 1200 debtors in *Notícias*. There was ample reason for those milking the financial sector to eliminate Siba-Siba.

> 24 December 2002. Emerging from an interview at the public prosecutor's office, Nyimpine Chissano refuses to speak to the press, telling reporters, 'I don't give interviews.'

> 9 January 2003. Nini Satar tells the court that the records of the mobile phone company M-Cel will confirm that Nyimpine Chissano was in contact with Anibalzinho in early 2001.

> 10 January 2003. Judge Paulino asks why the Satars' foreign exchange bureau, Unicambios, is still open.

If the illicit release of Anibalzinho was meant to prevent the trial from going ahead, it failed. As the trial continued, it took the lid off some of the more sordid corners of the Mozambican economy. The legal foreign-exchange dealings of Unicambios were just a front for the loan-sharking operations of Nini Satar. The Satars, Nyimpine Chissano and Candida Cossa all talked of hundreds of thousands of dollars, millions of rands, billions of meticais, as if these were sums that everyone has in their pocket. At one point, Nini Satar remarked that he considered five or ten thousand dollars 'derisory amounts'. Day after day, the Mozambican public had, on their TV screens and radio sets, glimpses into the shadow economy of contraband and stolen cars, of short-term loans issued at extortionate interest rates, and of threats to those who fail to pay up.

> 13 January 2003. The prosecution sums up and demands the maximum sentence for all six accused. The Cardoso family lawyer, Lucinda Cruz, declares:
>> The live broadcasts of this trial have achieved what Carlos Cardoso was unable to do while alive. They have carried his voice to the most remote parts of

Mozambique. And it has made us aware that we were losing the moral values that are universally recognised, regardless of political regime or religious creed.

The main motive for the murder was the obvious one: Carlos Cardoso was a journalist who denounced abuses, who did not shut up, who would not forget any matter, who insisted on following what he regarded as most important, and who would not allow any of the illegalities he had written about to fall into oblivion. Carlos Cardoso was a pain, he was obstinate, he was really inconvenient. The only way for any criminal to go on practising crimes with impunity was to silence Carlos Cardoso. And the only way to silence Carlos Cardoso was to kill him.

The fact that Carlos Cardoso was an incorruptible journalist, a journalist who would never shut up about any crime, the fact that Carlos Cardoso would never stop insisting that the BCM 14-million-dollar fraud be brought to trial was, if not the only reason, at least one of the motives that led to his death.

As for Nyimpine Chissano and all the others who have been accused here by the defendants, it will be up to civil society and to the friends of Carlos Cardoso to demand that the investigation continue, that their responsibility be seriously ascertained, and, if applicable, that they be tried and sentenced. Once again, it will be up to civil society and the mass media to ensure that this investigation is not forgotten, and that this case does not join the heap of other cases that have ground to a halt in the various stages of criminal investigation.

The legal system is going through a serious crisis of legitimacy, credibility and trust among the citizens. We think this trial has helped restore some hope. We know it is not easy, under the country's present conditions, to fight against organised crime. But we are convinced that this trial has been the first sign of firmness by the legal system in this combat. That first sign, which Carlos Cardoso thought could be given by bringing the BCM fraud to trial, has in the end been given by the trial of his own assassins.

The second case file, in which Nyimpine Chissano is a suspect, follows its course in the Maputo city branch of the public prosecutor's office. In January 2003, some prosecutors were reportedly in favour of the preventive detention of Chissano, others were not. They started the meticulous work of checking on mobile phone records, looking for a pattern of contacts between Chissano, the Satars and others involved in the case. When rumours circulated that the case was shelved, Joaquim Madeira peremptorily denied it.

30 January 2003. The South African police arrest Anibalzinho on the outskirts of Pretoria. The operation is carried out in coordination with Joaquim Madeira's office: Manhenje is not informed until Anibalzinho is in a South African police station. The illicit release has served its function of keeping Anibalzinho out of circulation, and his mouth shut, during the trial.

31 January 2003. Judge Paulino reads the verdict and sentence. The court sentences Anibalzinho to 28 years and 6 months; Manuel Fernandes and Carlitos Rachid to 23 years and 6 months; Nini Satar to 24 years; Ayob Satar to 23 years and 3 months; and Vicente Ramaya to 23 years and 6 months. The defendants are ordered to pay compensation of 14 billion meticais (US$588 000) to Carlos Cardoso's children, and 500 million meticais to his injured driver, Carlos Manjate. The defence lawyers announce their intention to appeal.

The extradition is rapid, and Anibalzinho arrives in Maputo on the evening of 31 January, returning at once to the top-security prison.

Carlos Cardoso,
June 2000.

Paul Fauvet

And 31 January 2003 seems as good a date as any to end this narrative. History has no simple conclusions, and there are always loose ends. Appeals will go up to the Supreme Court and, regardless of the decisions there, the Satars and Ramaya will certainly be in the dock again when the cases of the BCM fraud and the attempt on Albano Silva's life are heard.

Nyimpine Chissano may, or may not, be arrested. Further trials, deriving from the revelations made during the Cardoso murder trial, might take place. Much will depend on whether Mozambican society maintains the pressure for a clean and credible judicial system. Nothing is guaranteed, for there is a deep truth in that oldest of Frelimo slogans – *A Luta Continua* (The Struggle Continues).

Notes

CHAPTER 1

I am indebted to Stelios Comninos, José Manuel and Milena Cardoso, and Dee Malcomess for their e-mail communications concerning this period in Cardoso's life.

Cardoso's articles on Witbank, '*A ordem natural das coisas*', were published in *Notícias* between 13 and 18 August 1983. An English summary of his experiences in South Africa, entitled 'Memories of racism', was published in the feature service of the Agência de Informação de Moçambique (AIM) in the same year.

CHAPTER 2

Many of Cardoso's friends at Wits delved into their memories for this chapter. I am particularly indebted to Patrick Fitzgerald for gathering several people together for a long evening of reminiscing in Johannesburg, and to Glynis O'Hara for her e-mail correspondence.

Cardoso kept the key documents concerning his deportation, including press cuttings and the deportation order itself. They are all in his personal archive.

1   The *Star*, Johannesburg, 25 April 1974.
2   The founder of the PAIGC of Guinea-Bissau, assassinated by the Portuguese in 1973.

CHAPTER 3

1   Machado da Graça, 1994.
2   Cardoso gave this interview on 17 November 2000 to a university research student, Emidio Machiana, who kindly offered me a transcript, from which these quotes are taken.
3   The original nationalist movement, the Zimbabwe African People's Union (Zapu) of Joshua Nkomo, had split, with the creation of the rival Zimbabwe African National Union (Zanu), led by Ndabaningi Sithole. Both had guerrilla armies, respectively Zipra and Zanla. Zanu went through further convulsions in

1975–76, with the expulsion of Sithole and the election of Robert Mugabe as the new leader. For a more detailed analysis of the Zimbabwean movements and Mozambique's relations to them, see Christie, 1988.

4 For the genesis of the MNR/Renamo, see Flower, 1987, and Martin and Johnson, 1986.

Chapter 4

1 Machado da Graça, 1994, p. 62.
2 Magaia, 1994, p. 45.
3 Cardoso's account of this meeting is contained in a long letter to Rebelo, a draft of which is in his personal archive. It may never have been sent, since Rebelo cannot recall receiving it.
4 Machado da Graça, 1996, p. 179.
5 These plays are still occasionally retransmitted by Radio Mozambique. So, years after his death, Cardoso's voice can still be heard on radio dramas.

Chapter 6

1 Leaked documents on US–South African relations published in *Transafrica News Report*, Special Edition, August 1981.
2 Slovo, 1997, p. 263.

Chapter 7

1 I am indebted to José Mota Lopes, who transcribed the relevant pages of his diary and e-mailed them to me.
2 The red tin containing the 100 scraps of paper is in Nina Berg's possession. Shortly after leaving Machava, Cardoso transcribed the entire prison diary into a notebook and this more legible version has been used for this chapter.
3 Unfortunately, this letter has not survived (at least, I could not find it in Cardoso's archive), and we do not know if he ever sent it.

Chapter 8

1 The justification given for the *lei de chicotada* was popular concern about rising crime. Brigades preparing the Frelimo congress found, across the country, anger at perceived leniency towards criminals. So, rather than lead the masses, in this instance Frelimo decided to follow them.
2 Maiopuè's enthusiasm for Frelimo proved short-lived. In the late 1990s he formed a tiny opposition party, Pamomo, that allied with Renamo. He was a key adviser to Renamo leader Afonso Dhlakama in abortive negotiations with the government in early 2001.

CHAPTER 9

1   See Hanlon, 1991, p. 29. As he put it, 'At least 100 000 people starved to death, waiting for the donors to accept Mozambique's turn to the west.'

2   The text of the agreement, the speeches at Nkomati, and a host of supporting documentation were conveniently gathered together by the ministry of information into a book entitled *Pela Paz: Acordo de Nkomati* (Maputo, 1984).

CHAPTER 10

1   Ministry of Information, 1985.

2   The *Star*, Johannesburg, 20 September 1985; *Business Day*, Johannesburg, 20 September 1985.

CHAPTER 11

1   The Frelimo guerrilla army in the war for independence was called the FPLM (Forças Populares para a Libertação de Moçambique – People's Forces for the Liberation of Mozambique). This name was kept for a few years after independence. But the army was gradually structured as a regular force, ranks were introduced in 1980, and it was renamed the FAM (Forças Armadas de Moçambique). Yet plenty of people kept on using the old name, and often, even in official discourse, to avoid any confusion, the armed forces were called the FAM/FPLM.

CHAPTER 12

1   The *Star*, Johannesburg, 8 October 1986.

2   Probably the Portuguese journalist Augusto de Carvalho.

CHAPTER 13

1   The *Sunday Star* of 26 October 1986 headlined its piece 'South African monitors paid little heed to Machel flight'. Had the *Star* reporters bothered to search their archives, they would have found the material on the Mariepskop installation in the *Star* of 8 February 1975, and further information on the Devon computer centre in the issue of 29 November 1975. The 1979 South African Defence White Paper spoke explicitly of modernising the air-defence radars.

2   Mozambique has never closed the file on Mbuzini. As this book was being written, new evidence emerged. A former member of an apartheid death squad, the innocuously named Civil Cooperation Bureau (CCB), Hans Louw, currently serving a 28-year jail term for murder, claimed he was part of a 'clean-up team' whose job was to go to the crash site and finish off the Mozambican president if he survived the crash. The backup was not needed because the false beacon worked perfectly and Machel died on impact.

Chapter 15

1 The *Star*, Johannesburg, 10 December 1987.
2 Cardoso was shown the full file of Angolan complaints in the ministry of information, and copied them into his notebook.
3 My own notes from Chissano's impromptu airport speech.

Chapter 16

1 *Chapa-cem*: the slang term for the privately owned minibuses and other vehicles that provided much of Maputo's passenger transport after liberalisation of the economy began in 1987. The poorly maintained and overcrowded vehicles, with their overworked drivers, brought death to the roads and substantial profits to their owners. They were one of the clearest examples of 'savage accumulation', of capitalism without rules.
2 'General Statute of State Functionaries', the rulebook for civil servants and other state employees.

Chapter 18

1 Salomão Moyana, interviewed by Eduardo Namburete, in Mazula, 1995, p. 268.
2 Dirk Salomons: *Probing the Successful Application of Leverage in Support of Mozambique's Quest for Peace*, New York, 2000. This was kept well hidden from the press: Cardoso was one of the few who suspected that something was being plotted. It is, however, doubtful that there could have been a successful coup: the soldiers wanted to leave the army and were in no mood for adventures.
3 Coal from the mines at Moatize, in Tete, could not be exported because Renamo destroyed the railway to Beira. At Marromeu, Renamo destroyed the most modern sugar mill in the country, and at Caia a key electricity substation was blown up.
4 *Domingo* never admitted that it had been deceived by a forgery. Indeed, 10 years later it was still protesting that the document was genuine (even though nothing in the supposed plan for a return to war ever came to pass).

Chapter 20

1 The reference is to a traditional ceremony to placate the ancestors, involving sprinkling alcoholic drinks on the ground (and often the slaughter of goats and chickens, mercifully dispensed with in *Metical*'s case).

Chapter 22

1 The truth about Nyimpine Chissano's relation to the Austral Bank did not come out until almost two years after Cardoso's death. In August 2002, *Savana* reported that Austral hired Nyimpine, despite his youth and his inexperience, as

a consultant at a salary of US$3000 a month, a contract that was cancelled only after the bank's near-collapse in April 2001.

2   Three years later, honest businesses still claim they face delays in attempting to claim VAT rebates. Dishonest ones still offer clients a choice: they can buy goods with a receipt and pay VAT, or without a receipt and without VAT.

CHAPTER 23

1   This seems another instance of donor complicity in corruption, witting or not. After Cardoso's death, Joe Hanlon also wrote to the governments concerned, asking whether the money had ever been repaid. He too received no answer.

2   The Portuguese acronym PGR stands for both the attorney-general himself and for the institution. Under the attorney-general is the public prosecutor's office.

3   ANC militant Robert McBride, convicted for the Magoo Bar bombing, became a senior foreign ministry official under the first South African democratic government. He was arrested in Mozambique on trumped-up espionage charges while undertaking an apparently freelance investigation into arms trafficking.

4   Lusa news item, 1 February 2003.

Sources

The main primary material is the work of Cardoso himself. Cardoso wrote prolifically, and his published articles can be found, depending on the period, in *Tempo*, *Notícias*, the AIM wire service, *Mediafax*, and *Metical*. All copies of *Metical*, from its first issue on 25 June 1997 to its last on 26 December 2001, are available on a CD-ROM issued by the Maputo company Pandora Box. Unfortunately no such thorough job has been done with *Mediafax*, and the Mediacoop archives contain gaps.

Cardoso published one slim volume of poetry, *Directo ao Assunto*, in 1985. His experimental paintings survive for a large audience because the photographer José Cabral took slides of them: 40 were published on the second anniversary of Cardoso's death under the title used for the 1991 exhibition, *Os Habitantes do Forno*.

Among the other significant sources consulted are the following:

Christie, Iain: *Machel of Mozambique*, Zimbabwe Publishing House, Harare 1988.

Flower, Ken: *Serving Secretly: An intelligence chief on record, Rhodesia into Zimbabwe 1964–1981*, Murray, London 1987.

Hanlon, Joseph: *Mozambique: Who calls the shots?*, James Currey, Oxford 1991.

Hanlon, Joseph: *Peace without Profit: How the IMF blocks rebuilding in Mozambique*, James Currey, Oxford 1996.

Lima, Fernando: *1975–2000 Moçambique: Revolução e liberalismo: Das dogmas, das lutas e dos sonhos*, unpublished paper, Lisbon 2000.

Machado da Graça, João: *A Talhe de Foice*, Casa Velha, Maputo 1994.

Machiana, Emídio: *A Revista 'Tempo' e a Revolução Moçambicana: Da mobilização popular ao problema da critica na informação 1974–1977*, Promedia, Maputo, 2002.

Magaia, Albino: *Informação em Moçambique: A força da palavra*, Publicações Notícias, Maputo 1994.

Martin, David and Johnson, Phyllis: *Destructive Engagement: Southern Africa at war*, Zimbabwe Publishing House, Harare 1986.

Mazula, Brazão (editor and publisher): *Moçambique: Eleições, democracia e desenvolvimento*, privately printed, Maputo 1995.

Ministry of Information: *Pela Paz: Acordo de Nkomati*, Maputo 1984.

Ministry of Information: *Documentos da Gorongosa (extractos)*, Maputo 1985.

Ministry of Information: *Fazer da Informação um Destacamento Avançado da Luta de Classes e na Revolução: Documentos do primeiro seminário nacional de informação*, Maputo 1977.

Ribeiro, Fatima and Sopa, António (eds.): *140 Anos de Imprensa em Moçambique: Estudos e relatos,* Amolp (Mozambican Portuguese Language Association), Maputo, 1996.

Slovo, Gillian: *Every Secret Thing*, Abacus, London 1997.

Sopa, António (ed.): *Samora: Homem do povo*, Maguezo, Maputo 2001.

Vasconcelos, Leite de: *Pela Boca Morre o Peixe*, Associação dos Amigos de Leite de Vasconcelos, Maputo 1999.

Index